Acclaim for *Yeargin on Management*

Bill Yeargin, through his writing and speaking, has become a leading management force. In my years of experience, Bill stands out as the person who best communicates effective management concepts. He is truly a rare resource!

Paul Dodson, Co-founder,
International Marina Institute

Yeargin gives solid, clear and useful information. Bill has a unique way of helping his readers see the big picture. His columns are always the first I read!

Larry Halgren, Former President
- Halgren Consulting Group
- President, International Marina Institute

Yeargin's columns are first-rate information from an expert with first-hand knowledge!

JJ Marie, CEO - Zodiac North America

Yeargin's columns educate in a practical, useful and easy to read style. I like to call Bill's tips the "golden nuggets" of successful leadership!

Gregg Kenney, CEO - Flagship Marinas

The usefulness of *Yeargin'.s* columns to both my business and personal life is invaluable. His columns are always the first I read. Bill is THE source of excellent management information, period!

Skip Moyer, President
- American Boat and Yacht Council (retired)

Reading a *Yeargin* column is like an instant wake up call. Bill's column is my monthly management refresher course!

Dennis Nixon, Dean and Professor
- University of Rhode Island Co-founder,
International Marina Institute

Bill Yeargin is a no-nonsense guy! His columns challenge managers to continually improve while presenting a common-sense approach to solving everyday management problems.

Dennis Kissman, CEO
- Marina Management Services

Yeargin's columns are a combination of straightforward "how-to" lessons and thought-provoking questions every manager should ask. They are equally effective for managers in any industry!

Bill Slansky, President
- National Marine Distributors Association CEO
- Land and Sea Distributing

Yeargin's columns effectively focus on skills that professionals need. He gives his readers an effective way to take inventory of the management techniques they are using. Reading Bill's columns is time well spent!

Phil Keeter, President
- Marine Retailers Association of America

Bill's worldwide travels give his readers a unique global perspective. His columns are the "how-to" from someone who talks the talk and walks the walk! I find Bill's columns both powerful and relevant to all aspects of my life, both professional and personal.

Pat Kearns, President
- Recreational Marine Experts Group

Yeargin's inspiring management commentary helps me as both an individual and as a business owner. Bill's insight and direct, no-nonsense approach to a variety of relevant business topics offers good, sound thinking, usually coupled with a compelling challenge for change. A great read!

Wanda Kenton Smith, CEO
- Kenton Smith Advertising & Public Relations

Yeargin's columns provide practical advice for managers. While managers in any size of company can benefit from his writings, Bill effectively distills his topics down for the small business person and provides advice that can be understood and implemented by anyone.

Thom Dammrich, **President**
- National Marine Manufacturers Association

At a time when American organizations desperately need to energize people and produce leaders at all levels, *Yeargin* provides an empowering philosophy for leadership that is the best guarantee of success in business - a perfect blend of wisdom, insight and practical experience.

James L. Frye, **CMM - Executive Director**,
Association of Marina Industries

Yeargin's fix on the pulse of today's management issues is truly refreshing. Bill has a keen understanding of how today's business leaders must push their organizations to embrace continuous improvement. His insights are concise, thought-provoking and certainly relevant in today's business climate.

Neal Harrell, **President**
- Brooks Marine Group

I have had the opportunity to work side by side with *Bill Yeargin* for the past 18 years. Bill 'practices what he preaches' and does it with both class and style!

Jim Bronstien, President - Bron Properties

Yeargin's writing and advice is incisive, accurate and readable. His columns provide essential tools for today's professionals.

Mick Bettesworth, CMM and Development Director
- MDL Marinas (UK)

Yeargin's columns are concise, on target and educational. They are a must-read for every manager. *Yeargin on Management* should be on every CEO's desk.

Dave Fielding, CEO
- Hospice of Palm Beach County

Drawing on a wealth of experience and a long record of success, *Yeargin* provides his readers with a management veteran's perspective on both issues that impact organizations and best practices of effective leaders. His cogent style, compelling insights and thoughtful advice ensure that managers will read his columns again and again.

Jim Ellis, President - Boat U.S.

Yeargin's writing and perspective about management issues is invaluable. His columns keep me connected to the trends that affect the foundation of solid corporate communications and marketing.

Amy Halsted, President - The Halsted Agency

At a practical and applied management level, *Yeargin on Management* is a virtual primer on how businesses can effectively work. This edition only strengthens its position on ABBRA's 'must read' list for its members.

Mark Amaral, **Managing Director**
-American Boat Builders and Repairers Association

Henry Ford represents innovation in the automotive industry, Bill Gates in software. Think of innovation in proven powerful management techniques, and *Bill Yeargin* comes to mind. Combining profound insights with practical ideas, *Yeargin's* columns are a must read for all managers.

Alison Pruitt, **Executive Director**
- Marine Industries Association of Palm Beach County

Yeargin on Management

FIFTH EDITION

Bill Yeargin

Published in the United States by
Ignite Press
5070 N 6th St. #189
Fresno, CA 93710
www.IgnitePress.us

ISBN: 978-1-953655-23-3 (Amazon Print)
ISBN: 978-1-953655-24-0 (IngramSpark)
ISBN: 978-1-953655-25-7 (E-book)

Table of Contents

Introduction 1

Chapter 1   June 1995
Want Profits? Boost Teamwork 5

Chapter 2   September 1995
Employee Reviews: A Right of Passage 9

Chapter 3   October 1995
Know Your Numbers 13

Chapter 4   November 1995
Reporting Dollars Makes Sense 15

Chapter 5   January 1996
Seven Ways to Improve Your Hiring 19

Chapter 6   February 1996
Firing Someone? Follow These Rules 23

Chapter 7   March 1996
Are You Trapped in a Paradigm? 27

Chapter 8   April 1996
Improving Your Use of Time 31

Chapter 9   May 1996
Creating the Mission Statement 35

Chapter 10   June 1996
Preparing Your Strategic Plan 39

Chapter 11   July 1996
Managing Your Vendors 43

Chapter 12   August 1996
Staff Meetings: The Why and How 47

Chapter 13   September 1996
Tapping Computer Power Effectively 51

Chapter 14   October 1996
Cost Management Costs Little 55

TABLE OF CONTENTS

Chapter 15   November 1996
              Task Forces Create Solutions 59

Chapter 16   January 1997
              Taking Inventory: A Necessary Evil 63

Chapter 17   February 1997
              What is Your Company's Culture? 67

Chapter 18   March 1997
              Avoid the Collection Headache 71

Chapter 19   April 1997
              Happy Customers, Happy Company 75

Chapter 20   May 1997
              Manager's Tunnel Vision: An "Inbred" Disease 79

Chapter 21   June 1997
              Don't "De-motivate" Your Employees 83

Chapter 22   July 1997
              Manage Cash Flow to Thrive 87

Chapter 23   August 1997
              Create a "Personal" Mission Statement 91

Chapter 24   September 1997
              Reading for Management's Sake 95

Chapter 25   October 1997
              If You Criticize, Make it Constructive 99

Chapter 26   January 1998
              Be Accountable to Accounts Payable 103

Chapter 27   February 1998
              Think "Out of the Box" for Solutions 107

Chapter 28   March 1998
              Make Honesty and Integrity Your Standard 111

Chapter 29   April 1998
              Positive Reinforcement Motivates Employees 115

Chapter 30   May 1998
              Let Optimism Drive Your Business 119

TABLE OF CONTENTS

Chapter 31   June 1998
             Promote the Power of Teamwork 123

Chapter 32   July 1998
             How to Get an A+ in Employee Training 127

Chapter 33   August 1998
             Do as The Europeans Do: Think Long-Term 131

Chapter 34   September 1998
             Nonverbal Communication Speaks Volumes 135

Chapter 35   October 1998
             Plan on Becoming a Great Manager 139

Chapter 36   November 1998
             Goals Kick Start Your Marine Business 143

Chapter 37   December 1998
             Know Your Employees' Emotional Temperament 147

Chapter 38   January 1999
             No "Quick-Fix" for Customer Service Problems 151

Chapter 39   February 1999
             Retain Customers by Resolving Complaints 155

Chapter 40   March 1999
             Energized Employees are more Profit-Driven 159

Chapter 41   April 1999
             Take Control of Your Time 163

Chapter 42   May 1999
             Customer Service Tips from Japan 165

Chapter 43   June 1999
             Read to Succeed 169

Chapter 44   July 1999
             Let Meetings be a Tool for Good Communication 173

Chapter 45   January 2000
             Of "Cheese" and Change-
             A Parable for our Industry 175

TABLE OF CONTENTS

Chapter 46   February 2000
             Information Age Spawns the
             "Knowledge Manager" 179

Chapter 47   March 2000
             The Golden Rule Applies to Your Employees, Too 183

Chapter 48   April 2000
             Is Your Management Style Cutting into
             Your Profits? 187

Chapter 49   May 2000
             Ability to Focus Helps Build Profits, Efficiency 191

Chapter 50   June 2000
             Keep Your Employees - Treat Them Like Volunteers 195

Chapter 51   July 2000
             Manage Your Time Better and Quit
             "Putting Out Fires" 199

Chapter 52   August 2000
             Capital Budget Time Means Tough
             Decisions Await You 203

Chapter 53   September 2000
             How Valuable is Training? Think About a 33-1 Return ...207

Chapter 54   October 2000
             Get Feedback, Set Goals In Employee Evaluations. 211

Chapter 55   November 2000
             Saving a Miffed Customer:
             I Call it "Fumble Recovery" 215

Chapter 56   December 2000
             Knowing isn't Enough - You Need The DO Part, Too 219

Chapter 57   January 2001
             A Leader Supplies a Vision, A Manager Implements It ... 223

Chapter 58   February 2001
             Give Staffers Autonomy, They'll Give You Results 227

Chapter 59   March 2001
             Some Personality Traits You Just Cannot Change 231

TABLE OF CONTENTS

Chapter 60   April 2001
              Some Boat Show Exhibitors Must
              Have Money to Burn 235

Chapter 61   May 2001
              Have a Global Mindset? No? You'd Better Get One 239

Chapter 62   June 2001
              A Strategic Plan Will Serve as Your Business Roadmap .. 243

Chapter 63   July 2001
              Staying Ahead of "Entropy" Means Steadily Improving ..247

Chapter 64   August 2001
              How to Cut Costs and Stay Positioned for a Recovery 251

Chapter 65   September 2001
              Essentials of Leadership: Vision, Talent and Focus 255

Chapter 66   October 2001
              Column On Leadership Hit Home for Readers 259

Chapter 67   November 2001
              An Instant 8-Step Formula for Better Business Letters ... 263

Chapter 68   December 2001
              Seven Simple Steps to Reducing Premiums 267

Chapter 69   January 2002
              "Jack" is an Instant Classic, but Then, it's Jack Welch 271

Chapter 70   February 2002
              A Good Leader Gets Focused;
              A Great Leader Stays Focused 275

Chapter 71   March 2002
              Attributes of Leadership: What the Leaders Think 279

Chapter 72   April 2002
              A Very Fine Line Separates Champions from The Pack .. 283

Chapter 73   May 2002
              It's a Karma Of Business: Integrity Pays Dividends 287

Chapter 74   June 2002
              Even with a Good Accountant,
              You Need Your Own Scorecard 291

TABLE OF CONTENTS

Chapter 75   July 2002
              Creating a Climate of Cheer Will Pay Off in
              the Long Run 295

Chapter 76   August 2002
              As the Economy Heats Up, So Will the War for Talent .. 299

Chapter 77   September 2002
              Accounting/Ceo Scandals Put the Spotlight on Trust 303

Chapter 78   October 2002
              Sound Management Tips for a Fast-Food Operator 307

Chapter 79   November 2002
              Your Most Valuable Asset? It Could be Your Brand 311

Chapter 80   December 2002
              The Manager of the Future Will Exhibit These Qualities 315

Chapter 81   January 2003
              Catching a Vision Opens up a
              Whole World of Potential 319

Chapter 82   February 2003
              Work as a Team: Send Your Business to the Big Leagues 323

Chapter 83   March 2003
              Do Your Research Before You Come to Your Decision 327

Chapter 84   April 2003
              All Work, No Play Seldom Brings the Desired Result 331

Chapter 85   May 2003
              E-Mail is a Wonderful Tool if You Use it the Right Way 335

Chapter 86   June 2003
              A Positive Outlook is Key to Management Success 339

Chapter 87   July 2003
              Significance and Success: One Leads You to the Other .. 343

Chapter 88   August 2003
              Managing the Intangibles: A True Measure of Success 347

Chapter 89   September 2003
              The Leadership Investment that Won a Super Bowl Title 351

TABLE OF CONTENTS

Chapter 90   October 2003
              There's More to a Budget Than an Annual Headache 355

Chapter 91   November 2003
              You Can't Change Outcomes without
              Changing Methods 359

Chapter 92   December 2003
              It's the Season for Lists: Here's One for Managers 363

Chapter 93   January 2004
              New Year's Resolutions: Why Goal-Setting Can Fail 367

Chapter 94   February 2004
              Choices you Make Today are Keys to your Future 371

Chapter 95   March 2004
              Project Management: It's Not as Scary as you Think 375

Chapter 96   April 2004
              Solid Planning Beats out a Crystal Ball Every Time 379

Chapter 97   May 2004
              Follow these Six Pointers to Build an Energized Team ... 383

Chapter 98   June 2004
              The Best Listeners Make the Best Communicators 387

Chapter 99   July 2004
              5 Steps to Help you Keep a Project Under Control 391

Chapter 100   August 2004
              100 Columns in 3 Words: Vision, Talent and Focus 395

Chapter 101   September 2004
              The Chronic Complainers: They're Not Always Wrong .. 399

Chapter 102   October 2004
              Learn Public Speaking Skills;
              It's a Sure-Fire Stature Builder 403

Chapter 103   November 2004
              Delayed Gratification: Taking Profits Now
              Can Cost You Later 407

Chapter 104   December 2004
              Keeping Employees Safe Keeps Bottom Line Healthy 411

TABLE OF CONTENTS

Chapter 105   January 2005
              Our Industry's Future Rides on February Jobs Summit .. 415

Chapter 106   February 2005
              Help Keep Catastrophe at Bay With an
              Updated Disaster Plan 419

Chapter 107   March 2005
              Diagnosing and Stemming Your
              Company's Brain Drain 423

Chapter 108   April 2005
              Don't Personalize Criticism Even If
              It's Not Constructive 427

Chapter 109   May 2005
              In Business as in Sports, Capture the Momentum 431

Chapter 110   June 2005
              Are You Drowning in Detail and
              Missing the Big Picture? 435

Chapter 111   July 2005
              Clearly Defined Expectations Eliminate
              Office Frustrations 439

Chapter 112   August 2005
              Effective Communication:
              A Skill That can be Learned 443

Chapter 113   September 2005
              You Can Go With Your Gut, But Back It Up With Data 447

Chapter 114   October 2005
              Try Revisiting "The 7 Habits";
              It Will Be Time Well Invested 451

Chapter 115   November 2005
              Don't be a "Dumb" Manager;
              It Hurts You, Your Company 455

Chapter 116   December 2005
              Don't Leave a Career Behind at
              the Office Holiday Party 459

Chapter 117   January 2006
              Eliminate Waste from Your Operations 463

TABLE OF CONTENTS

Chapter 118   September 2017
               Technology and Globalization 467

Chapter 119   July 2018
               Technological Change Will
               Reset Global Power Structure 471

Chapter 120   March 2019
               Reading = Success 473

Chapter 121   March 2020
               Good Things Will Happen 477

Chapter 122   March 2020
               Leadership During Crisis 479

Chapter 123   April 2020
               Don't Restart - Reset Your Business 481

Chapter 124   May 2020
               Crisis Management 483

Chapter 125   June 2020
               The Way Forward 485

Chapter 126   August 2020
               Busting the Creativity Myth 489

Chapter 127   August 2020
               Innovation Made Easy 493

Chapter 128   October 2020
               Leadership Made Easy 499

Chapter 129   November 2020
               Truth or Consequences? 505

Chapter 130   November 2020
               Expecting the Unexpected 509

ABOUT THE AUTHOR.. 513

Index by Topic

Boat Shows

Chapter 60   April 2001
              Some Boat Show Exhibitors Must
              Have Money to Burn 235

Brand Management

Chapter 79   November 2002
              Your Most Valuable Asset? It Could be Your Brand 311

Communication

Chapter 12   August 1996
              Staff Meetings: The Why and How 47

Chapter 34   September 1998
              Nonverbal Communication Speaks Volumes 135

Chapter 44   July 1999
              Let Meetings be a Tool for Good Communication 173

Chapter 85   May 2003
              E-Mail is a Wonderful Tool if You Use it the Right Way 335

Chapter 112   August 2005
              Effective Communication: A Skill That can be Learned . 443

Change

Chapter 45   January 2000
              Of "Cheese" and Change-A Parable for our Industry 175

Chapter 121   March 2020
              Good Things Will Happen 477

Chapter 123   April 2020
              Don't Restart - Reset Your Business 481

Chapter 127   August 2020
              Innovation Made Easy 493

Customers

Chapter 19   April 1997
              Happy Customers, Happy Company 75

Chapter 38   January 1999
              No "Quick-Fix" for Customer Service Problems 151

Chapter 39   February 1999
              Retain Customers by Resolving Complaints 155

Chapter 42   May 1999
              Customer Service Tips from Japan 165

Chapter 55   November 2000
              Saving a Miffed Customer:
              I Call it "Fumble Recovery" 215

Financial/Accounting

Chapter 3   October 1995
              Know Your Numbers 13

Chapter 4   November 1995
              Reporting Dollars Makes Sense 15

Chapter 14   October 1996
              Cost Management Costs Little 55

Chapter 16   January 1997
              Taking Inventory: A Necessary Evil 63

Chapter 18   March 1997
              Avoid the Collection Headache 71

Chapter 22   July 1997
              Manage Cash Flow to Thrive 87

Chapter 26   January 1998
              Be Accountable to Accounts Payable 103

Chapter 52   August 2000
Capital Budget Time Means Tough
Decisions Await You 203

Chapter 64   August 2001
How to Cut Costs and Stay Positioned for a Recovery 251

Chapter 74   June 2002
Even with a Good Accountant,
You Need Your Own Scorecard 291

Chapter 90   October 2003
There's More to a Budget Than an Annual Headache 355

General Management

Chapter 15   November 1996
Task Forces Create Solutions 59

Chapter 17   February 1997
What is Your Company's Culture? 67

Chapter 20   May 1997
Manager's Tunnel Vision: An "Inbred" Disease 79

Chapter 27   February 1998
Think "Out of the Box" for Solutions 107

Chapter 30   May 1998
Let Optimism Drive Your Business 119

Chapter 36   November 1998
Goals Kick Start Your Marine Business 143

Chapter 48   April 2000
Is Your Management Style Cutting into
Your Profits? 187

Chapter 49   May 2000
Ability to Focus Helps Build Profits, Efficiency 191

Chapter 63   July 2001
Staying Ahead of "Entropy" Means Steadily Improving ..247

Chapter 70   February 2002
              A Good Leader Gets Focused;
              A Great Leader Stays Focused 275

Chapter 78   October 2002
              Sound Management Tips for a Fast-Food Operator 307

Chapter 80   December 2002
              The Manager of the Future Will Exhibit These Qualities 315

Chapter 83   March 2003
              Do Your Research Before You Come to Your Decision 327

Chapter 86   June 2003
              A Positive Outlook is Key to Management Success 339

Chapter 89   September 2003
              The Leadership Investment that Won a Super Bowl Title 351

Chapter 91   November 2003
              You Can't Change Outcomes without
              Changing Methods 359

Chapter 92   December 2003
              It's the Season for Lists: Here's One for Managers 363

Chapter 100   August 2004
              100 Columns in 3 Words: Vision, Talent and Focus 395

Chapter 106   February 2005
              Help Keep Catastrophe at Bay With an
              Updated Disaster Plan 419

Chapter 109   May 2005
              In Business as in Sports, Capture the Momentum 431

Chapter 113   September 2005
              You Can Go With Your Gut, But Back It Up With Data 447

Chapter 115   November 2005
              Don't be a "Dumb" Manager;
              It Hurts You, Your Company 455

Chapter 117   January 2006
              Eliminate Waste from Your Operations 463

Chapter 122   March 2020
              Leadership During Crisis 479

Chapter 124   May 2020
              Crisis Management 483

Chapter 125   June 2020
              The Way Forward 485

Chapter 128   October 2020
              Leadership Made Easy 499

Globalization

Chapter 61   May 2001
              Have a Global Mindset? No? You'd Better Get One 239

Chapter 118   September 2017
              Technology and Globalization 467

Chapter 119   July 2018
              Technological Change Will
              Reset Global Power Structure 471

Hiring/Firing

Chapter 5   January 1996
              Seven Ways to Improve Your Hiring 19

Chapter 6   February 1996
              Firing Someone? Follow These Rules 23

Information Management

Chapter 13   September 1996
              Tapping Computer Power Effectively 51

Chapter 46   February 2000
              Information Age Spawns the "Knowledge Manager" 179

Insurance

Chapter 68   December 2001
Seven Simple Steps to Reducing Premiums 267

Managing Employees

Chapter 2   September 1995
Employee Reviews: A Right of Passage 9

Chapter 21   June 1997
Don't "De-motivate" Your Employees 83

Chapter 25   October 1997
If You Criticize, Make it Constructive 99

Chapter 29   April 1998
Positive Reinforcement Motivates Employees 115

Chapter 37   December 1998
Know Your Employees' Emotional Temperament 147

Chapter 40   March 1999
Energized Employees are more Profit-Driven 159

Chapter 47   March 2000
The Golden Rule Applies to Your Employees, Too 183

Chapter 50   June 2000
Keep Your Employees - Treat Them Like Volunteers 195

Chapter 54   October 2000
Get Feedback, Set Goals In Employee Evaluations. 211

Chapter 58   February 2001
Give Staffers Autonomy, They'll Give You Results 227

Chapter 59   March 2001
Some Personality Traits You Just Cannot Change 231

Chapter 75   July 2002
Creating a Climate of Cheer Will Pay Off in
the Long Run 295

Chapter 76   August 2002
As the Economy Heats Up, So Will the War for Talent .. 299

Chapter 101   September 2004
      The Chronic Complainers: They're Not Always Wrong .. 399

Chapter 104   December 2004
      Keeping Employees Safe Keeps Bottom Line Healthy 411

Chapter 107   March 2005
      Diagnosing and Stemming Your
      Company's Brain Drain 423

Chapter 108   April 2005
      Don't Personalize Criticism Even If
      It's Not Constructive 427

Chapter 111   July 2005
      Clearly Defined Expectations
      Eliminate Office Frustrations 439

Personal Development

Chapter 7   March 1996
      Are You Trapped in a Paradigm? 27

Chapter 8   April 1996
      Improving Your Use of Time 31

Chapter 23   August 1997
      Create a "Personal" Mission Statement 91

Chapter 24   September 1997
      Reading for Management's Sake 95

Chapter 28   March 1998
      Make Honesty and Integrity Your Standard 111

Chapter 41   April 1999
      Take Control of Your Time 163

Chapter 43   June 1999
      Read to Succeed 169

Chapter 51   July 2000
      Manage Your Time Better and Quit "Putting Out Fires" 199

Chapter 56   December 2000
      Knowing isn't Enough - You Need The DO Part, Too 219

Chapter 65   September 2001
              Essentials of Leadership: Vision, Talent and Focus 255

Chapter 66   October 2001
              Column On Leadership Hit Home for Readers 259

Chapter 67   November 2001
              An Instant 8-Step Formula for Better Business Letters ... 263

Chapter 69   January 2002
              "Jack" is an Instant Classic, but Then, it's Jack Welch 271

Chapter 71   March 2002
              Attributes of Leadership: What the Leaders Think 279

Chapter 72   April 2002
              A Very Fine Line Separates Champions from The Pack .. 283

Chapter 73   May 2002
              It's a Karma Of Business: Integrity Pays Dividends 287

Chapter 77   September 2002
              Accounting/Ceo Scandals Put the Spotlight on Trust 303

Chapter 81   January 2003
              Catching a Vision Opens up a
              Whole World of Potential 319

Chapter 84   April 2003
              All Work, No Play Seldom Brings the Desired Result 331

Chapter 87   July 2003
              Significance and Success: One Leads You to the Other .. 343

Chapter 93   January 2004
              New Year's Resolutions: Why Goal-Setting Can Fail 367

Chapter 94   February 2004
              Choices you Make Today are Keys to your Future 371

Chapter 102   October 2004
              Learn Public Speaking Skills;
              It's a Sure-Fire Stature Builder 403

Chapter 110   June 2005
              Are You Drowning in Detail
              and Missing the Big Picture? 435

Chapter 114 October 2005
Try Revisiting "The 7 Habits";
It Will Be Time Well Invested 451

Chapter 116 December 2005
Don't Leave a Career Behind at the
Office Holiday Party 459

Chapter 120 March 2019
Reading = Success 473

Chapter 126 August 2020
Busting the Creativity Myth 489

Chapter 129 November 2020
Truth or Consequences? 505

Project Management

Chapter 95 March 2004
Project Management: It's Not as Scary as you Think 375

Chapter 96 April 2004
Solid Planning Beats out a Crystal Ball Every Time 379

Chapter 97 May 2004
Follow these Six Pointers to Build an Energized Team ... 383

Chapter 98 June 2004
The Best Listeners Make the Best Communicators 387

Chapter 99 July 2004
5 Steps to Help you Keep a Project Under Control 391

Strategic Management

Chapter 9 May 1996
Creating the Mission Statement 35

Chapter 10 June 1996
Preparing Your Strategic Plan 39

Chapter 33 August 1998
Do as The Europeans Do: Think Long-Term 131

Chapter 35   October 1998
              Plan on Becoming a Great Manager 139

Chapter 57   January 2001
              A Leader Supplies a Vision, A Manager Implements It ... 223

Chapter 61   May 2001
              Have a Global Mindset? No? You'd Better Get One 239

Chapter 62   June 2001
              A Strategic Plan Will Serve as Your Business Roadmap .. 243

Chapter 88   August 2003
              Managing the Intangibles: A True Measure of Success 347

Chapter 103   November 2004
              Delayed Gratification: Taking Profits Now
              Can Cost You Later 407

Chapter 105   January 2005
              Our Industry's Future Rides on February Jobs Summit .. 415

Chapter 130   November 2020
              Expecting the Unexpected 509

Teamwork

Chapter 1   June 1995
              Want Profits? Boost Teamwork 5

Chapter 31   June 1998
              Promote the Power of Teamwork 123

Chapter 82   February 2003
              Work as a Team: Send Your Business to the Big Leagues 323

Training

Chapter 32   July 1998
              How to Get an A+ in Employee Training 127

Chapter 53   September 2000
              How Valuable is Training? Think About a 33-1 Return ...207

Vendor Management

Chapter 11   July 1996

        Managing Your Vendors 43

Introduction

Several years ago I was invited to speak at a marine industry conference in Newport, Rhode Island. The purpose of my presentation was to share what I was doing from a management perspective at Rybovich, my employer in West Palm Beach, Florida.

Rybovich is a world-renowned sportfish manufacturer and yacht service facility. Prior to my presentation in Rhode Island, the company went through a merger of three relatively equal organizations. Rybovich also successfully weathered the recession of the early '90s. The conference attendees in Newport were eager to hear about what we had done at our company to transition through these difficult times.

After my presentation, the editor of an industry trade magazine approached me and asked if I would be interested in writing a monthly management column for his publication. He said he was impressed by what he heard me say at the conference and thought I should share what I was doing on a broader basis.

Over ten years later, those monthly columns have been a huge success. People regularly tell me that the columns are an enormous help to them as they deal with the management problems they face on a day-to-day basis.

On many occasions, these same readers have asked when I was going to publish a book based on the information I have shared in my columns. When pressed, I always responded, "Someday." A couple of years ago, I realized that the time for the book had come and decided to publish all of my previous columns at one time. That was the First Edition of this book. This Fifth Edition of *Yeargin on Management* includes my first one-hundred seventeen columns.

I consider this book similar to a management "toolbox" because it gives managers the "tools" they need in specific areas of management without going into long, drawn-out detail. In other words, I want to give managers "tools" they can learn quickly and put to work immediately in their businesses to improve their effectiveness and profitability.

There are many management "tools" provided in this book that you will find helpful, however, if I had to summarize the columns I have written over the years I would say that their theme has been that successful managers have three attributes that others do not have; ***Vision, Talent and Focus.*** One of the columns in this book (Chapter 65-September 2001) deals specifically with this perspective. Incidentally, that column on vision, talent and focus drew, by far, the largest reader response I have ever received.

To help put this book in perspective, I would like to share a golf analogy that some people reading this introduction may have previously heard me share at one of my marine industry presentations.

What's Your Score?

At the risk of alienating vast numbers of readers, I must admit that I have never really enjoyed playing golf. I simply don't have the patience to dedicate large blocks of time to become good at it. And since I haven't played much golf over the years, I am not very good at it. And, since I am not very good, I don't play often.

But there is one statistical quirk about golf that I find very interesting. I have noticed a disproportionate relationship between the average per-round score of the PGA tour players and the money they earn. The difference between players who win millions of dollars a year and those who earn significantly less is about two strokes per round. In other words, the players who perform just a little better make significantly bigger bucks!

Both sports and life in general are full of similar analogies. People can achieve disproportionately positive results by doing things just a little better.

This same principle is true for business managers. The best ones get dramatically better results by doing things just a little bit differently from others. Their employees, customers, and bosses perceive them to be much better managers. And chances are, their financial results reflect in a big way the little things they are doing better.

The Same the World Over

I have done a fair amount of traveling both in the United States and internationally speaking to managers who are trying to improve their "score." Whether it's in Europe, Asia, Australia, South America, or here in the United States, I have learned that most managers spend the bulk of their time dealing with the same problems.

"How can I be more effective with my customers?" and "How can I help my employees handle change?" are two of the questions I hear often. Other popular queries relate to time management, focus, building a management team and instituting a corporate culture. Managers are concerned about issues of productivity-specifically, getting people to accomplish more in their eight-hour days.

While these problems are the same worldwide, so are the solutions. As I stated above, the three attributes necessary to be a successful manager are Vision, Talent, and Focus. The purpose of this book is to provide you with tips and techniques you can use to improve your Vision, Talent and Focus, and perhaps more importantly, help you improve your management "score" by just a little bit so you too can realize the substantially better results that go along with that higher score.

Finally, I have tried to share my experience and knowledge as I have written these columns. However, I have also grown substantially while writing. I hope this book helps you as much as it has helped me.

Bill Yeargin

Chapter 1
WANT PROFITS? BOOST TEAMWORK
June 1995

You have a salesperson, a service manager or a marina manager, who generally does a great job. In fact, they know they are doing a great job, so much so that they can be downright difficult to work with. They believe themselves to be irreplaceable, and sometimes you even have to wonder yourself how you could do without them. Surprisingly, this employee probably does not fit into your company's long-term future. Team players are what a business needs to achieve lasting success.

Your employees have different backgrounds, temperaments, education levels and experience. These differences give your employees distinct perspectives on what needs to be done in your company. The essence of teamwork is using these differences to create synergy, not discord.

Basically, synergy means 1+1=3. You can achieve this synergy best by encouraging everyone to focus on their own roles. The human body is a great analogy for this. The hands, brain, heart, liver, feet, etc., are all important parts, but they have their own roles. If these parts were to fight with each other, or with each other's roles, the body would not achieve its objectives and could possibly die. This also holds true within your company.

How do you know if your employees are working together as a team? A big part of it is intuitive, however, there are signs you can look for. Do your employees trust each other? Do they have common goals and focus? Are the inevitable conflicts that arise easily resolved? Do your employees understand each others' temperament? Do they understand and work off each others' strengths and weaknesses? If you answered "yes" to each question above, your company may be operating as a team.

No matter how you answer these questions, teamwork is a topic that should be constantly addressed, and there are several things that you can do to encourage your employees to function as a team:

- **Constantly emphasize teamwork.** Half the battle is won if your employees honestly believe that teamwork is important to you. Talk about it at all your formal meetings and during informal discussions. Have your employees tell you why they think teamwork is important. Remind them that to be treated like a teammate, they must act like a teammate. It can be uncomfortable when you first start emphasizing teamwork. Don't worry about that. Stick with it until teamwork becomes part of your company's culture.

- **Keep employees focused on your goals/objectives.** If you keep everyone in your organization focused on common objectives or goals, it is much more likely that they will operate as a team. If you have a mission statement for your organization - and it's a good idea to develop one if you don't - it should specifically include a reference to teams or teamwork.

- **Reward based on teamwork.** Set up your incentive plans so that they pay out based on team performance. Avoid incentive plans that encourage people to be focused on their individual performance at team expense. Some companies have eliminated their employee-of-the-month programs in order to promote improved teamwork.

- **Educate your employees on teamwork.** The best person to do this is you. If you are uncomfortable teaching, there are videos that can be shown to your employees that do a great job emphasizing the importance of teamwork. Read this article at your next staff meeting. Your employees probably already think that they personally are team players. Encourage them to consider what they can learn from teamwork, not just what those around them can learn.

When emphasizing teamwork, you are not looking for uniformity - you are looking for unity. There is a big difference. You don't want a company in which everyone thinks alike. You do want a company in which employees use their differences to the organization's advantage.

Some may say that teamwork won't work because everyone just wants to look out for themselves. Teamwork is not inconsistent with the idea of people looking out for themselves. In fact, team players are helping themselves by being a team player. Team players are not trying to get a bigger piece of the pie, they are trying to get a bigger pie.

Competition today is war. If your employees are competing internally, instead of focusing this energy on external competition, your company's very survival could be at risk. Getting your employees to work together as a team can have a dramatic impact on your profitability. Teamwork is not just some esoteric idea; it is a powerful and underutilized concept that can unleash the hidden resources in companies. There is no limit to what can be accomplished when it does not matter who gets the credit for success.

Chapter 2
EMPLOYEE REVIEWS:
A RIGHT OF PASSAGE
September 1995

Just for a moment, put yourself into your employees' shoes. Would you be a better worker if you received honest feedback about your performance and were given goals for the next 12 months?

The answer is obvious. Of course you would!

Fortunately, there is a process that helps you give your employees the information they need to be more effective. It's the annual performance evaluation, the purpose of which is to focus on the future. Unfortunately, most managers focus too much on past performances. Problems, mistakes and "lessons-to-be-learned" should be handled in your daily communications as these situations arise. You've wasted the time of both you and your employee if you focus primarily on the past. Employees should leave the evaluation thinking about their future and your expectations of them.

How you conduct the evaluation will affect the future success of both you and your employee. The first step to ensuring successful performance evaluations is to have a good evaluation form. Ideally, the form would be developed in-house and tailored to your company. There are also many pre-printed forms available, however, be sure to select one that has relevance to your employees. You may want to ask some of your colleagues at other companies what they are using. Perhaps it would work for you, too.

Below are some ideas to keep in mind as you complete the evaluation form.

- **Do it on time.** The process may be a nuisance to you, but it is very significant to the employee. Show them respect and courtesy by doing the evaluation on time.
- **Determine your objective in advance.** What do you want to accomplish during the evaluation? Your objective should be related to the goals you set for the employee.
- **Choose your words carefully.** What you write on the evaluation form in passing will be taken very seriously by your employee. After completing the review, read it from the employee's perspective.
- **Stay objective.** Don't let personalities or personal preferences affect your evaluation. Whether or not you are "buddies" with the employee should not influence the review.

Once you have completed the evaluation form, it's time for the hard part: meeting with the employee. Some tips for the actual employee review are as follows:

- **Save the pay review for a future meeting.** If you discuss pay during the evaluation, it will dominate the employee's thoughts and make it more difficult for you to accomplish your objective. Tell employees beforehand that you will be discussing performance only and not pay.
- **Establish and maintain rapport.** Start with some small talk and make the employee comfortable. This will be easier if you have done a good job of communicating with the employee during the year.

- **Be a good listener.** The evaluation meeting is also a good time for you to learn some things.
- **Avoid arguments.** Keep the conversation constructive. No one ever wins an argument during a performance evaluation.
- **Focus on performance.** Avoid any focus on personalities.
- **Emphasize the employee's strengths.** Still, you must be honest about their weaknesses.
- **Focus on the future.** The employee's future and your goals for them should dominate the meeting.
- **End on a positive note.** Make sure the employee leaves the evaluation feeling good, not demoralized. You want the employee to leave the meeting feeling that if they follow your suggestions, their future with the company will be bright.

Many managers don't like doing performance evaluations because the process is awkward at best. Often even the best evaluator is more uncomfortable than the employee is. Don't let this awkwardness keep you from achieving the benefits the performance evaluation process offers.

Another complaint about performance evaluations is that they take up a lot of time. As a manager, your time is valuable, but be careful not to let tasks that absorb much of your day replace something as important as this.

Business today is tough, and we need every advantage that is available. The effective use of performance evaluations can help develop your company's employees into the high performance team of professionals you need in the 1990s.

Chapter 3
KNOW YOUR NUMBERS
October 1995

You know your market; you take good care of your customers, and your employees think you're a great boss. You pour your heart into the company, working long hours and making personal sacrifices. Still as hard as you've tried, you don't really have a good grasp of the "financials." You're not exactly sure what the numbers mean or even what to expect.

Are you in trouble? You bet!

Should you run out to your local college and sign up for an accounting class? Sure, if you have the interest, but it is not necessary. There are, however, some things you must do if you want your company to survive.

- **Hire a financial expert.** This person does not have to be an employee, but he or she must be someone you can count on to provide solid financial guidance. The preferable choice is a CPA who stays up-to-date on current financial and accounting issues.
- **Produce timely and detailed financial reports.** Your CPA or financial expert should provide comprehensive financial statements by the tenth of each month. If you wait longer, the statements become useless, like an old newspaper. The statements should include a balance sheet, income statement, statement

of cash flows and a summary of key financial indicators. If you have good financial statements but don't understand them, spend time with your financial adviser and learn how to read your basic financial indicators.

- **Prepare a budget.** Accountants can provide you with information about what has happened in the past, but you also need information about your future. Each month, your budget should be compared to your actual results. This is called variance analysis, and it serves as an early warning system to help identify problems in your business.

- **Watch your cash.** It is amazing how many companies aren't sure how much cash they have at the end of the day. Get a daily cash report and be sure it is reconciled to your bank statement on a monthly basis.

- **Watch your inventory.** Because inventory is not an income statement expense, it may seem harmless to purchase. But inventory can build up on your balance sheet and kill your cash flow. Review your inventory monthly and adjust accordingly.

- **Review unbilled revenue.** If you have a busy service operation, don't be surprised if cash is tight. Insist on a report at least weekly, showing revenue earned on service work that has not yet been billed to the customer. Don't be shy about asking your customers for deposits or progress payments on service work.

- **Keep a close eye on your receivables.** Ask for a report at least monthly of accounts outstanding more than 30 days, including a summary of what is being done to collect each account. Be persistent, after all, it's your money.

Insist on the above information from your financial advisor. It's just the basics, so don't accept excuses about why it can't be provided to you. If you want your business to survive, you must have a good system to track your success.

Chapter 4
REPORTING DOLLARS MAKES SENSE
November 1995

Does it make you cringe to think about your company's financial information becoming known to your employees? If so, you are not alone. In fact, odds are that most of the people reading this column either own or work for a company that is very protective of its "numbers." Yet today, despite years of trying to guard this information many business owners are becoming open with their employees regarding the financial results of the company. These owners realize the powerful benefits of sharing financial information throughout their organization.

Last spring I had the opportunity to speak at the annual conference of the American Boat Builders and Repairers Association. During the conference there was an interesting round table discussion of whether financial information should be revealed to employees. Marine business owners expressed strong and sincere opinions on both sides of this issue. Those arguing for sharing the financial information talked about educating and empowering employees to be more effective. The owners arguing against sharing the numbers mentioned perceived dangers of employees, customers or competitors getting the information.

What do you really need to be afraid of? Most of your customers own boats because they are successful in their businesses. They want the best service at a good price. If you can provide that and still make good money, more power to you! As for your competitors, if they are astute, they can already project your financial results with a 10 percent margin of error. The remainder of your competitors will not understand the information and are going to be left behind by your managerial prowess anyway. So, don't let a little concern hold your team back from its potential.

As managers and owners, we are always trying to instill in our employees an ownership mentality. Sharing financial information not only helps accomplish this objective but also aids employees in understanding that every action, no matter how small has a financial impact on the company.

It is important to realize that employees are theorizing about your financial results anyway. It's only natural. Wouldn't you if you were in their shoes? Usually, their uninformed guesses, which typically estimate your profit to be a lot higher than it actually is, are more dangerous than the accurate information ever would be.

So once you get over the psychological hurdle and decide to share some of your financial information, what do you need to do? The following are some pointers that will help you:

- **Educate.** You must teach your employees how to understand the financial information. Explain what contribution margin and other key financial concepts are. If you are uncomfortable teaching this information, have someone else who is knowledgeable and a good teacher do it. However you decide to do it, it is important that your employees learn how to interpret the information you will provide them.
- **Instill accountability.** Your employees should realize that having good numbers is not just the boss' job - it is everyone's responsibility.
- **Reward the results.** Instill as part of your corporate culture that rewards are based on results, not just effort.

- **Shoot straight.** Do not play games with the numbers. If data sharing is to be effective for your company, it is imperative that you maintain your credibility.
- **Be consistent.** Don't present the information only when it is very good or very bad. Give the information monthly or quarterly in a consistent format. This will help reinforce the importance of what you are presenting.

At first, presenting this information may be uncomfortable, but there are a number of effective ways to communicate it. At Rybovich we have one of the bigger companies in our industry with 170 employees. We provide a detailed monthly financial presentation to division heads and department supervisors. We then rely on these managers to carry the information back to their employees. The method you choose to present the information is not as important as the fact that you are presenting it.

Presenting financial information is not just some textbook management technique. It is a specific way to improve your profits. Educating and informing your employees will always result in higher performance from them.

Chapter 5
SEVEN WAYS TO IMPROVE YOUR HIRING
January 1996

It's natural for you as a manager to wonder about the future of your company. Will you be able to compete in the years to come? Will you have the strong team that is necessary to accomplish your objectives? Will you be able to achieve the financial results that are necessary to ensure your long-term future? The answers to these questions are not a matter of luck or fate; they are a direct result of the hiring decisions that you make today.

Bad hiring decisions have resulted in the decline and eventual collapse of many companies. This results partly from the fact that hiring new employees is tough. It involves making commitments that impact your company's customer satisfaction, productivity, effectiveness and ultimately, its financial results for years. These are commitments that can cost your company hundreds of thousands of dollars in pay and benefits over a career. Yet, despite these significant ramifications, many managers do not recognize the long-term impact that each new hire will have on their company. Because your company's future will be limited by the quality of the employees you hire today, you must have procedures in place to ensure that you are making good decisions. Outlined below are some steps you can take to improve your odds of hiring the best employees.

- **Develop a thorough application form.** Your employment application form should be designed to obtain all the information you need. The form should require educational background, work experience, references and current information about the applicant. Be sure the form asks for information in chronological order, this will help you identify gaps of time the applicant may not want you to know about.
- **Verify the information.** Studies have shown that many people are not honest on their employment application or resume. If you find the applicant has been dishonest, end your consideration of them immediately.
- **Check references.** Most people will not list someone as a reference unless they are confident of receiving a good recommendation. Try to speak to people from their prior companies who were not listed. If the applicant is applying for a managerial position, speak with someone who worked for the applicant. Some companies, fearing legal repercussions, will refuse to give out information beyond dates of employment, title and salary.
- **Ask tough questions.** Ask questions the applicant has not prepared to answer, such as who are your heroes? What did you dislike about your least favorite boss? What are three of your weak points? What is the best decision you ever made? The worst? What are you doing to improve yourself? Where do you see yourself in 3, 5, 10 years?
- **Get a second opinion.** Ask someone else in your organization to interview the applicant. You may be missing something that is obvious and could be identified by someone you trust.
- **Consider the applicant's "profile."** Do you want someone assertive and results oriented, for example, or more agreeable and unassuming? Someone socially-oriented or more reserved? Someone with a good sense of urgency or someone more patient and relaxed? Someone detail-oriented or more informal?

At Rybovich, we use a tool called the "Predictive Index" to help answer these questions. It is a quick word selection exercise that evaluates with amazing accuracy whether the applicant fits the position. Whether or not you use a formal evaluation tool, it is important that you consider the applicant's profile for the position they're going to fill.

- **Take your time.** Many times we have an immediate need when we are hiring, but always wait at least a day after the first interview before you hire someone. What seems so sure during the excitement of the interview may not be such a good idea after you have a day to think about it.

Finally, in today's litigious environment, it is imperative that you have a good understanding of the legal boundaries of the hiring process. You must have a good legal resource who can counsel you with accurate and timely information. Some of the hot topics these days include appropriate interview questions, discriminatory practices and hiring the disabled. If you have not been to a class or seminar on hiring legalities, look for one immediately. Don't take this area of the law lightly.

If you expect your company to meet or exceed your expectations, you need to hire people who are as committed to success as you are. If you have not been successful in selecting quality personnel, the above steps will help you screen more effectively and put together a team that will ensure your future success.

Chapter 6
FIRING SOMEONE?
FOLLOW THESE RULES
February 1996

I recently had the unpleasant experience of sitting through the firing of an employee. The manager doing the firing was well-trained and had the best of intentions, but, unfortunately, the meeting included almost everything you should avoid when terminating an employee.

The manager started by stating how difficult it is to be a supervisor and how you sometimes have to make really tough decisions. He then went into a speech about how the employee had really tried hard despite his well-documented problems. This was all before the manager told the soon-to-be-ex-employee that he was fired.

The employee sat in bewilderment trying to figure out what was going on while the manager finally meandered to his point. I didn't intervene, but I wanted to put both the manager and employee out of their misery.

As a manager, firing an employee is one of the most difficult tasks you will face. It is very awkward and uncomfortable. I have witnessed many terminations in which it seemed like the person doing the firing was more distraught than the person being fired.

Despite this difficulty, there are times when firing an employee is perfectly justifiable or even a business necessity. In fact, companies that never fire anyone probably have deadwood in their organization that is holding them back from peak performance and ultimately increased profits.

Before you fire an employee, be sure that you have your reasons well-documented. If you are laying off the employee for general business reasons, such as a sales slowdown, cost-cutting or restructuring, be sure you document your rationale. If you are firing the employee for cause, it is best if you have used progressive discipline including written warnings that the employee's job is in jeopardy. There are plenty of legal problems related to firing an employee so if you have any doubt about your justification, be sure to check with an employment attorney.

When it comes time to hold the actual meeting with the employee, you should follow a few simple rules:

- **Maintain eye contact.** This shows that despite the employee's termination, you still respect him or her as an individual. It also indicates that you are being honest with them regarding the reasons for their termination.

- **Have a second person join you in the meeting.** This will ensure that there is no future disagreement over what was said during the meeting.

- **Get right to the point.** Avoid small talk when firing an employee. You are not trying to make a friend, you are firing someone, so get to the point and tell the employee why you are meeting. This is not to suggest that you should be rude, but small talk only makes the manager feel better, not the person being fired.

- **Don't argue.** After you terminate the employee, let them say whatever they would like or ask any questions. Answer the questions as concisely as possible and end the meeting. Prolonged discussion at this point is useless. Regardless of how emotional the employee gets, avoid arguing at all costs. Arguing accomplishes nothing and just increases the hard feelings. You will never win an argument with someone who has just been fired.

- **Support the company.** Even if you do not completely understand your company's reason for the firing, the time to express your ambivalence is not during the termination meeting. It may make you feel better, but it just confuses the employee and adds to his or her bitterness.
- **Put their severance in writing.** Employees understandably have a million things going through their minds during the termination meetings, so you can't expect them to remember every detail of their severance arrangement. As a courtesy, you should put the arrangement in writing so they can review it later.
- **Spare the employee's dignity.** The termination meeting is not the time to be critical of the employee. Though it can be difficult, try to allow the employee to save face as much as possible.
- **Make it effective immediately.** In most cases, the day of the termination meeting should be the employee's last day. An employee is not likely to be productive after the firing and their presence will keep reminding the remaining employees about what happened. Go ahead and pay the employee for whatever extra days you were going to let them work and let him or her leave. Ex-employees generally prefer to just take the pay and not come in and face everyone anyway.

Firing an employee is never easy but sometimes you must do it to ensure your company's survival. Following the practices outlined above can help you through this very difficult but necessary management responsibility.

Chapter 7
ARE YOU TRAPPED IN A PARADIGM?
March 1996

The devil you know is better than the devil you don't know. This is a common way of thinking for many managers, but, unfortunately, it's an attitude that often leads to negative paradigms.

The word paradigm (pronounced "par-a-dime") has become a frequently used part of management vocabulary. A paradigm is the lens or frame of reference that you use to view what is happening around you. If a paradigm is negative, it can blind you to important developments or opportunities in your company, industry or market.

The best example I have heard of a negative paradigm occurred in the Swiss watch industry. Thirty years ago, the Swiss dominated the worldwide watch market. They were comfortable, and there was no end to their superiority in sight. Then a Swiss watchmaker developed a new concept in time keeping- the quartz watch. The response he received to his new idea was surprising. Swiss managers downplayed the development and even failed to legally protect it. They chose instead to hold onto the negative paradigm that people want watches they wind. Things had gone so well for the Swiss managers for so long that they were not about to change, and they ignored the new idea. The result was devastating. Japanese and American companies successfully marketed quartz technology, basically destroying the Swiss watchmaking industry.

If a negative paradigm can destroy a national industry, it can certainly destroy your business. As a manager, you must ensure that they don't impair your company's short term profits or your long-term results.

How do you know whether your company is a potential victim of negative paradigms? Below are some key phrases that are indicative of negative paradigms. If you hear them used at your company, watch out! You could be headed for trouble.

- **"We have always done it this way."** This phrase is certain trouble. All companies, no matter how successful, must continue to look for ways to improve.
- **"It's policy."** Policy and structure are important; however, they can be changed. Don't let your company get caught in a bureaucratic trap. Be the master, not the slave, of your policy.
- **"We tried it before."** How much enthusiasm was there for the idea when you tried it? Could it be tried a better way or with more ardor?
- **"Our problems are different."** The more I learn about businesses, the more I realize that most companies have similar problems. Don't fall into the trap of thinking that your company is so special that no one else's problems are like yours.
- **"I know it won't work."** Another sure danger sign. This phrase not only reflects a negative paradigm but becomes a self-fulfilling prophecy.
- **"We don't do it that way."** You need to be open to change. Maybe you should do it that way.
- **"We're doing okay now."** You'd better be looking over your shoulder, because with this attitude, there is probably a competitor coming right up behind you.

If it is common to hear these phrases at your company, you need a plan to help your organization break out of its negative paradigms.

Here are some things you can do to help your company get back on the right track:

- **Lead by example.** Be sure that you don't communicate negative paradigms. Be sure the people you work with know that you are always open to new and better ideas.
- **Discuss negative paradigms.** Have a brainstorming session to put together a list of the negative paradigms pervading your company. Get everyone at the meeting to commit to not letting the identified paradigms hold back your business.
- **Focus on continuous improvement.** A constant search for better ways to do things will naturally break negative paradigms. This focus must be pushed throughout all levels of your organization in staff meetings, internal newsletters, individual meetings or any other means of employee communication.
- **Send your employees to training.** Hearing outsiders' perspectives at training sessions can help both you and your employees break out of negative paradigms. Your employees will also meet their peers at these sessions, and others may help them see your issues from a much broader perspective.
- **Be creative.** It's hard to stay trapped by negative paradigms if you are forcing yourself to be creative.

To be profitable in today's competitive environment, you need every advantage available. The most successful companies break out of their negative paradigms by constantly looking at their businesses from a fresh perspective.

Chapter 8
IMPROVING YOUR USE OF TIME
April 1996

Do you ever feel like there are just not enough hours in the day? Do you sometimes find it impossible to get everything done regardless of how hard you work? Do you feel as though your schedule is out of control? If you answered "yes" to any of these questions, you may be in the majority of managers who have problems with time management.

It is hard to understand why so many managers who want to improve their time management skills won't make the effort to do so. They probably think it would take too much time. These managers fail to realize what a dramatic impact improved time management can have on their effectiveness. Whether you are an owner or employee, this improved effectiveness can significantly increase both your value to your company and the enjoyment you get from your job.

Unfortunately, though the benefits are obvious, time management remains a mystery to most managers. Actually, it is not a mystery at all. There are several specific things that you can do to better manage your time:

- **Discontinue low-priority tasks.** Most people with time-management problems do not know how to differentiate tasks that are *important* from those that are *immediate.*

  To discontinue low-priority tasks you must know what

your high priorities are. You can't manage your time effectively unless you know what you are working toward. This requires setting goals and being willing to say no to tasks that are not important to your objectives. Although it is hard to avoid all the distractions that eat up your day, you must focus your time on items that have long-term importance to your company.

Another way to discontinue low-priority tasks is to improve your daily planning. If you are in a reactive state you probably have problems with time management. One great time-saving technique is to spend the last few minutes at work every day planning the next day.

- **Delegate.** Have someone who works for you do it. Seems simple, doesn't it? Then why aren't more managers effective delegators? Why do so many managers feel like they have to do everything? Why do they often micro-manage simple tasks?

    Effective delegation requires investing in your people - an investment that will develop the talents of your employees so you can rely on them to handle problems like you would. This short-term investment can save you significant time and dollars over the years.

    Another reason managers give for not delegating is that "it is just easier to do it myself." These managers are usually right in the short run, but in the long run they are hurting themselves. Invest the time to teach your employee once, and it will save you many multiples of that time later on.

- **Get organized.** Time invested in staying organized will also pay off in multiples. Don't be a packrat. Throw out things that are unnecessary. If you touch a piece of paper, deal with it; don't put it aside to deal with later. Keep your work area clean and organized. These suggestions may seem simple, but they can have a big impact on improving your time management.

- **Use time-management tools.** If you do not have a "to do" list, you almost certainly have time-management problems. Have a master task list with everything you need to do listed. You should also have a daily "to do" list that you generate each evening when you do your planning for the next day.

  You also should have a daily calendar. Don't try to keep your schedule in your head.

- **Focus on results.** Effective time managers stay focused on results. Don't get carried away with all the tasks you are doing and forget the result you are working toward. It is not important how many hours you work. What you get done is much more important. Concentrate on finishing tasks.

  Part of being results-oriented is avoiding procrastination and focusing on things you *can* control. There is no need to spend your valuable time worrying about or focusing on things you *can't* control. It will be a lot less frustrating for you also.

You have a choice. You can work like crazy, always be in a frenzy, and complain about not being able to get everything done. Or you can be a manager who gets more done in less time and is always in control. By following the steps above you will become a master of one of the hottest management skills of the '90s: effective time management.

Chapter 9
CREATING THE MISSION STATEMENT
May 1996

That man is on a mission. We are on a mission. I am on a mission. What do you think about when you read those words? You may think of someone who is very focused and determined to accomplish their objective. You probably also think of someone who has a high probability of achieving their desired results.

Wouldn't it be great if you could capture the intensity and focus of someone on a mission in your business? Do you think it would improve your profits if your employees were on a mission? Of course it would, and you can do it - probably more easily than you think. The first step in capturing this power to improve your profits is to develop a written mission statement.

People on a mission know that it is difficult to achieve success until you define success. A mission statement not only defines success but also provides valuable direction to help you develop strategy, look for opportunities and deal with your customers and employees - all things that will improve your profits.

If you think a mission statement could help your company, don't hesitate to write one and implement it. The following steps can help you get started:

- **Ask the tough questions.** Where do you want to go? How do you want to get there? What business are you in? What culture do you want to encourage? What is important to you? Who is important? Answering these questions is tougher than it may at first appear. Force yourself to answer them. It will be healthy for you and your company.

- **Identify important factors.** Identify these factors based on your answers to the above questions. At our business, we determined that we wanted to be recognized worldwide as the premier company in the recreational marine industry. We wanted to acquire this recognition by emphasizing continuous improvement, teamwork, results-orientation and customer satisfaction with equal emphasis on results for employees and owners. Once this step is complete you will know the important factors to include in your mission statement.

- **Review other mission statements.** Call numerous companies and have them email you a copy of their mission statement. Your mission statement should be original to your company; however, this process can help you with brainstorming and provide you with numerous ideas as you begin writing.

- **Begin writing drafts.** Take all the information you have gathered and begin writing drafts. Don't worry about getting it right the first time. Write a draft and let it sit for a day before you look at it again. Write another draft independent of the first. Get comments on your drafts from others in your company and from outsiders whom you trust.

- **Finalize the mission statement.** Pull together the best of your ideas in a concise easy-to-understand mission statement. Try to get your ideas across in a few words but don't be afraid to show some emotion. Be sure the final mission statement captures the essence of what you want to accomplish in your business. It should be a mission statement that makes you proud.

After writing your mission statement you must communicate it to your employees. The best way to introduce the mission statement is in an employee meeting represented by a top officer or owner of the company. Go over the mission statement in detail during that meeting and give each employee a laminated wallet-size copy. At our firm, we also had small magnetic copies made so our employees could put them on their toolbox or refrigerator. Make signs of the mission statement to hang around the company. Include it in your employee handbook and employee newsletter. Regardless of the method you choose, it is imperative that you do an excellent job communicating the new mission statement to your employees.

It is also important to communicate your mission statement to your customers. You can do this through your customer newsletter, boat show displays or by including it with a customer mailing. Posting the mission statement or sign in the customer areas of your business also will help get out your message. Sharing your mission statement with your customers makes them feel valuable. It also gives them an idea of your goals and what they can expect from your organization.

Some managers don't want a mission statement because they are afraid it will constrain them. A mission statement is not a leash, it is an energizer. If you want your company to become a high-performance organization then create a mission statement. You will be surprised at the results as your organization starts redirecting the energy that it had been using to figure out what its mission was. Use this newly available energy to generate outstanding results for your company that will make customers and competitors alike say, "that man (or woman) is on a mission!"

Chapter 10
PREPARING YOUR STRATEGIC PLAN
June 1996

Most managers I speak with in our industry agree that a strategic plan can have a direct impact on a company's effectiveness and profits. They also acknowledge that a strategic plan can provide the vision and goals that every company needs. Despite this, it is interesting that many of these same managers do not have a strategic plan for their own businesses.

What causes managers who understand the importance of a strategic plan to avoid preparing one for their operation? Many believe that the strategic planning process is onerous and lengthy, and they may not even be sure how to go about it. This is unfortunate because preparing a strategic plan can be easy if you follow the right steps.

The first step in preparing a strategic plan is to understand its purpose: to improve your company's future results by helping you make better decisions today. This month's results, for example, are primarily the result of prior months' decisions. Therefore, if you want to positively impact your company's future results, the time to take action is today. A strategic plan helps you look at the future and decide what to do today to impact it.

The second step in preparing a strategic plan is to conduct a situation analysis, which is a summary of the company as it stands today. It should include a clear identification of your market, competition and all aspects of your business. A situation analysis should also include a summary of your company's financial condition and organization. Because you know your business well, this may seem unnecessary, but do it anyway. A situation analysis forces you to think about your business in ways you may not normally consider.

After preparing the situation analysis, the next step is to prepare a SWOT (strengths, weaknesses, opportunities and threats) analysis. An effective way to compile this is to list your company's strengths and weaknesses and then list the opportunities and threats associated with each. The more detailed you can be the better. One good way to get this data is to give your company's managers a questionnaire soliciting the information you need. After you obtain this information, you can summarize it concisely for inclusion in your strategic plan.

The next and most important step is to prepare your plan of action, which should be based on the information you gathered in the situation and SWOT analysis. It should include 10 key areas on which you need to focus. Identify the steps you need to take to help you achieve your objectives in each area. This is the heart and soul of your strategic plan because it provides the road map you follow to strengthen your operation.

The last step is preparing the executive summary that goes at the beginning of your strategic plan. This is a brief synopsis of your plan that summarizes its key points in one or two pages.

After you have completed these steps, bind the strategic plan in a folder with tabs for each of the sections. This will give your plan a professional appearance and make it easy to use.

These five steps are the basics of a strategic plan. In addition, there are other important things you should consider as you prepare the plan for your company:

- **Planned obsolescence.** Work on improvements that will obsolete what you do well today. Do not spend a lot of time getting better at something that won't be needed in the future.
- **Be creative.** Don't think that you can use today's solutions to solve tomorrow's problems.
- **Government regulation.** Don't complain about it; just get good at dealing with it. While others are complaining about something they cannot change, firms adept at dealing with government regulation will be gaining a real competitive advantage.
- **Focus.** Don't do something you can't be good at, and stay focused on those things that give you a real advantage in the long run. The wider your portfolio of advantages, the less risk you face in competitive battles.
- **Mission statement.** It is much easier to prepare a strategic plan if you have a mission statement (see page 49, May issue).
- **Competitive intelligence.** Learn as much as you can about your competition.
- **Think globally.** Your company either is or will be impacted by international market trends and developments.
- **Be realistic.** Try to minimize the gap between your desires and the most likely performance.

Whether your business is large or small, strategic planning is imperative. The process you go through to prepare is indispensable. It forces you to think about and deal with issues that you may not have otherwise considered.

The future of your company is not a mystery. It's a direct result of the actions you are taking today. Developing a strategic plan can go a long way toward brightening that future considerably.

Chapter 11
MANAGING YOUR VENDORS
July 1996

When you think of your vendors, what comes to mind? Before you answer the question, consider your vendors in the broadest sense. This includes suppliers of inventory, outside purchases and subcontractors.

If you are like most managers, you probably have a "love-hate" relationship with your vendors. You love them because they provide you with the essential elements of your business, but you also hate to be reliant on others for your success.

Successful businesses today are taking a very proactive approach to vendor management. They realize that vendors are an important link to providing customers the service they demand. Business managers also realize that a small improvement in vendor management can have a dramatic impact on a company's bottom line. This potent combination of improved customer service and profits attracts managers that are aggressively managing their companies.

Almost every company can improve their vendor management. Even if you believe your company is doing a good job in this area, you probably have room for improvement. Here are some steps that can help you improve your vendor management.

- **Remember, you are the customer.** This can easily be forgotten in the typical vendor relationship. You probably do a great job staying focused on your end retail customer, but don't forget that to the vendor you are the customer. You should demand to be treated like a customer and not like a middleman.

- **Identify your top vendors.** Many companies fail to specifically identify their largest vendors. At least annually, you should prepare a list of your top vendors in order of the dollar amount spent with them. You may be surprised who makes the list. This list should be used to help set priorities about whom you deal with when managing your vendors.

- **Visit your top vendors.** Visits can be a powerful tool for vendor management. You will be surprised how much you can learn about a vendor, their operations and your relationship with them during a one- to two-hour visit to their facility. This may require that you set aside three or four days for an extended visit and consultation, but the time spent will be well worth it.

- **Get the best price.** Use your improved relationship with the vendor to negotiate a good price for the items you are purchasing. If your cash flow permits, one very effective way to get vendor price concessions is to provide earlier payment. Remember, you won't get what you don't ask for, so be aggressive when shopping for a price. Also, don't rubber-stamp vendor invoices for payment, review them closely, just like your customers do.

- **Make them earn their money.** Have high expectations for your vendors. Hold your vendors to the same standards that your customers expect you to uphold.

- **If you give a credit, get a credit.** If you have to adjust a customer invoice because of a vendor problem, insist that the vendor give you an equal credit. If the vendor caused the problem, they should pay for the problem.

- **Ask vendors for training.** Your vendors have access, through their own organizations and the manufacturers that they purchase from, to training that can significantly help your team.

Don't be shy about asking your vendors to provide or arrange cost-free employee development. In some cases you may even want to open up this training to your customers.

- **Insist on continual improvement.** Ask your vendors to keep you updated on what they are doing to improve their operations and the service or products that they provide to you. Look for vendors who consider continual improvement an important part of their company's culture.

If you do all of the above it can have a significant positive impact on your business. However, there is another important component of vendor management that can't be left out. In fact, this component is critical in making the items listed above work; you must reward your vendors.

Vendors must know that if they are fair to you, and do the above, you will do your best to take care of and be loyal to them. Give vendors that are good to you exclusive parts of your business. Don't penny-pinch them on the little things if overall you are getting excellent pricing. Annually, hold a vendor appreciation lunch for your best vendors. Let them know that you appreciate their effort to help your business.

Rewarding your vendors is not inconsistent with the other steps above. It is part of an overall effective vendor management strategy and can make the other steps work more smoothly.

Effective vendor management is an important ingredient to the success of your business, but it is often overlooked. Give it the attention it deserves, and you will find that your operation has a powerful new support system.

Chapter 12
STAFF MEETINGS: THE WHY AND HOW
August 1996

At the bottom of almost every management problem is a communication problem. On the surface, communication seems simple, but for many managers, it is their biggest problem. If you are interested in communicating more effectively with your employees, consider holding regular staff meetings.

As simple as it seems, busy managers often overlook the benefits that can come from the effective use of regular staff meetings. Many of these managers do not feel comfortable communicating in a staff meeting environment and some even question the time devoted to these meetings.

Despite these concerns, regular staff meetings have many benefits. They send your employees the message that it is important to you to keep them updated and remind them of the important things going on around them. Meetings also remind employees what they have to say to you and their peers is important.

Regular staff meetings also can minimize speculation by an uninformed workforce. Employee speculation can be dangerous to your organization, but speculate is exactly what they will do if you are not communicating effectively. And the worst part is that employee speculation is almost always worse than the facts.

Many managers think that there are not enough topics to discuss in regular staff meetings. I usually find the opposite. Some topics you may want to consider for your staff meeting include:

- **Birthdays and anniversaries.** This may seem silly to you but most people love to be recognized.
- **Vacations.** Discussing vacation dates keeps everyone updated on the upcoming schedule and helps you plan for employee absences.
- **Upcoming training.** Hopefully, training is an important part of your company's culture. Use your staff meetings to stay focused on continuous improvement.
- **Changes in policies and procedures.** Update your team on both implemented and proposed changes. This also can help you reduce the number of memos, which are often very impersonal.
- **Other upcoming events.** Boat shows are a good example of an upcoming event you will want to discuss. Any other upcoming or internal events are also good topics for staff meetings.
- **Customer happenings.** Customers coming or going, potential or consummated sales or any other customer information is good to discuss. Customer preferences are also a good topic for these meetings.
- **Other important topics.** Use this time to update your staff on any other topics of interest or events related to the company.

After identifying topics you want to cover, you need to develop a format that maximizes the effectiveness of the meetings. You want your employees to believe that the meetings are productive. Some ways to do so include:

- **Hold staff meetings regularly.** I suggest weekly, but set up a schedule that works for your organization. Let everyone know the schedule so there is no need to call people every time you hold a meeting.

- **Keep them motivational.** This is a good time to focus on team building and sales.
- **Keep them fun.** The meetings should be interesting enough to keep people looking forward to them. You don't need to be comic but, when possible, keep it light.
- **Communicate clearly.** Employees will take you literally so be sure you are clear and direct in your communication. Also, be honest in your communication. Don't play mental games with your employees.
- **Look forward.** Staff meetings should focus on the future. It's OK to discuss the past but only as a point of reference regarding what you should do in the future. Unfortunately, many managers frequently make the mistake of focusing on the past when they should be focusing on the future.
- **Roundtable.** Go around the table and give everyone an opportunity to update the group on what they are working on or to ask questions.
- **Listen carefully.** Listening in staff meetings is as important as talking. By listening carefully you can pick up ideas to help your organization.

It is important that you keep information flowing in your organization. If your staff meeting is with supervisors, be sure that they take the information from your meeting and communicate it back to their employees. It is important that supervisors do more than just sit on the information you have provided them.

If you can get all of your employees operating in sync, your company's effectiveness will increase dramatically. The skillful use of staff meetings is a management tool that can help you and your team coordinate your energies, focus your effort and achieve the success your company deserves.

Chapter 13
TAPPING COMPUTER POWER
EFFECTIVELY
September 1996

The Road Ahead is a fascinating book about the future world of computers authored by Microsoft's chairman and founder, Bill Gates. I recently finished reading it with great interest.

It's clear that the future is going to be exciting. Computer capabilities are doubling every 18 months, and while no one knows what the exact results will be, one thing is certain: it will impact us all. Within 20 years, we will look back at today and wonder how we did without all the new technology that will be developed.

While it is interesting to think about future developments, most managers worry about the best way to manage information technology today. The environment is everything but stagnant and frequently confusing. Do I buy today or do I wait until the next technology breakthrough? Should I upgrade even if my current system works well? Do I need to be an expert myself or should I rely on others? These are all questions that managers consider every day. Below are some ideas that will help you when dealing with these and other computer issues:

- **Use an expert.** Even if you are skilled at working with computers, they can consume a lot of time. There are many computer consultants who can work with your system and allow you to focus on the bigger issues of running your business. Perhaps there is someone in your area who can help you with both hardware and software issues. If not, you may need one person for each. Also, there are a lot of people posing as experts who are not really that knowledgeable. Be sure to check references before you hire your experts.

- **Don't be afraid.** It's amazing to watch your children use a computer. My daughters, Erin and Amanda (ages 6 and 4), astonish me sometimes with their prowess. I believe that a big reason kids do so well on computers is that they are not afraid. If you are not computer savvy, just dig right in. Everything will be fine. Believe me.

- **Be familiar with the Internet.** Use of the "information highway" is growing at a phenomenal pace. You don't need to be an expert but you better be familiar with how others in the marine industry, including your competitors, are using the Internet. Many of them are trying to use the Internet as a marketing tool. If you are not already accessing it, you will be surprised at how much information is available to you.

- **Look for computer uses.** Look for ways to use a computer to improve the productivity of your business. At Rybovich, productivity improvements have allowed us to do twice the business with 20 percent fewer administrative staff. In addition to these savings, the operational uses for computers are limitless. Scheduling, CAD, CAM and other programs are helping many companies produce a better product with few resources.

- **Have a system that is customer-sensitive.** There has been a lot of discussion in the management world over the past few years regarding the importance of customer service. Your computer system is no exception. Ask your customers their opinion of your systems and, if necessary, make changes.

- **Don't feel pressed to have the latest.** If you are not careful, keeping up with the latest technology can be both intoxicating and addictive. If your system is accomplishing your objectives, don't feel like you have to be constantly upgrading. If you stay focused on always having the latest and greatest, it can be very distracting to your business.

- **Keep your employees trained.** As with any part of our business, it is important to train your employees well. I have seen many occasions when someone has used a program for years without realizing its best features. Along with the traveling computer seminars, many local colleges and computer stores offer inexpensive classes that can be as short as a half day. These classes can open up a whole new world to your employees.

- **Don't be a slave to your system.** A good system should be liberating, not enslaving. You have a problem if you hear people at our company saying things like, "That's a great idea but our systems won't let us do it." Be sure that you have a system that is flexible and can be changed to implement good ideas. You also need to be sure that the person in your company managing the information system is open to change. Unfortunately, many companies have people managing their computer systems who act like a demagogue instead of team players.

- **Back-up your files.** Today, this seems like very elementary advice, but it is still important. Back-up your system daily.

Your company's computer system can be your best tool or your worst nightmare. It can either improve your profits or cost you money. Good management of your system will provide you with benefits that will help keep your company consistently profitable for years to come.

Chapter 14
COST MANAGEMENT COSTS LITTLE
October 1996

Are the costs of operating your business too high? Do you understand the cost structure of your company? Unless you keep a close eye on business expenditures, your company's cost structure is probably too high.

Reducing your cost structure can be difficult. Most managers will acknowledge that you can justify or rationalize almost any expense, which can lead to big problems in cost management.

Unfortunately, once you've wasted dollars on unnecessary expenses, they will never be recouped, and this waste often compounds yearly. This lost revenue can significantly reduce the amount of money you have to invest in your company's future. When you waste expense dollars it also reduces the amount of profit available to be shared among owners and employees.

A hidden cause of an excessive cost structure - one that many managers don't realize - is its customer impact. Customers will pay a fair price for your product but they will only pay for the value you create, not resources you waste.

If you force customers to pay a higher price to cover your excessive expense levels, it will have a negative long-term impact because they won't come back and pay your high prices again.

You also take the risk of having a closely operating competitor enter the market and steal your customers away. To be competitive you must have a cost structure that allows you to offer attractive pricing.

Even though it seems simple, cost-cutting can be difficult. Following are some ideas that can help you take a fresh look at your company's cost structure:

- **Have a "zero-based" budget. A** budget will force you to take a detailed look at your expenses at least annually. More importantly, a zero-based budget looks at each expense independent of what was spent in past years. Don't just take last year's expense and adjust it; start with the question, "Do we need to spend this at all?"
- **Be creative.** Look at each expense and consider what would happen if you didn't spend that money. Consider ways to avoid the expense and save money.
- **Reduce fixed costs.** These stay the same regardless of sales levels. Variable costs directly correlate to sales amounts. In most cases, you should try to convert your fixed costs to variable.

For example, consider using temporary employees to help you during your busy season, instead of hiring someone you must pay and give benefits to all year. Reducing your company's fixed costs can be a big step toward ensuring long-term profitability.

Don't worship the "sacred cows," kill them. You must be prepared to eliminate waste regardless of where it's found. If you want to operate "lean and mean," cut costs everywhere in your organization.

- **Have good cost information.** You should have an accounting system that provides good cost information quickly. This information should include itemized costs that are meaningful to you, the manager. If your accounting system or manager isn't providing you with good information, find out why.

- **Compare your costs to others'.** Find out what other boatyards, dealerships or marinas are spending. Ask some of your peers or contacts - with whom you have a good relationship - what they regularly spend on their business.
- **Search out published financial information**. Trade magazines regularly publish financial statistics of interest to boating businesses. Universities with business schools may have them too.
- **Stay focused on costs.** This may be the most important factor. Many managers think about costs only when they review their monthly financial statements. If you stay focused on your cost structure every day, most other expense-related concerns will fall into place by themselves.

Many managers bristle at the idea of cost-cutting. They may argue that it's impossible to grow a company through cost reduction. Though there is truth to this argument, you'd better have an appropriate cost structure for your sales levels or prepare to go out of business before your company even gets a chance to grow.

Your company must live within its means. While cost management requires a continuous focus, if you stay vigilant, your company will have the opportunity to improve its long term prospects and - in some cases - even ensure its survival.

Chapter 15
TASK FORCES CREATE SOLUTIONS
November 1996

At a recent boat show, I spoke with someone in the boating industry who runs a well respected company. We discussed an issue that has been plaguing his company.

It wasn't a big issue, but one that - if solved - could make the lives of his employees and customers a little easier. He had intended to deal with the problem before, but just didn't take the time to focus on it.

Does your company have nagging problems like this that just won't go away? Do you have a management issue that you just can't seem to solve?

Unfortunately, these avoidable problems can result in substantial amounts of lost profit. Many of these problems could be resolved by using a "task force."

I imagine some readers are already cringing. A task force may seem like a "bureaucratic animal" created only to waste time in meetings, instead of solving problems. Sure, it can turn into that, if not properly managed.

However, a properly managed task force can be a powerful source of solutions for your company, providing you with the focus you need to get through difficult problems.

A task force is a group of people who meet periodically to focus on a specific problem. They meet until they resolve the problem and then the group is dissolved. Taskforce groups have been used successfully to reduce costs, improve communication within a company, effectively spend budgeted funds and make invoices easier for customers to understand.

If you would like to implement task force groups in your company, follow these steps:

- **Identify the problem.** Select a problem that you've wanted to focus on, but haven't had the time to devote to. If the topic is one that generates employee interest and excitement, your task force may have a greater chance of success.
- **Select the task force group.** Choose employees who are closest to the problem and would most like to see it resolved. You also may want to pick an "outsider" who can offer the group a broader perspective, or someone who will spread the enthusiasm of the group.
- **Identify the goal.** Be specific and make sure the goal is attainable. Write the goal down and emphasize it at the beginning and end of every task force meeting. If the group begins to lose focus during the meetings, go over the goal again.
- **Identify the issues.** The group should list all the problems that need to be solved to achieve the goal. Don't cut this step out or limit it, and don't worry if the list is exhaustive.
- **Brainstorm.** Everyone in the group should have a chance to list all of their possible solutions. All solutions should be considered and none should be criticized at this step. Try to be creative when identifying possible solutions.
- **Create a plan of action.** This is a "to do" list of the solutions that you want to implement. It is imperative that you achieve accountability by assigning someone responsible for every item on the list, with a firm completion date.

- **Follow up.** Meet with the task force team a few weeks after creating your plan of action to ensure that it is being properly carried out.
- **Keep the meetings short.** Never let them go over an hour. If you meet for a full hour, quit wherever you are, and schedule another meeting for the next week. Err on the side of making the meetings too short rather than too long.
- **Dissolve the group.** After the problem has been solved, end the task force. Don't let it drag out. You should form a completely new task force for any further problems you want to tackle.

These steps work best if employees know the task force is important to you, their boss. Make it important and reinforce it with your words and actions. Create the expectation that the task force will achieve its stated goal.

Don't waste any more of your company's resources dealing with a problem that can be resolved. Create a task force to deal with it and move on to bigger and better things.

Chapter 16
TAKING INVENTORY: A NECESSARY EVIL
January 1997

When was the last time you counted your company's inventory? If a year has passed since your last count, you may have a problem. Assessing inventory at least annually is considered a necessary exercise by most well-run companies.

Despite its importance, taking a physical inventory can strike fear in the heart of many managers. Granted, it is a difficult process, but counting your inventory can benefit your company in many ways.

An inventory can help you improve the accuracy of your costing, provide better financial information, ensure your tax returns are accurate and help identify possible internal control problems.

It can also improve cash flow. You probably have a large cash investment in your inventory and an accurate count can help you identify areas to reduce stock.

The following ideas can be helpful when you are ready to begin.

- **Reduce your inventory before the count.** Make the process as easy as possible by purchasing nothing but essentials for a few weeks before the count.
- **Get help if you need it.** If you are not comfortable managing the inventory count yourself, ask your accountant - or someone else with experience in this area to help you.

- **Formalize your procedures.** Write out your procedures and distribute them to everyone participating in the count. It is important that everyone understands not only what needs to be done but also why they are doing it.
- **Control your count sheets.** Number the count sheets before you begin counting and be sure to account for all sheets at the end of the count. Missing sheets can result in an inaccurate count.
- **Count "floor to sheet."** When your staff is counting inventory, have them "sweep" the floor (proceed from one side of the room or area to another) and record all quantities on the count sheets.

  Resist the temptations to simply run computer printouts of items in stock, and then have your staff just go check to see if all the items are on the shelf. This is a sure way to miss items that should be counted.
- **Mark off counted areas.** After you have counted certain areas mark them off with tape to ensure no one counts that area again.
- **Audit the counts.** Have someone responsible for checking the counts. They should be directed to take any variances seriously. Research every variance and if you find problems, you may need to recount.

Remember that test counts are just a sample, so you must do more than just fix the problems found. Consider how these problems may carry over in the overall count.

- **Segregate obsolete items.** An accurate inventory count for accounting purposes should not include obsolete items. However, you should keep a separate list of these items so they can be promptly liquidated.

- **Obtain good inventory software.** Once you have taken the counts, you should have them input into an inventory program that will summarize the information.
- **Manage the input process.** Be sure the counts are input correctly. Control the input of sheets and audit this process as you did the counts.
- **Get a good "cutoff."** Cutoff refers to the importance of ensuring that you record on your books - in the proper period - all sales and deliveries received before or after your count.

Effective communication to employees before and during the count can make the inventory process go smoothly. Be sure that all employees know their role in the process.

After you have finished the count, your accountant should compare it to what you have on your books and help you summarize and analyze the results.

The process of counting your inventory may bring to light issues you might not have previously considered. In some cases, this may be the most important reason to take a count.

For example, you may find that your company stocks parts for an engine line you no longer service, or you might find items you didn't know you carried. In general, taking an inventory can help you assess how effectively your operation manages its inventory.

Chapter 17
WHAT IS YOUR COMPANY'S CULTURE?
February 1997

We all know stories of owners who seemed to work hard but lost their companies anyway. Their companies went out of business despite their best intentions.

As hard as it is to think about, the same can happen to you if you don't successfully manage your company's culture.

Your company's culture is probably not something you think about regularly, even though it reflects the core beliefs of your employees. The culture is not necessarily the beliefs espoused by the owners or management but instead is what the employees actually accept.

It is the soul of a company, what is actually important in the business and what is truly driving the organization. It can be negative or positive but every company has a culture.

You may be wondering how you can find out what your company's culture is. Your real company culture is what a new employee learns during the first few days on break or at lunch.

It is what your other employees tell this new employee about what is important at the company. In fact, it may be much easier for a new employee to learn your real company culture than it will be for you.

Regardless of your current culture, one thing is sure: if you don't actively manage your company culture, it probably will evolve into something that you don't want it to be.

Answer the following question as honestly as you can. "Which of the following three concepts is more important to the success of our company: taking care of customers, taking care of employees, or taking care of your company's owners?"

If you picked customers, you are in good company. I have asked this question in the past when speaking to industry groups and almost always most of the hands go up for customers. While customer service is obviously important, it is not the "correct" answer.

The most effective company cultures treat customers, employees and owners equally. Maybe it was a bit of a trick question, but it makes the point. If you want your company to be successful, take all three groups mentioned into equal consideration.

By overly favoring customers, you may alienate the employees you rely on and give away the owner's rightful return. If you treat employees better than other groups, you may not receive the necessary customer service and financial return. If you focus on the owners' needs more than customers' or employees' needs, customer service will suffer.

When considering these ideas many managers' first reaction is to reduce work in whichever of these three areas they emphasize the most. That's the wrong approach.

Instead, increase your emphasis in the other two areas so all three are equal. Once they are equal you can work on increasing your emphasis in all three.

Other ways you can develop an effective company culture are:

- **Stay focused on culture.** Accept the importance of your company's culture. When making decisions regarding your company, be sure they are consistent with the culture you want to maintain.
- **Use your mission statement.** When developing our company mission statement, we made sure that customers, employees and owners were all included.

- **Discuss financial results.** Share the financial results of the company. It helps everyone keep things in perspective.
- **Communicate.** At the root of almost every management problem is a communication problem. Use every opportunity to communicate to your employees the importance of taking care of customers and owners. At the same time be sure to emphasize with owners the importance of taking care of employees.
- **Train, train, train.** The more you develop your employees, the better off your company will be. Try to get your employees to "see the big picture."

Most managers in our industry consider themselves too busy to sit around and contemplate their company's culture. If you internalize the above concepts it will not take much time at all. Instead, it becomes a part of you and the way you do business.

Don't expect an overnight change in your company's culture once you begin to focus on it. Culture changes take time but are well worth the effort in the long run. Commit the time and watch the results.

Chapter 18
AVOID THE COLLECTION HEADACHE
March 1997

It probably seems like you never run out of management issues to consider. You struggle to keep up with all the latest ideas. You work to keep your customers, employees, and owners happy, and try to stay focused on profits. With everything you must consider it's easy to forget that your company must eventually get paid for its services and sales.

There is no good management reason to grant customers credit. However, there may be some good marketing reasons to do so. If you don't have a good marketing reason, discontinue all credit policies.

If you do grant credit, it's likely that your company has collection problems. You will always find that some of your customers get in over their heads financially, and other customers just don't pay at all. Regardless of the reason, you need to have a good collection program in place. Our company's collection program has resulted in a de minimis bad debt expense for several years.

To reduce your chance of bad debt expense, consider implementing the following:

- **Have a good credit application.** This provides you with information about your customers. It should ask customers for their address, phone, social security number and credit references. It also should include language that makes the customers personally liable for charges if they use a corporation.

- **Be sure to verify all the information** your customer gives you and to check their credit references. If you find discrepancies, don't grant them credit.

- **Run a credit report.** It is fairly inexpensive to find a credit agency that can provide you with information about customers who want credit. When you sign up for the service, be sure that the agency provides you with training on how to use the information.

- **Make one person in your company responsible for handling collections.** Theresa handles the collections at our company. She is persistent and effective because it is her responsibility to collect on debts owed to the company, and she is accountable.

    You must have one person who is responsible to collect your receivables. If several people are responsible for this duty, ultimately no one will be responsible.

- **Check your aging weekly.** Frequently review your receivables aging to look for problems. Experience in doing this will give you an intuitive sense for accounts that can turn into problems.

- **Have a past-due list.** This list should include past-due accounts, any notes regarding the accounts and steps taken to collect them. It should be reviewed frequently by an officer of your company.

- **Send collection notices quickly.** You should send personalized collection letters to customers immediately after their account becomes past due. State in the letter that this account is past due, the amount due and that you expect immediate payment. Keep it short, clear and specific. Many times this letter will be all the collection effort that is needed.

- **Follow up with a phone call.** If you don't get an immediate response to your letter, call the customer. Ask them to send a payment today. If they cannot send a check today, ask them what it will take, specifically, to settle the account. Keep calling until you get it resolved.

- **Speak to the right person.** When making your collection calls be sure to find the right person to pursue. Ask point blank, "Do you have the authority to approve this for payment today?" If they don't, find the right person.

- **Watch for warning signs.** You may have a good customer who starts paying slowly; who is no longer reachable, telephone messages unreturned and frequent excuses. If you start getting warning signs, be prepared to get aggressive with your collection techniques.

- **Get outside help.** Hopefully your collection problems won't get this far. This is when you need a collection agency or attorney to help you collect. Good collection agencies seem hard to find, but most will work on a contingency. This means that if they don't collect, you don't pay. Ask other marine industry firms in your area who they use for their collection needs.

- **Get a legal review.** Have your attorney review your collection process to be sure you are doing everything within the law. Every state has different laws that apply in this area, so find an attorney who is familiar with your state's regulations.

Your attorney can also help you with legalities such as UCC filings, personal guarantees and letters of credit. Be sure to ask your attorney if there is anything else you should consider.

Chapter 19
HAPPY CUSTOMERS, HAPPY COMPANY
April 1997

Would your company's profits improve if its customer service improved? If your company is like most others, even small improvements in customer service can result in big increases in profits.

No matter how well you understand the importance of customer service, it will not be part of your company's culture until your employees understand its importance. Even if your employees do understand how crucial customer service is, it is still your job to show them the steps they need to take to keep your customers happy.

Keep customers happy by exceeding their expectations. The movies I enjoy the most are the ones for which I have no expectations before I go to see them. However, I am frequently disappointed by movies that my friends have raved about. My expectations cause my disappointment.

If you can exceed your customers' expectations, you will always provide good service. This can be tough for those of us who work for companies with great reputations. Customers come to us with high expectations, so we must work hard to exceed them.

You may have heard the phrase, "The customer's perception is reality." To deliver good customer service, you must control the customer's perception.

First impressions stick, or as the saying goes, "You don't get a second chance to make a first impression." Your company's and employees' appearances are always important. You should be clean, neat and smiling. Don't forget that you can say more with nonverbal communication than with words.

You must also properly train your employees in good customer service. Instruct your supervisors to train employees as follows:

- **Have a good attitude.** No matter what else is happening, employees must always present an upbeat attitude to customers.
- **Make the customers feel important.** Compliment customers and use their first names frequently. Everyone loves to hear their name used. This will help employees establish rapport with customers. Many customers will return to certain companies because they like the employees there and because the employees make them feel important.
- **Listen carefully.** You can easily learn your customers' expectations if you listen carefully. Most customers will share them with you if they get the chance.

    You can also learn about other opportunities to serve the customer - and generate sales - by listening carefully. Everyone likes to be listened to, especially someone who is paying you to work for them.
- **Imagine that you're the customer.** If you would be satisfied with the service your company offers, most likely your customers will also be satisfied. However, you have to be careful. You must honestly put yourself in their situation and not approach it from your point-of-view as a business owner or manager.
- **Take personal responsibility.** Every employee in your company must take responsibility to exceed your customers' expectations. This is why some companies deliberately don't have a quality control inspector - because they want all employees to be responsible for ensuring customer satisfaction.

- **Recover "fumbles."** During a football game, what happens when there is a fumble? Everyone dives for it! The same thing should happen in your company if there is a customer problem. Every employee from the top down should dive in until the customer is happy. It's better to have too many people working on the problem than not enough.
- **Don't leave customers hanging.** Never leave them waiting for something either. Always be sure that every customer encounter has closure.

If you follow these steps, your customers will leave feeling good about your organization and its employees. You may also want to monitor customer satisfaction. The best way I know is to mail surveys to all customers after you have served them.

The survey should be sent with a cover letter thanking them for their business and explaining the purpose of the survey. It also should include a self-addressed, stamped envelope to make it easy for customers to respond. You can easily develop this survey by simply asking customers what is important to them and whether they would rate your company as successful in the area of customer service.

Finally, never forget that the customer, not us, is the judge of good customer service. No matter how hard we try, if the customer isn't happy, we have failed. However, if you take the time to follow the above steps, you may find that your customers are happy and your profits will improve.

Chapter 20
MANAGER'S TUNNEL VISION:
AN "INBRED" DISEASE
May 1997

I've been lucky. I have had the opportunity to visit all 50 U.S. states and over twenty countries. My wife and I love to travel and visit new places with our daughters.

One reason that I love to travel is because of how it changes my perspective. For example, the first time I visited New York City I expected to be robbed and to witness a murder.

"Scared" did not completely describe how I felt. However, I learned that the "Big Apple" is quite different from what I thought it would be. In fact, I love visiting this city and have re-visited it probably 20 times. I broadened my perspective.

The same thing can happen to you as a manager. If you are not careful, it can be easy to manage with a distorted perspective.

The most common form of distorted management perspective occurs when companies or their managers become "inbred." An inbred manager is one who rarely ventures outside the organization or beyond their horizons.

Unfortunately, it is easy to become complacent over the years as you become comfortable in your position, especially if your results are good. However, the long-term results of being inbred can be disastrous.

Your organization may wake up one day to find that its more

progressive competitors have passed it by. Managers who let this happen are often replaced.

Don't let this happen to you. Continually take steps to broaden your managerial horizons. Here are a few tips to help you.

- **Continue your education.** Take advantage of your local community college or technical schools to learn more about business or technical topics. Usually these courses are inexpensive but still provide valuable knowledge and insight.

   Also, keep an eye out for traveling seminars that come through your area. They are usually one-day seminars, and my company has found many of them useful for managers and employees.

- **Network in your industry.** Get to know other managers. Many times ideas shared over lunch can be helpful to you and your lunch partner. You will probably find the other managers' problems are similar to yours. Sometimes it's nice to know that you're not the only one dealing with problems.

- **Network outside your industry.** Companies outside your industry have many good ideas that can be used by our company. Don't think that your own industry is unique.

- **Go to boat shows.** This may seem obvious, but if you are not in sales it may be easy to justify skipping some shows in your area. Boat shows can be a great way to broaden your horizons.

- **Visit competitors.** Be sure to know what is going on with your competitors. Sometimes just strolling through their location can give you some great ideas to implement at your business.

- **Attend industry conferences.** This can be a good way to network, attend a boat show and seminars and visit competitors all at once.

- **Read.** Your local bookstore may have a number of good books that can help you. Even if you are not a big reader, force yourself to occasionally read a work-related book. Trade magazines can also be a good source of industry information and new ideas.

- **Talk with employees.** Employees have a funny way of broadening your perspective in a hurry. Listen to their comments. Many times they know what is really happening in your company.

You may find that it can be exhilarating to expand your horizons. It feels good to learn new things and implement them in your company, especially when they have an impact on your bottom line.

Be sure to give your employees many of the same opportunities to grow that you allow yourself. It will help keep their morale high and increase their effectiveness and value to your company.

Business today is competitive and tough, especially in the boating industry. Profits don't come easily. If you want to stay competitive and profitable, be sure you continually improve. It will help you and your company achieve the success you deserve.

Chapter 21
DON'T "DE-MOTIVATE" YOUR EMPLOYEES
June 1997

Odds are that you want to be successful. However, no matter how badly you want to be successful, you will not achieve success without the cooperation and support of your employees.

Sounds tough? Well, maybe it is, but there is no denying that your company's profits, customer service and overall success depend on the people who work for you. If you have motivated employees, success will come easy; if your employees are not motivated, you probably have a tough road ahead of you.

Unfortunately, motivating employees is very complicated. Every employee is different and every manager has their own individual style. It can be difficult finding the right combination of management techniques to keep your employees motivated and your company on the right track.

Sometimes it helps to put yourself into your employees' shoes. Try to think about what would motivate you. After dealing with an employee, think to yourself, "How would I react if a boss treated me like I just treated that employee?"

Chances are that the employee's reaction is close to what yours would be. Just because you're a manager does not mean that your emotional or motivational needs have changed.

It is much easier to "de-motivate" employees than it is to motivate them. Managers are people, too, and it's a good bet that you have your share of bad days.

It is hard to constantly be a great motivator. Despite this, there are some things that you can do to avoid de-motivating your employees, such as:

- **Avoid making veiled comments.** Some managers like to make their critical points indirectly. They try to be subtle and even joke or kid with employees to make their point.

  Don't do this, for it can be confusing and discouraging to employees. If you need to communicate something to your employees, be direct. Of course, you should be diplomatic. But think about it - don't you prefer people to be direct with you?

- **Don't focus only on small details.** It is frustrating to employees when they explain a problem or proposal to you and instead of dealing with the "big picture," you nitpick about a small detail. It is tempting to do this when you are not sure how to handle the issue the employee has brought to your attention. It is much better to say that you want to think about the issue than to put off your decision by picking on a detail.

- **Don't change for the sake of change alone.** If an employee brings you a proposal, don't change it unless it is necessary. Avoid feeling as though you must put your imprint on the proposal by making small changes.

It can be discouraging to employees when you make small changes to their proposals or work that are not important. You're the boss and both you and the employee know that you can make whatever change you want, so let the employee work with their idea. Of course, you have a responsibility to correct errors, but for the sake of the employee try to avoid being picky.

There are some steps you can take to help motivate employees, such as:

- **Be supportive.** Find things employees are doing in their jobs that you can praise. Positive reinforcement is a wonderful management tool. Try not to be negative, even on topics unrelated to employees.
- **Encourage creativity and risk-taking.** Reward and reinforce new ideas. Encourage employees to come to you with new ways of doing things. One of the worst things you can do is to make someone regret talking to you, even if they are being critical of you.
- **Be consistent.** We all have good and bad days. However, one of the best things you can do to ensure positive employee motivation is to be consistent.
- **Offer chances to improve.** Another way you can motivate employees is to offer them chances to improve. This can be achieved through training or learning a new responsibility within the company.

Obviously, there are many more ways to keep your employees motivated. However, by implementing these ideas you can take a big step toward having a motivated workforce that will certainly improve your company's results. These ideas are simple ways to improve not only your company's profits, but also your performance as a manager.

Chapter 22
MANAGE CASH FLOW TO THRIVE
July 1997

You have probably heard the phrase "cash is king." Cash is the lifeblood of your business and ultimately is the most important measurement of your success.

Many companies have been profitable - as measured by generally accepted accounting principles - only to find that they had to close their doors. This is because they did not properly manage their cash flow.

Unfortunately, the same thing can happen to you. Each month you may review financial statements that show a profit without realizing that you are on the verge of losing your company because of poor cash flow management.

Managing your cash flow is not always easy. Odds are that you are not an accountant, and the terms such as "working capital," "payables," "receivables" and "capitalization of assets" are confusing.

Fortunately, accountants don't have a lock on the best ways to manage your company's cash flow. Any manager can effectively manage a company's cash flow by focusing on a few important factors.

When many managers think of cash flow management they think about slowing disbursements. That can be only one aspect of managing your cash.

There are other simple steps you can take to better manage your cash flow and help ensure the long-term viability of your business:

- **Monthly reporting.** Your monthly financial statements should include a statement of cash flow, which shows you where your cash comes from and where it is going. It should be in a format that is useful and easy for you to understand.
- **Daily reporting.** Your company should have an end-of-the-day cash report, listing all cash received and all disbursements made during the day.

  An end-of-the-day cash balance can then be calculated on the report by adding the day's activity to the prior day's cash balance. This daily report should be reconciled to your general ledger at least weekly. Review this report closely and ask for details of any unusual items.
- **Bank reconciliation.** Reconcile your bank statements to your general ledger each month. Be sure that the person who prepares this reconciliation is not responsible either for cash receipts or disbursements. A monthly bank reconciliation is imperative - don't let it slide.
- **Forecast cash.** The process of forecasting your cash needs is as important as the actual reports that you generate. You must look ahead to determine your cash needs. By making projections, it will force you to think ahead about many aspects of your business.
- **Manage acquisitions.** Avoid acquiring long-term assets with short-term operating cash. Some assets rightfully have a payback period of several years. Typically, you will want to lease or finance these long-term asset purchases.
- **Line of credit.** Even if you don't use it, you will need to have a line of credit. Plan for the unexpected. A line of credit is also a good way to build a relationship with your local bank.
- **Deposits.** When you have to put out money in advance, don't be shy about asking your customers for deposits. It not only improves your cash flow, but also helps secure the sale.

- **Invest short-term cash.** If you have a sizable short-term cash balance, ask your banker how to best use it. Some banks will use this balance to credit toward your bank fees. Another option is to consider investing it in overnight securities. Your banker should be able to help you decide the best way to handle these funds.
- **Collect, collect, collect.** You are in business to get paid, so don't be shy about collecting your money.
- **Manage discounts.** Most of the time, it makes sense to take discounts offered by your vendors. Ask any vendor not presently giving you a discount what they can offer you. Be sure to delay payments to vendors that will not offer you a discount.

As you manage your cash, keep in mind that a declining cash balance does not necessarily mean that business is bad. Frequently, it means that business is great. Companies typically see their cash balances drop as their sales grow.

Accounts receivable, inventories and unbilled work all increase along with your expenses when sales take off. The effect can be a real cash crunch.

Your company's long-term survival may depend upon how well you manage your cash flow today. Follow the above steps and improve the odds of your company's future being both long and profitable.

Chapter 23
CREATE A "PERSONAL" MISSION STATEMENT
August 1997

I find it extremely gratifying when I can help someone through my columns or management speeches. I am not a consultant; I write and speak for "fun" and to be helpful, not to make a living. This fact made a recent experience I had all the more meaningful.

After I finished speaking about customer service at an American Boat Builders and Repairers Association (ABBRA) conference in Annapolis, MD., several people in the audience approached me. One of them was a man whom I consider to be a leader in our industry. I was anxious to talk to him because I respect his opinion and I was curious about his thoughts on my presentation.

Before he made any comment about the presentation, he mentioned a speech I had made nearly two years ago at a conference in Newport, RI. At the time, I had discussed the importance of having a "personal mission statement" and reviewing it regularly. He said that my comments on that topic had helped him immensely.

Afterward, I couldn't stop thinking about this man's comment, even though we had only discussed this briefly. On the flight home the next day, I continued to think about it.

I hate to admit it, but the reason his comment haunted me was that

I have been somewhat remiss recently in reviewing my own personal mission statement. It had been at least three months since I had read it.

Shortly after arriving home, I pulled out my personal mission statement. It invigorated me to read it. I realized again the power that such a document can have on your life.

Many people drive through life without such a roadmap and get nowhere. This is my roadmap, and I knew that by following it, I was becoming a better and more productive person. It excited me.

I have written and spoken about the importance of having a mission statement and a strategic plan for your business. It is equally important to have one for yourself. It will make both your personal and business life significantly more productive.

Creating your personal mission statement is relatively easy. It is a matter of identifying major areas of your life and listing your goals in each of those areas. Areas I have listed are:

- **Family.** This section includes not only my family goals, but also my goals for my daughters. This area is important. If you are having problems at home, it is almost impossible to keep them from affecting you on your job.

- **Career.** Studies have shown that people who have career goals are much more likely to be successful professionally. This section should cover not only future positions you would like to obtain, but also objectives you would like to accomplish in your current position.

- **Community service.** By the way, there is nothing wrong with directing your involvement in community service in such a way that provides you with business opportunities.

- **Self-improvement.** I believe that everyone should be focused on improving themselves. Don't be stagnant or content. You should constantly be looking for opportunities to improve both your business and personal skills.

Read books, take a class or seminar or just try something new, but always stay focused on making yourself better. It will make you feel better and will protect both your job and your company.

- **Financial.** These are your goals regarding your savings, retirement funds, home, debt and your children's college tuition. Time flies, and it is never too early to think about these topics.

After you have identified your goals in each of these areas, summarize them in a typewritten form. You now have a personal mission statement. Be sure to put it in a place that forces you to review it frequently. You will be surprised at the difference it can make in your life.

Having a personal mission statement and staying focused on it can make your entire life - not just the business part - more productive and satisfying.

I haven't read the personal mission statement of the man who made the comment to me after my recent seminar. However, by knowing him, I would guess that he has something in his mission statement about helping others. His brief comment was certainly a helpful reminder to me, and, hopefully, by reading this column, I will be helpful to you.

Chapter 24
READING FOR MANAGEMENT'S SAKE
September 1997

I love to read. In fact, I read close to a hundred books a year. While only 10 or 15 percent of these books relate to business, I try to read about a dozen books a year on various management topics.

Reading is a great way to improve your management skills and effectiveness. It is a cheap and easy way not only to broaden your horizons but also to pick up new ideas that will help you directly and immediately.

People frequently ask me to recommend books that they can read to help them become better managers. Following is a list of some of the books - with their author's last names in parentheses - that I have found helpful as a manager:

- *The 7 Habits of Highly Effective People* (Covey) - This is the only book I have read twice. It does a great job of identifying principles that you can implement to improve your effectiveness in all areas of your life.
- *The Great Game of Business* (Stack) - This is an excellent book that not only explains the benefits of unleashing and empowering your employees but also tells you how to do it. The book also makes a strong argument for why you should share your company's financial information with your employees.

- *Emotional Intelligence* (Goleman) - This book will give you insight into the emotional aspects of managing employees. It explains why you sometimes have problems with your smart employees, while those employees who are not as smart excel.

- *Learned Optimism* (Seligman) - This book is more than just another positive mental attitude book, it explains the importance of dealing with people from an optimistic perspective. It includes a test to measure your level of optimism and explains how you can break out of the cycle of defeat.

- *Control your Destiny or Some Else Will* (Welch) - General Electric Chief Executive Officer Jack Welch shares his secrets of success.

- *The Wall Street Journal on Managing* (Asian) - This book is a compilation of management articles from the "Managers Journal" column published in the *Wall Street Journal.*

- *Return on Quality* (Rust, Zahorik, Keiningham) - Have you ever wondered if your quality program is really paying off? This book gives you the tools you need to figure that out. Many companies have implemented quality programs only to be disappointed with the financial results. The authors demonstrate not only the importance of creating an accountable quality program but also how to create one that allows you to measure its results.

- *The Super Chiefs* (Heller) - This book profiles many of today's most successful CEOs and discusses their methods of achieving peak performance from their organizations. You 'll find it full of ideas that you can use to improve the performance of yourself and your organization.

- *The Best of Chief Executive* (Donlon) - This is a compilation of articles published in *Chief Executive* magazine. The articles offer sound advice on a wide range of topics.

- **One Minute Manager** (Blanchard) - This book proves that it is possible to simplistically convey a very powerful management message. Everyone who manages people should read it.
- *The Virtual Corporation* (Davido & Malone)-Through their study of successful and competitive companies, the authors of this book have created a synthesis of ideas that will help your company improve its performance.
- **Brain Longevity** (Khalsa) - Once I started reading this book I couldn't put it down. I have recommended it to several other people who - when they read it - had the same comment. Even though it is not a management book, it may be the most important book on this list.

Much of your management success depends on your ability to stay at peak mental performance. This book gives you specific suggestions to help you improve your concentration, energy level and learning ability.

These are some of my favorites; they may or may not be for you. You probably also have a favorite management book that has been helpful to you. If you wish to share its title, send me the name of the book and its author. I'll read your suggestions and compile another list of recommendations for a future column.

In the meantime, try reading a few of these books. You are probably as busy as I am, but try to carve out a few minutes each day to improve yourself through reading. It will help you reach your potential as a manager and give you ideas to improve your company and its profitability.

Chapter 25
IF YOU CRITICIZE, MAKE IT CONSTRUCTIVE
October 1997

You have an employee who generally does an outstanding job. Your problem is that there is one thing that you want them to do differently.

You know that, despite being an excellent employee, their feelings get hurt easily. They are sensitive, and you are not sure how to correct them.

Or, you may have an employee who does not do a good job and is a real problem. You don't want to fire them, but you find it is almost impossible to correct their actions. This employee tends to get defensive and to blow up when you try to give them some constructive criticism.

Both of these situations are difficult. Giving employees effective criticism is one of the toughest jobs a manager must do. It is also one of the most important.

Criticizing employees is painstaking, for both the manager and the employee. The manager dreads it because they are not sure how the employee will react. The employee, despite their desire for feedback, whether good or bad, dreads it because criticism frequently gets delivered as a personal affront.

A study done by a psychology magazine reported that inept criticism is the main reason for conflict on the job. It is a managerial minefield.

Despite the difficulties, I have heard it said that feedback is the breakfast of champions, the lifeblood of a healthy organization. Your employees need feedback; without it they feel left in the dark and frustrated.

They cannot make you happy without your feedback. Unfortunately for managers, sometimes necessary feedback is negative.

When you must correct an employee:

- **Do it immediately.** Don't frustrate yourself by letting the problem fester. Usually, problems don't correct themselves. It's not fair to you or the employee to postpone dealing with the situation.
- **Know your goal.** Before you speak with an employee, be sure that you know what you want to accomplish. Don't expect the employee to know what to do if you don't even know.
- **Avoid personal attacks.** This is probably the most important point. Focus on the employee's work ethic or character. If the employee perceives the criticism as a personal affront, you will accomplish nothing and probably magnify the problem.
- **Be specific.** Limit the criticism to the specific points you want corrected. Be sure the employee knows that the criticism is not pervasive, but is limited to a specific behavior.
- **Do it quickly.** Don't belabor your point or get caught up in listening to yourself talk. Say what needs to be said and move on. The employee will pick up the problem quickly and does not want or need to be told repeatedly.
- **Offer a solution.** Don't leave the employee wondering what they should do. Be specific in what you want them to do, don't be ambiguous. If you think it would be helpful, put your solution in writing.

- **Be optimistic.** Avoid being adversarial at all costs. Be as positive as you can and focus on the future. Explain to the employee the benefits of making the change you want.
- **Do it in person.** Never criticize an employee by memo. Of course, it is fine to follow up a face-to-face meeting in writing, or give the employee something in writing when you meet. But don't try to get off that easy because it rarely works. If the employee is in another city or state, at least discuss the criticism on the phone.
- **Put yourself in their situation.** Just because you are the boss doesn't really make you any different as a person. Most times the meeting in which you correct an employee will go smoothly if you treat the employee how you would want to be treated.

The suggestions I've listed work better if you have a good, ongoing relationship with your employees and they trust you. You don't need to be your employees' "best buddy," but you should have a friendly relationship built on good communication.

How we correct our employees is one of the most important factors in determining how content they are in their jobs. In a nutshell, employees just want to feel they are treated fairly. When you treat employees fairly, it results in higher productivity levels - and that means higher profits for your company.

Chapter 26
BE ACCOUNTABLE TO
ACCOUNTS PAYABLE
January 1998

There is one part of your business that can be easy to ignore, even though it affects your cash flow, profits, tax liability, accuracy of financial information, vendor relationships and, ultimately, even your customer satisfaction.

Accounts payable is not the most exciting part of your business, but it is important.

Before you shut me out and turn the page, think about it. Don't many of your company's business transactions pass over the desk of the person who handles your payables? If so, it deserves your attention.

Unfortunately, accounts payable is something that managers like to ignore. Most managers consider it a backroom or accounting function that takes care of itself. Astute managers recognize its importance and institute procedures that ensure it is managed properly.

Some steps you can take to ensure your accounts payable are properly managed are:

- **Hire good personnel.** As with most management issues, it is much easier to do a good job if you have someone good at doing it. Make sure one of your best administrative employees handles accounts payable. At our company, our accounts payable person seems to make the job easy.

- **Take discounts.** In most cases, it makes good financial sense to take offered discounts. If a vendor does not offer a discount, ask for one. If they do offer a discount, negotiate a better one. You are the vendor's customer, in many cases you will get what you request.
- **Stretch payments.** If a vendor does not offer you a discount, delay your payment to preserve your cash flow. Of course, you must balance the timing of your payment with the importance of keeping good relationships with your vendors.
- **Proper authorization.** The most important authorization takes place before purchasing an item or service. Be sure that you have good purchasing controls in place, including type of authorized purchases and dollar limits by position. After you receive products or services, be sure the proper person authorizes the invoice indicating receipt and quality of the purchase before making payment. No check should ever be written without proper approvals.
- **Minimize manual checks.** These are checks, usually COD, written outside of your normal payment cycle. Whenever possible, limit them by using vendors who will allow you to pay on credit. Writing manual checks can be costly and very distracting to your organization.
- **Systemize payments.** Limit your check runs to twice a month. At our company, we pay all discounted invoices on the 10th of the month and run all other checks on the 20th.
- **Define your reimbursement policy.** Be specific about what types of expenses employees can submit for reimbursement and who approves those reimbursements.
- **Automate.** Accounts payable is one area of your business that should definitely be automated. It is also probably one of the easiest places to automate.

- **Ask for credits when due.** Be aggressive when requesting credits, and be sure that you have a system to follow up on credits that are due your company. Don't count on your vendors to remember.
- **Be careful of tax implications.** There are federal income tax implications related to your accounts payable. You may need to send out IRS 1099 forms and get the related W-9 forms.

  Be careful if you are using independent contractors. IRS rules defining the qualifications for independent contract status are stringent. If you are unclear on any of these tax issues, get advice from your certified public accountant today.
- **Have record retention guidelines.** You should have formal procedures stating how long you keep both your accounts payable and other files.
- **Stay neat and organized.** Don't leave your accounts payable files in a mess. Have your staff file forms daily and keep the files neat. This will make it much easier to find the information you need.

All of us are looking for ways to improve our companies' financial results. Following the above procedures can help you in numerous ways, all of which will ultimately improve your profits and protect your most important asset - your cash.

Show this column to your chief financial officer, controller, payables clerk or anyone else involved in managing your payment cycle. Ask them to follow these procedures. If they tell you they cannot follow them, you may want to find an accounting team that can.

You work hard in your business. Effective management of your accounts payable can help you tum all of your efforts into even better results for you and your company.

Chapter 27
THINK "OUT OF THE BOX"
FOR SOLUTIONS
February 1998

I have never considered myself a daredevil. In fact, most people who know me well would tell you that I am a pretty conservative guy. Despite this reputation, I recently lived out a longtime dream to go skydiving.

The beginning skydiver has two different options when making their first jump. The first is called tandem jumping, which means that you jump out of an airplane attached to an experienced skydiver. Basically, you go for a ride.

I chose the second way, which is called accelerated free fall. This type of skydive required an eight-hour course at the end of which I jumped from a plane at an altitude of 12,500 feet. What a rush!

It was interesting to notice the change in my perspective during the weeks that followed the skydive. Tasks that previously seemed difficult suddenly seemed easy. Projects that were previously intimidating suddenly lost their power to cause me anxiety. I had stretched my boundaries and broadened my horizons. I had gotten "out of the box."

"Getting out of the box" is a phrase used to describe the effort of expanding one's horizons or seeing things from a fresh perspective. The "box" refers to our negative paradigms and the ruts that we sometimes get into.

For some people getting out of the box is virtually impossible. These people hate change and are very uncomfortable doing anything new. This puts them at a significant disadvantage in the workplace.

Effective managers try to see things from a fresh perspective and are constantly looking for new and better ideas. These managers do not mind the temporary uncomfortable feeling that results from going out on a limb. In fact, sometimes they thrive on it.

By looking at things from a fresh perspective, you can give yourself and your company a great competitive advantage. Below are some ways that can help you get out of the box:

- **Look for new experiences.** There's a big difference between 20 years of experience and one year of experience done 20 times over. No matter how comfortable you are, don't let yourself get in the rut of doing the same thing for years and years. Look for new ways of doing things.
- **Look for new technologies.** Sometimes new technology can be intimidating. Keep looking for new ways to improve your productivity through technology. Trade periodicals, educational seminars and boat shows are great places to learn what is new.
- **Listen carefully.** You can frequently pick up new ideas just by listening. Don't be someone who just likes to listen to themselves.
- **Promote continuous improvement.** Make sure that your entire organization is focused on improving.
- **Embrace change.** Don't be afraid of change, encourage it.
- **Encourage new ideas.** Most managers think they encourage their employees to present new ideas. However, if you are critical of your employees' ideas, they will stop presenting them. Find something positive to say, no matter how outlandish the idea.
- **Try to look at things with a fresh perspective.** The best

time for a new perspective is right after you come back from a holiday.

- **Don't punish people for trying.** Show employees appreciation for trying to make a good faith effort, even if they fail.
- **Allow yourself to dream.** No one can hold you back like you can hold yourself back. Don't limit yourself by your own thinking.
- **Believe in yourself and your team.** Don't let a lack of self-confidence keep you from being creative.
- **Network.** Meet with others from the boating industry and from other industries. You will be surprised at the new ideas you can pick up.

If you are feeling overwhelmed or wondering how you'll get everything done, the above is especially for you. Odds are you just need to get "out of the box II and look at things from a fresh perspective.

Everyone can identify problems, but it is those who are willing to "get out of the box" that develop solutions that will make them and their companies successful.

Try thinking of a problem you have had for some time, but have not been able to solve. Next, think of totally fresh, even outlandish, solutions. The solution you need may be right at your fingertips, but requires looking at it from a slightly different perspective.

Chapter 28
MAKE HONESTY AND INTEGRITY
YOUR STANDARD
March 1998

The past year has been difficult for my family. After many years of suffering from Parkinson's disease, my father had a brain hemorrhage. Unfortunately, this combination of problems has set my dad on a path that will probably end his life too soon.

I don't want to set an overly somber tone for this column, but as I look back on his life I believe that we can learn valuable lessons by examining his business experiences. You see, my dad was successful in business and has an impeccable reputation for honesty and leadership.

Like my dad, I believe that effective management must be based on complete honesty and integrity. These attributes are also the building blocks of true leadership.

I believe that our industry has a good reputation for honesty. Many of our businesses are "mom and pop" operations that try to be above board. In general, we try hard to give people that we deal with a "fair shake." We realize that long-term success is built on long term relationships.

These attitudes are not only morally and ethically right, but they are also smart business. Companies and managers that demonstrate high ethics will always come out on top in the long run.

As managers, we have the responsibility to set the ethical tone for our organization. Following are some things you can do to help ensure that your company and its employees are on the right track:

- **Prepare to deal with ethics.** Don't get caught off-guard when an ethical issue comes up. Believe me, these types of issues will come up from time to time and you need to be ready to deal with them. Anticipate potential ethical dilemmas and instruct your employees on how to deal with them before a problem occurs.
- **Be consistent.** A lifetime reputation may be lost in a day. Never let the people around you see you compromise your standards.
- **Be honest.** This does not mean that you should not be diplomatic, but, in the end, you must be honest. Your employees, customers and others must know you are honest and trustworthy.
- **Don't cover up mistakes.** Covering up your mistakes takes more effort than acknowledging them. If you deny or hide mistakes, when they are eventually discovered it makes them significantly harder to deal with.

  Be quick to apologize if you do make a mistake, and set the situation right.
- **Give others proper credit.** Stealing ideas from others or accepting praise that belongs to others is a quick way to lose your integrity. You can rarely get away with this and others realize you cannot be trusted.
- **Don't be a "blamer."** Be willing to accept responsibility when things go wrong.
- **Reinforce integrity with your employees.** Be sure that your employees know you expect nothing but the highest integrity from them. Be clear when communicating your standards.
- **Don't lower your standards or those of your facility.** Don't make any exceptions.

Preaching integrity is much easier than practicing it. Unfortunately, the people who work for you will easily become discouraged if you say one thing and do another. Be sure not to allow exceptions when implementing ethical standards at your marina and boatyard.

Keep focused on long-term consequences. Once your integrity is lost it is very difficult to get it back. Small inconveniences today - for the sake of maintaining your integrity - will pay large dividends in the long run.

Sometimes it can be hard to maintain your standards, especially if you see others around you seemingly getting away with having low standards. However, a person with integrity is someone who does the right thing even when they know that they can get away with doing the wrong thing. Having high standards makes it easier to live with yourself and is good for your business.

I know that my dad does not regret maintaining his standards and I know that you won't either.

Chapter 29
POSITIVE REINFORCEMENT
MOTIVATES EMPLOYEES
April 1998

Those of you who know me well know how important my two daughters, Erin and Amanda, are to me.

Even though I was lucky to have an incredible example in my father, when Erin was born I felt very inadequate. I had no idea how to be a good father, or what my new baby required of me. I'm sure many of you reading this felt the same way after the birth of your first child.

In an effort to become more secure in my new role, I did what I always do when I feel inadequate: I read like crazy. I have no idea how many parenting books I've read in the past seven years, but it's a lot.

And it wasn't until just recently that I made the connection between managing and being a good parent. It hit me during lunch with a friend when we were talking about ways we could become better fathers. Being an effective parent and being an effective manager requires similar skills.

Now, before you think I've lost my mind, let me clarify by saying that no employee wants to be treated like a child, and effective managers don't treat their employees like children. But I think that after reading this column, you will agree that there are many parenting principles used by successful managers. Some of these principles are as follows:

- **Acceptance.** Acceptance of our kids must be unconditional; acceptance of your employees must be conditional, but clear. It is always interesting to me when an excellent employee says something that indicates that they are wondering about their security at the company. Even your best employees will do it. Good employees will work much better if they feel accepted by you and secure in their position.

- **Availability.** Your employees must know that they are important to you, and the best way to prove it is through your availability. Make time for everyone on your team, and remember that their problems can't be arranged around your schedule.

- **Positive reinforcement.** You should be praising your best employees 20 to 30 times for each time you correct them. Positive feedback is the breakfast of champions.

    Many managers are afraid that if they praise their employees, the employees will get big egos and become unbearable. That's just not how it works. I have found that the more liberal you are with your praise, the less you have to correct. Praising your employees is a great way to build up their loyalty to you and increase their reluctance to let you down.

- **Relationships.** Remember that those who are lower than you on the organization chart are equal as persons. I know that sounds obvious, but many times managers don't act like it is true. You don't need to be your employees' best friend, but you should have a relationship with them that reflects their importance.

- **Clear expectations.** You should be very clear regarding what you expect from your employees. Even if they do not agree with you, they will respect you for being clear and appreciate knowing what they need to do.

- **Keep your word.** Sometimes it is hard to keep your word, but you have to do it. Your credibility is one of the most important things you have as a manager.

- **Open communication.** Your employees must feel free to talk to you about anything. Never make an employee regret coming to you and being honest about a problem or issue.
- **Discipline.** No one likes to do it, but you must be willing to deal with problems and be willing to discipline if necessary. All talk and no action is a quick road to being ineffective. However, it is also important to note that if you follow the previous steps, you will have much less need to discipline.

One effective way to apply the above principles as a manager is to treat your employees exactly as you want to be treated by your boss. Odds are that your employees are motivated by many of the same things that motivate you. And, don't worry if you don't get immediate results. As with any relationship, it takes time to absorb changes.

All of us want our kids to be successful, and the same should be true of our employees. If your employees are successful, it will help make you individually successful and have a positive impact on the profits of your company.

Try implementing the above principles and watch the results. You will find that besides the benefits to you and your company, your employees will appreciate the way that you are treating them. And you don't have to worry about your employees asking to borrow your car for a date.

Chapter 30
LET OPTIMISM DRIVE YOUR BUSINESS
May 1998

Years ago when I was in college the philosophy of "positive mental at-titude" (PMA) was at the height of its popularity. I have to admit that I read many books on this topic and found them quite interesting. I'll also admit that I had a sticker made for my dormitory desk that simply read "PMA" - it served as a reminder to me when times were tough.

Despite its enormous popularity, positive thinking eventually start-ed to become unfashionable. Of course, there are still many people who preach PMA and many more that use it. However, most people eventually realized that just telling themselves that things are going to go right will not make them go right. While PMA thinking can cer-tainly help you feel better, it is no guarantee of success.

While positive thinking continues to be a help to me, there is an-other concept - one that is closely related to the PMA philosophy - that goes a step further. "Optimistic management" can help you succeed by having a dramatically positive impact on your effectiveness as a manager. By increasing your effectiveness, this concept can help in-crease your productivity and ability to motivate people, thus increasing your profits.

Psychologists have determined that optimistic people are physical-ly and mentally healthier, and get more of what they want from life.

I have also observed that optimistic people are generally more effective managers.

As a manager, you set the tone for your employees. Do you want optimistic "can-do" people working for you? If so, you need to lead by example. It is almost impossible for the people on a team to be optimistic if their leader is not.

Because employees look to you for direction, their moods will be significantly affected by your mood. However, this can be difficult and is a big responsibility. You probably do not always feel like being optimistic, yet good managers are almost always upbeat around their employees.

Maybe optimistic management does not come easy to you. Following are some tips to help you be a more optimistic - and effective - manager:

- **Always be "up."** This is not easy but it is always necessary to stay positive and enthusiastic when dealing with your employees.
- **Praise freely.** Some managers are uncomfortable doing this, but I've found that for every reason there is to correct an employee, there are probably 10 reasons to praise them. If you are not close to this ratio, reevaluate your style. Another interesting thing I have learned is that the more generous you are with praise, the less you have to criticize. Employees who are often praised will try harder not to let you down.
- **Never personalize criticism.** When you are correcting an employee focus on the behavior that needs to be changed - not the person. If you devalue an employee you and your company are the ones that will pay the price.
- **Expand positive developments.** When good things happen, try to use them to build positive momentum. You want to build this positive momentum in a way that is far reaching and long-lasting.

- **Limit the scope of setbacks.** When something goes wrong in your operation it is easy for people to generalize and think that everything is going wrong. Don't let this happen. When something bad happens don't just wait for it to go away, address it. Give people the whole story and explain that the problem only relates to this specific issue. Reassure them that everything else is going fine.
- **Look beyond bad times.** When you go through tough times with your team, stay focused on your more positive future. Keep reminding everyone that the tough times are temporary. If you let people dwell on the tough times it can become part of your team's permanent mind-set.

To learn more about the impact of optimism on people, read the book *Learned Optimism* by Martin Segilman. It is not a management book, but it has a lot of general optimism principles that you'll find useful.

Chapter 31
PROMOTE THE POWER OF TEAMWORK
June 1998

There is nothing more important in management than teamwork. The effective manager focuses on teamwork and does everything possible to promote it. Unfortunately, many managers, while aware of the concept of teamwork, are completely unaware of its power.

Teamwork is something that does not come naturally for many people, especially Americans. I know that it doesn't come easy for me. The "Rugged Individualist" is a big part of the American persona, and we tend to carry that into the workplace. Despite this, many great things are accomplished by teams. Except in unusual cases, exceptional performance in the workplace is almost always the result of a team effort.

As a manager, you need to be focused on creating and sustaining your team. The first step - which is an important one - is to continuously emphasize teamwork with your employees. Following are some ways to help your group function as a team:

- **Hire good people.** This may seem obvious but all great team leaders have this key skill. Great team leaders hire people with different perspectives and skills and are willing to hire people that are smarter than themselves.
- **Have team goals.** Many managers make the mistake of focusing on what they don't want employees to do when they

should be focusing on what they do want employees to do. Every highly effective team has a mission. Your mission should be in writing, preferably in the form of a formal mission statement. Identify objectives and keep your team focused on them.

- **Be a leader, not a friend.** It is much more important to do what is right and earn your employees' trust and respect than to be everyone's friend. Popularity dissipates quickly but trust and respect will continue to work for you even when people disagree with your decisions.

- **Communicate.** Remember that the most important part of communication is listening. Your employees must know they can talk to you without recourse. Encourage open discussion among your employees and use the information you gather to help build your team. Also, be sure to keep your team updated. Consider weekly staff meetings.

- **Manage failure and problems.** There is nothing like a properly managed problem or failure to bring people together. Don't overly criticize employees who try something new and fail. The ability to fail when trying something new can be a significant boost to your team's creativity. Also, use problems to bring your team together, not tear them apart.

- **Don't micromanage.** You should be a goal-setter, decision-maker and facilitator. Let your team solve its own problems and work as they see fit. It is important that your team get results, not that you are always there.

- **Be optimistic.** Believe in yourself and your team. Optimistic people, even with unwarranted optimism, accomplish more than realists.

- **Be loyal.** Your team should know that you will always look out for them and defend them from outside attacks.

- **Have fun.** It's fun to be a part of a great team. Don't get uptight if your employees are having fun. They must stay focused on the team's mission and follow company rules, however, if they can have fun while doing that, great! Employees who enjoy coming to work are significantly more productive than those who dread it.

In addition to the above items, be sure to hold your team account-able. However, remember to give credit where credit is due and always celebrate success.

I wrote a column on teamwork a few years ago that discussed other issues, including the importance of having on your team employees with different perspectives than yours, the importance of synergy and ways to determine if your employees are functioning as a team. If you would like a copy of the original column, contact me - I would be happy to send it.

Chapter 32
HOW TO GET AN A+ IN
EMPLOYEE TRAINING
July 1998

Take a moment to focus on your boat dealership's or marina's training program. If you don't have one, start one. If you do have an employee-training program, review and enhance it. Though it is admittedly hard to quantify the benefits, an employee-training program is one of the best investments you can make.

I recently reviewed our company's employee training program and I've concluded that we are doing a good job. Rarely a week goes by that we do not have one or more employees in an external or internal training session. We definitely try to live up to the first two words of our mission statement: "continuously improve."

Many companies, however, fall short when it comes to offering their employees the training opportunities that they need. By doing this, these companies fail in an important area of their own development. When I ask managers in our industry why they don't offer their employees more training opportunities, I frequently get the same answer. Many managers are reluctant to pay for employee training because they fear losing them to another job.

A Powerful Message

Though I have never seen this fear of losing good employees turn into a real problem, I have to admit that I used to struggle with how to respond to it. Not any more. About four years ago, I went to hear Zig Ziglar speak and he said something that has stuck with me since then. "One thing worse than training employees and losing them is not training employees and keeping them," said Ziglar. Now that is powerful.

Your company should constantly be looking for opportunities to develop its employees. Following are some ideas that can help:

- **Have a "development mentality."** Make training important. Always look for training opportunities. Believe in the benefits of training. Focus on continuous improvement.
- **Watch for industry opportunities.** The American Boat and Yacht Council (ABYC), the American Boat Builders and Repairers Association (ABBRA) and other industry groups offer educational programs. For example, I recently had the opportunity to speak at the annual meeting of the ABYC. What an impressive meeting and group. I was familiar with ABYC but unaware of what a great job they are doing regarding the technical training of our industry. Skip Moyer, Pat Kearns and their entire team deserve kudos!

  Industry events such as the International Marine Trades Exhibit & Conference (IMTEC) and the International Boatbuilders' Exhibition & Conference (IBEX) also offer good training opportunities. Watch your mail and industry periodicals for specific boat industry training programs.
- **Do in-house sessions.** Have someone in your organization with a specific expertise put on a training session to share that expertise. Most employees will feel honored that you think highly enough of them to ask them to participate.

- **Rent training videos.** We've frequently used training videos as an aid to make a specific point. These videos are usually short, concise and often entertaining. They are an easy way to conduct effective training.
- **Use traveling seminars.** For the most part, these one-day seminars are excellent. They are inexpensive, effective and a good use of your employees' time. Generally, employees agree.
- **Attend American Manager Association (AMA) seminars.** The AMA offers one-day business seminars around the country - I've attended several and have never been disappointed.
- **Use vendors.** Ask your vendors about available training regarding their products. Usually vendors will jump at the chance to work with you.
- **Start a training library.** At our company, we have training books, tapes and other resources available to our employees. Find a company that offers good, inexpensive books that you could use to start your training library.

You'll find that your boat dealership or marina almost immediately will benefit from implementing these training program ideas. In addition, employees really appreciate the fact that you are investing in them through training.

They recognize that not all companies are willing to do that. Beside the specific benefits of a particular course, training will develop an employee's loyalty toward you and your boat dealership or marina that will pay off many times over.

Chapter 33
DO AS THE EUROPEANS DO:
THINK LONG-TERM
August 1998

Recently I had the opportunity to spend a week in Europe on business. During this week I attended a boat show and visited several European boatbuilders, boatyards, marine stores and marinas.

I'll grant you that drawing conclusions after spending a week visiting with our colleagues on "the Continent" is similar to drawing conclusions about the US boating industry after spending a week here. Many of us have yet to figure out what goes on in "the States" after a lifetime, much less a week, and I am sure that my friends in Europe would make the same point. However, I did make a number of interesting observations during my visit.

My first observation is the reinforcement of a point that I have made many times: as managers, we must occasionally get out of our comfort zone and see what others are doing. It's easy to get so busy with our day-to-day operations that we forget there is a big world out there. Sometimes it can be very humbling. However, when you allow yourself to see things from a different viewpoint your perspective almost always improves.

There are many domestic and international managers - both in and out of the boating industry - who share our challenges. It is interesting when I visit various companies to see how different managers deal with the same problems in equally effective but distinctly different ways. No one has the lock on good ideas.

As a manager, you should take advantage of every opportunity to broaden your horizons. Get outside of your comfort zone. See what others are doing inside and outside of the boating industry by networking with colleagues, attending industry events and visiting other locations. When you return to your business look at what you are doing through a fresh set of eyes - it can only help you.

My second observation relates to the European manager's time reference, or time horizon, when making decisions. They appear to be much more long-term focused than many American managers.

In fact, one European manager stated he was terminating an alliance relationship with an American counterpart because of this issue. His comment was, "We look at issues on a 50- to 100-year time horizon, not a one- to two-year time horizon."

The European managers were generally reluctant to say anything negative about American managers, however, when pressed this was always their concern. Their perception that American companies are too focused on the current year's profits and not on whether the company will be alive and stronger for the next generation.

After seeing European managers' operations I believe they are right. As American managers, we need to be more long-term focused.

I was also impressed by the emphasis on training. One manager said to me, "The continuous improvement learning curve has no end."

Employees are trained in both formal and informal training programs and in apprenticeship programs. Employers consider employees as lifetime partners so there is not a problem justifying training expenses. I was surprised when one boatbuilder told me how much his company spent each year on training.

My final observation relates to planning. I was impressed with the amount of planning that I observed. A lot of time is invested upfront to save time in the long run and to make sure that a job is done right the first time.

Many managers in the United States frequently find it easy to say that they don't have time to plan. The European managers I spoke with would argue that time invested in planning actually reduces the total time spent on a project. Plus, as the old saying goes, "If you don't have the time to plan and do it right the first time, where will you ever find the time to fix it?"

This column is not intended in any way to knock American management. I am as patriotic as anyone; I may be biased but I believe that the United States has the world's most effective managers. However, I also know that effective managers use every opportunity to learn new things from every source possible.

Consider the above observations and I think that you'll find some points that you can build on to help improve both your company's productivity and profitability.

Chapter 34
NONVERBAL COMMUNICATION
SPEAKS VOLUMES
September 1998

Communication problems are at the core of many management problems. This is not unique to the boating industry: communication has traditionally been a major stumbling block to management effectiveness in all industries.

Many managers have trouble with communication because they ignore the most important element of communication - nonverbal communication.

Studies have shown that nonverbal communication may constitute as much as 93 percent of the message that you are sending. It is much more powerful than the verbal portion of your message and many managers underestimate its importance. You may have a very powerful verbal message but if it conflicts with your nonverbal signals, it will be almost impossible for you to communicate your point effectively.

Last year I taught a one-day seminar for the American Boat Builders and Repairers Association (ABBRA) called "Becoming the Indispensable Employee." During the seminar, we discussed nonverbal communication and many of the participants were amazed at its impact. One participant in particular said that he had been frustrated for years by his lack of ability to communicate. He said that while he believed that he was saying what needed to be said he was probably sending a wide range of conflicting nonverbal messages. He said he believed that his overall effectiveness could increase significantly by focusing on and improving his nonverbal communication skills.

How effective is your nonverbal communication? Are your nonverbal messages conflicting with your verbal communication? If you are not focused on your nonverbal communication, odds are that it could use improvement. Odds are also good that you could be sending the wrong message to your employees, customers and boss.

Following are some things that you can do to help improve your nonverbal skills.

- **Get a good book.** There are many books at your local library or bookstore on nonverbal communication. Read one. You'll be amazed at how easy it is to pick up tips to improve in this area.
- **Be a good listener.** Most people think of communication as talking. A big part of effective communication requires good listening. When someone else is talking, listen carefully and don't be thinking ahead to your response.
- **Maintain** eye **contact.** This shows respect for and interest in the person with whom you are communicating. I always worry about someone who won't look me in the eye when we're speaking.
- **Watch your posture.** How you stand and sit, and hold your arms and legs, has a significant impact on the message you send. For example, if you cross your arms while listening it sends the message that you don't care about what you are hearing. Position yourself in a way that shows interest in the person with whom you are communicating.
- **Transmit energy.** This is very hard sometimes; however, on the job you need to be up and positive all the time - even when you don't feel like it. Those around you are affected by your attitude. The key here is to leave others feeling good and energized

after encounters with you. Even if it doesn't come naturally to you, try to always be up and excited.

- **Don't wear your feelings.** If you're having a bad day, suffer alone. Resist the temptation to share your negative emotions with those around you.

Have you ever met someone who has a "presence" about them? We commonly refer to this bearing as "executive presence." People with an executive presence are people who combine the above with a positive attitude and leave other people feeling great. These are the kind of people others want to be around. Develop an executive presence by working on your nonverbal communication skills.

Most failures of nonverbal communication are the results of bad habits. I've heard that it takes 21 days to break a bad habit and - with effort - it can be done. Have someone you trust help you. Shoot a video of yourself in action to help you see yourself as others see you.

Some people are naturally excellent nonverbal communicators. With some practice, we too can refine our nonverbal skills. Watch it improve your relations with customers and employees, while improving your overall effectiveness to your company.

Chapter 35
PLAN ON BECOMING A GREAT MANAGER
October 1998

I recently was in California on business and had the opportunity to spend some time with the fund manager of one of the country's top-performing mutual funds

Given her company's track record, I had to ask for her secret to consistently choosing companies that outperform the broader markets and other fund managers' portfolios. I was intrigued by her response.

She said her secret was to look for companies that had great managers. Her definition of a great manager is simple. She said that based on her 30 years of experience choosing successful companies, a great manager is one who:

- Puts together a great plan.
- Executes the plan.
- Rarely deviates from the plan.

The next day as I returned home, I couldn't help but think about what I had heard, and about how many boatyard and marina managers would benefit from hearing it, too. It was so simple, but accurate. I believe that there are several lessons boatyard and marina managers can learn from her comments.

Planning Saves Time.

The first lesson relates to the importance of planning. For some reason, planning is something that some boatyard and marina managers do not like to do. Many say they are too busy to spend time planning.

The fact is that planning is a net time-saver. Time spent developing and communicating a plan almost always reduces the amount of time spent executing the plan.

Planning starts with a mission statement. Creating a strategic plan is next. Your boatyard or marina should have both of these. If you don't have these and you need help in creating them, drop me a note. I will be happy to send you copies of previous columns I have written on these topics.

Be Consistent and Persevere.

The second lesson relates to being consistent and persevering. Carry out your plan on a daily basis. Keep plodding until you have fully executed the plan. Do what you have to do to achieve this. Continually review your activities to ensure they are consistent with what needs to be done to execute your plan.

Think Results.

The third lesson relates to being results-oriented. Unfortunately, many boatyard and marina managers find it easy to be process-oriented. They get so caught up in their daily activities that they forget about the result. Stay focused on the result - without focusing on activities that are not pointing you toward your objective.

Boatyard and marina managers in the past have asked me what the most important thing is that someone can do to be a successful manager. That is a tough question because management is complex and there are many factors that go into determining if someone is successful. However, when pressed, I always answer managers can ensure their success by developing a results-orientation. Companies don't want a manager who works hard - they want managers who get results.

Stay on Course.

The fourth lesson is to avoid distractions. As a manager, it is easy to allow yourself to be distracted by something that is more interesting or appears to be a better opportunity. Don't allow it. Stay focused on carrying out your plan.

To some, these tips on how to be a great manager may sound simplistic. Whether they are simple or complex, the fact remains that many managers know exactly what to do - they just don't do it. It's not a deficiency of knowledge. It is a deficiency of execution. Boatyard and marina managers who use their knowledge have a significant advantage over those managers who have the knowledge but don't use it.

If we want to be the kind of managers that our boatyards and marinas need to remain profitable and viable as we enter the next millennium, we must consistently emphasize the fundamentals. We must execute what we know needs to be done. We must determine that we are not going to be good managers - we are going to be great managers. We must have great plans, execute those plans and rarely deviate from those plans.

Chapter 36
GOALS KICK START YOUR
MARINE BUSINESS
November 1998

While recently playing soccer with my two daughters, I saw an unexpected illustration of effective management that can be applied to the operation of a modem marina or boatyard.

My daughters were playing a game that helps them develop accuracy and leg strength in kicking. They take turns kicking the ball and the one who combines the most distance and accuracy gets a point. The first to get to 15 points wins.

As judge and scorekeeper, I found it interesting that the one who kicked second won the point almost 100 percent of the time. I realized that the second kicker did better each time because she had an objective or goal. The second kicker knew exactly where she needed to kick the ball to win the point.

Here was a powerful example of how goals get results.

As a manager in a marine business, you must use goals if you want to maximize your effectiveness and the productivity of your employees. Goals are powerful management tools. They give your employees direction and focus and almost always improve teamwork.

One of the best ways to use goals at your company is through a mission statement. A business that does not have a mission statement is violating one of the most basic rules of management.

Another important use of goals is in employee performance evaluation. Many managers mistakenly focus on the past in these uncomfortable exercises, but their real focus should be the future. Make sure your marina or boatyard employees receive goals for their next review period at the end of the evaluation.

Here are some other ways to use goals to manage your marine-business employees:

- **Set realistic goals.** For goals to be motivators, employees must have a reasonable shot at reaching them.
- **Put goals in writing.** Written down, they can be referred to often and put in a place that provides frequent reinforcement.
- **Share goal making.** Goals are much more effective if you and the employee create them together.
- **Set measurable goals.** Goals should be specific. Be sure you and the employee are clear on what constitutes an achieved goal.
- **Have a timetable.** Set the time frame within which you want the goals achieved. This is frequently an area of misunderstanding with employees. For example, your service manager may have thought he had a year to accomplish a goal, while you were thinking he would accomplish it in 30 days.
- **Identify obstacles.** Talk with employees about what may keep them from reaching their goals; help them identify ways to get around those obstacles.
- **Set specific responsibilities.** With a group goal, specifically identify who is responsible for accomplishing each part of the goal.

Employees can't be expected to know what you want done if you don't tell them. The best way to tell them is through goals. Once they have their goals, help them put together a plan to achieve them.

Try setting a couple of goals for marina/yard operation and see how the process works. You'll find it's a great way to improve your personal effectiveness, your employees' results and your profits.

Chapter 37
KNOW YOUR EMPLOYEES' EMOTIONAL TEMPERAMENT
December 1998

Golf is not a sport I enjoy. I'll admit that I rarely play the game, but when I do, it just doesn't appeal to me. Watching golf on television appeals to me even less than playing it.

I've often wondered what my dad, brother and friends see in this sport. I just cannot get into it.

Despite my aversion to this sport, I have thoroughly enjoyed watching the ascent of Tiger Woods to the top of the golfing world. He is an exceptional athlete whose career both on and off the course is gaining speed.

I also find it interesting to listen to people describe him. The one thing that has caught my attention the most is how almost everyone talks about Tiger's "mental toughness." He clearly appears to be someone who is emotionally in control.

Unfortunately, few marina operators/owners have degrees or any expertise in psychology. You are a manager, not a psychologist. Despite this, there is clearly an emotional aspect to managing your employees that you must consider to be an effective manager.

Every employee is different. Each is an individual who brings their own history to the job. That history results in an emotional temperament that you, as their supervisor, must manage. This is part of what makes management so challenging.

Effective managers frequently have good rapport with their employees that is helpful in learning and understanding their employees' emotional temperament. This rapport comes from trust.

If your employees trust you, they will be more likely to share things with you that will not only help them, but also will help you and your marina. If you do not earn your employees' trust, don't expect them to open up to you. The communication level in your organization will never exceed the trust level.

Some ideas to keep in mind as you try to manage the emotional aspects of your business are:

- **Acknowledge emotions.** They affect not only your employees' work but also your effectiveness as a manager, so you might as well acknowledge them. Employees have emotional factors in their lives that are impossible to separate from the workplace.

- **Recognize that everyone is different.** Every employee has their own emotional temperament. In your capacity as manager, you cannot expect to motivate all of your employees with the same techniques. Some employees will require lots of direction and correction; others may need just a little positive reinforcement.

- **Give effective criticism.** Give feedback to your employees; even negative feedback is an important part of management. However, if negative feedback is handled improperly it can backfire and be emotionally devastating to your employees.

    When correcting employees, focus with a constructive tone on the behavior that needs to be corrected and, at all costs, avoid personal attacks. Be specific regarding the problem and the solution to the problem. End the criticism on a positive note about the future.

- **Promote teamwork.** The best way I know how to develop an upbeat workplace is to promote teamwork. By its nature, teamwork results in an emotionally "up" atmosphere.
- **Value diversity.** We do not want teams of people working for us who all think the same way or have similar backgrounds. Diversity in our teams provides us with various perspectives, all of which can be helpful at different times.
- **Allow people to talk.** Your employees must be able to say what is on their minds without fear of reprisal. This will not only help you manage but also keep your employees from bottling up emotions that could explode at some future date. Don't let feedback from your employees irritate you; treat an employee who is willing to critique you as an ally. They can make you a better manager.
- **Allow some fun.** A little fun on the job can go a long way toward having an emotionally satisfying workplace.

Effectively managing your employees and their emotions can go a long way toward keeping your employees motivated. A motivated employee can complete several times more work than an unmotivated employee.

This will make you a more effective manager and will have a positive impact on your marina's revenues. You may even find that, in the long run, it takes fewer people to get the same work done.

Don't ignore an important part of management. Stay focused on the emotions of your team and reap the benefits for you, your employees and your marina.

Chapter 38
NO "QUICK-FIX" FOR CUSTOMER SERVICE PROBLEMS
January 1999

I recently asked several boatyard and marina managers what they considered their most difficult management problems. I expected their answers to be related to the supervision of employees. However, the problem most frequently mentioned related to the handling of customers.

Sometimes I think that problems related to customer service result from an unwillingness to make the commitment necessary to ensure great customer service. There is no "quick fix" to your boatyard or marina's customer service problems - whether they are repair related or otherwise.

Customer service is more than just carrying out steps or procedures. To rid yourself of "customer problems," you must be 100 percent committed to providing outstanding customer service.

Below are some general things that you can do to help improve your marine business's commitment to customer service:

- **Remain focused on customer service.** There are so many different issues that managers regularly must deal with that efforts to serve the customer are overlooked. Don't fall into that trap. Customer service is something that you must continually reinforce. For example, get to know your slip renters on a first-name basis. If that's too time-consuming, make sure you and your employees have a friendly presence on the dock.

- **Leave your baggage at the door.** Your customer does not care about your personal life. Therefore, your attitude toward your customers must not be impacted by it. Maintain an upbeat and pleasant attitude in front of customers.

- **Focus on and exceed customer expectations.** This is the key to great customer service.

- **Remember that the customer is the judge.** You may think that you did a good job but if the customer doesn't, you've got a problem. The long-term success of your marina or boatyard is based on what your customer thinks. Make every effort to address their complaints.

- **Don't take things personally.** Frustrated customers may say things that sound personal, but you must resist taking it that way. Instead, take action to address the source of their frustration.

- **Job security depends on customer service.** Remember, it's not the company that pays wages, it's the customers. Emphasize this point with your employees, from part time dockhands to your general manager.

- **Be result-focused.** Customers care more about results than invested effort. Focus on getting your customers the results they need.

If you or one of your employees unintentionally upsets a customer, keep in mind that an angry customer is an opportunity. Many times an angry customer will turn into your best customer if you handle the situation correctly and promptly resolve the problem.

Making customers happy is a challenge. However, we all know it's much easier to take care of your current customers than it is to find new ones. Every customer encounter is a moment of truth for your company.

Many marine businesses spend a lot of money marketing for new customers. What they may not realize is that keeping their current customers will have the maximum impact on their profits. Satisfied slip renters will encourage boating friends to visit - or do business with - your boatyard or marina.

The above items are general ideas on which we should focus. In a previous column, I wrote more about specific things that you and your employees can do to help ensure great customer service. Drop me a note and I'll send you that previous column.

Chapter 39
RETAIN CUSTOMERS BY RESOLVING COMPLAINTS
February 1999

Most marina and boatyard owners and managers know that the best way to meet customers' expectations is to exceed them.

However, speaking with a group of marina owners and operators at a recent International Marina Institute **(IMI)** meeting confirmed for me that it's tough to meet customers' demands all the time. Whether a problem-causing event is inside or outside of your control, your marina or boatyard occasionally will have to address upset customers.

The first thing to remember when you encounter upset customers is that you have a wonderful opportunity to make their situation right. Most customers won't inform you of their problems, sharing them only with those outside of your marine business. If you're fortunate enough to have a customer who asks you to address the problem, you have a chance to prove your facility's dedication to your customers.

For example, if a customer says that one of your employees treated them with disrespect, address the situation before your marina gets a reputation for being unfriendly. Take advantage of this opportunity and thank the customer for taking the time to make you aware of the problem.

Even those marina or boatyard managers who understand the importance of turning angry customers into happy customers have a tough time dealing with them. Below are some ideas to help you deal with a complaining customer:

- **Let customers talk uninterrupted.** If you get defensive or try to stop them before they are done complaining, it will just frustrate them and make them more difficult to handle.
- **Listen carefully rather than planning your response while the customer is still talking.** You cannot deal well with your customer's problem if you can't identify it clearly.
- **Understand the importance of your customer's viewpoint - whether you agree with it or not.** The customer's perception of your operation is the reality that will be shared with others.

For example, if a boater falls on a slippery dock - whether it is due to the customer's choice of improper footwear or your lack of dock care - the customer might tell others that your marina is unsafe or that the facility is not well-maintained.

By complaining, the customer has given you a chance to put up warning signs and to take other steps to prevent future injuries. This demonstrates to your customer that you are concerned for their safety. Handling a customer complaint properly is an inexpensive alternative to spending a lot of money on sales and marketing.

- **Don't make excuses.** Don't be defensive. Customers want results, not whining. Resolve the customer's problem.
- **Don't use form responses.** To make customers feel important, treat each one individually.
- **Always respond promptly.** If you have asked another of your boatyard's or marina's employees to solve the problem, personally follow up to be sure it has been done.

Use the above steps when handling customer complaints and watch your need for new marina or boatyard customers drop. By keeping your old customers happy, you will see a reduction in marketing expenses and a larger profit.

Chapter 40
ENERGIZED EMPLOYEES ARE MORE PROFIT-DRIVEN
March 1999

Many boatyards and marinas are running on empty, existing on the inertia of their past or even worse, the inertia of their bureaucracy.

Facilities that survive on this inertia often cruise along comfortably - until there is a change in their operation environment. Then, they find themselves in a tailspin. Boatyards or marinas that are energized - and most are energized by positive employees and working environments - can handle change better, remaining productive and profitable.

How to energize your facility

It can be difficult to energize your boatyard or marina. The current business environment, characterized by mergers, acquisitions and downsizing, causes many people to feel insecure in their jobs. It used to be that if you worked hard, were honest and had a good attitude, you had a job forever. While those traits are still important, almost everyone knows somebody with those attributes who has lost a job.

Despite the difficulties, it is your job as a marina or boatyard operator to keep your employees energized. The result will be huge improvements in morale and productivity. Energized employees are focused on accomplishing your facility's objectives.

Below are some things you can do to help keep your employees energized:

- **Make employees feel secure by giving them a future.** Focus your employee communications on the bright aspects of your facility's and employees' future.
- **Make people feel important.** This will motivate them to give their best.
- **Train employees.** If the training is good they will return to your marina or boatyard excited about the concepts they have learned and will be anxious to share their new ideas. Be sure that you are receptive to their new ideas if you want the energy to last.

For example, if your dockhands attend a seminar on best management practices on the fuel dock, be sure to encourage their sharing of the information with other fuel dock attendants.

- **Freely give information** - including financial results - to employees. Rumors are much more damaging than the truth. A good book on this topic is "The Great Game of Business," by Jack Stack. Employees who experience honesty are less likely to become de-energized by rumors.
- **Give feedback.** Employees want to know where they stand with their boss. If you give feedback openly and regularly employees won't waste time and energy worrying about their status on the job. Management by walking around accomplishes this: walk the yard or marina and compliment employees for what they're doing right.

More productive employees

- **Provide a pleasing environment.** Ancient philosophers identified "beauty" as one of the four fundamental dimensions of the human experience. This has an on-the-job impact. Employees are more productive in a nice working environment.

  Some boatyard repair shops are far from beautiful, but they can be pleasing. For example, in your boatyard's or marina's full-service repair shop, establish a system that ensures employees will find the tools they need when they need them. In setting up the system, get employee feedback so that they will be more likely to adhere to the system.

- **Be ethical.** It is energizing to employees to trust and respect their boss's integrity.

- **Be upbeat and positive.** This is a critical element to enhancing organizational energy. Employees subconsciously look to you for signals. Make sure that you are giving them the right ones. Try greeting your employees as you would your customers.

I recently told a group of our company's employees that everybody should have a job they enjoy. It should do more than provide a paycheck, it should add to your quality of life. You can accomplish this by energizing your facility.

Chapter 41
TAKE CONTROL OF YOUR TIME
April 1999

Time management has a tremendous impact on our quality of life. People who manage their time well tend to be much happier and satisfied than those who struggle with it.

While speaking about time management at the American Boat Builders and Repairers Association (ABBRA) Annual Conference and Meeting, January 13-16, I was reminded that many managers are looking for ways to increase their productivity and effectiveness.

Two signs that you are one of the many managers who could improve their time management skills are feelings that you don't have control over your own time and that there are not enough hours in the day to get everything done.

If this applies to you, here are some things you can do to take control of your time:

- **Develop a personal mission and prioritize your activities in relation to it.** This will help you differentiate between what is important and what can be set aside.
- **Delegate your tasks.** You can't do everything yourself. Once you've trained your marina or boatyard staff, let them show you what they can accomplish.
- **Focus on areas within your control.** Don't waste your time

worrying about things you can't change. If you follow this, your area of control will grow.

- **Keep a "to-do" list.** Use a master list to make up a short daily list for the next day before you end each workday. Keeping your responsibilities organized on paper frees up room for you to concentrate on the task at hand. Some marina or boatyard managers prefer to keep their to-do list on their electronic calendar. This is fine, too, as long as you have the satisfaction of deleting items from the list once they're completed.

- **Set up a filing system.** Establish a file for each month and put tasks with specific deadlines in the appropriate folder. Use these as follow-up folders as well. For example, if you have plans to winterize your docks in the fall, you would slip that task in the folder that best ensures you begin the project on time.

- **Remain organized.** Force yourself to clean your work area before you leave each night. This will get your morning off to a productive start.

- **Focus on results.** Finish what you've started instead of allowing other activities to distract you from your objective.

- **Buy a time management book.** Steven Covey's "Seven Habits of Highly Effective People" is one of many books available at your local bookstore or library that offers tips for you to use in becoming a more productive manager.

There are two types of boatyard and marina managers; those that give excuses why they cannot get everything done and those that actually accomplish their objectives.

Join the group that is getting things done. Develop your time management skills. As they improve, watch your profits and your quality of life rise.

Chapter 42
CUSTOMER SERVICE TIPS FROM JAPAN
May 1999

The Tokyo International Boat Show, held February 10-14 at the Tokyo International Exhibition Centre, was quite an experience.

As usual, I was on the lookout for new ideas or lessons that could be applied to the business of running a marina or boatyard. Fortunately, there were many.

The first and most obvious lesson related to the level of customer service experienced in Japan. Japanese businesses and their employees are committed to providing great customer service. On the boat show floor - and throughout my travels in Japan - I was treated with respect and made to feel comfortable in my business dealings. Employees were attentive, polite and pleasant.

I walked away from my business encounters knowing I would work with those companies again. We often remind our marina and boat-yard staff how important it is to respond to a customer in a timely and polite fashion; however, if we teach by example - and I don't think a trip to Japan is required - employees will see and feel the difference real commitment makes.

I was surprised that employees provide such outstanding customer service though there is a no-tipping policy in Japan. I think they do so because management establishes clear expectations for its employees, and nothing less will be accepted. I also witnessed management treating its employees with respect.

Although many boatyard and marina employees thrive on tips, they may work more efficiently and with a higher level of service when provided with clearly defined objectives delivered in a respectful manner.

The next lesson I learned is that different - or new - is not wrong. The Japanese culture, which is new to me, forced me to view things differently. Sometimes as managers we believe that any way but our way is the wrong way. However, my visit to the Tokyo boat show, and my communications with other marine industry managers, made me realize that I don't have a monopoly on the best ideas.

As managers of marinas and boatyards, we must be open to new ideas that come from our employees, customers, vendors and other industries. If we limit ourselves to one set of ideas, we hurt our business.

Be open to change in your facility. In fact, encourage it. Ask your marina or boatyard customers to rate your level of customer service, the quality of your workmanship and other areas of your business and customer-employee interactions. Then implement changes to improve areas of weakness.

The next lesson relates to continuous improvement. Consider training and education the process through which you can develop your employees and yourself. This is one of the best ways to ensure your marina and boatyard will meet all demands placed on it.

The last lesson related to getting out of your comfort zone. As marina and boatyard managers, you most likely spend a lot of time at your facility. However, to stay current and expand your horizons, you need to think big. To think big:

- Attend industry events and network with other marine industry professionals.
- Take a tour of marinas and yards either near your facility or in a different market.

- Get involved with political or community-related issues that touch home for you and your marina or boatyard.

For example, a no-wake ruling in water on which your facility is located may impact your marina or a ban on fishing from certain waters or certain fish may affect your boating customers. Keeping informed is to your business's benefit.

Chapter 43
READ TO SUCCEED
June 1999

Reading a good book is one of the simplest tools marina and boatyard managers can use to improve the skills and knowledge they rely on every day. I read close to 100 books a year. While only 12 to 15 of those books relate to business management, I always find a good business book refreshes my thinking.

As managers, we should be looking for little advantages that can give us a significant edge over our competitors, whether it is a new method to keep service customers coming back or a tip for inspiring hard work among your employees. It is hard to read a good business management book without picking up a few helpful ideas.

I frequently am asked to recommend books marina and boatyard managers should read to help them succeed in their jobs. With that in mind, I wrote a column recommending several books. The response was positive and several readers suggested to me books they found beneficial. The list below includes some of these suggestions along with some of the useful management books I've discovered.

- **"How to Win Friends and Influence People"** by Dale Carnegie. This classic book is a must-read for everyone.
- **"Clicking"** by Faith Popcorn & Lys Marigold. This book discusses 16 trends that affect our business and personal lives.

- **"Organizing Genius"** by Warren Bennis & Patricia Ward Biederman. This book gives great examples of effective teamwork and explains how to develop it at your boatyard or marina.
- **"Why Employees Don't Do What They're Supposed to Do"** by Ferdinand F. Fournies. Written more than 10 years ago, this book recently had resurgence in popularity. It is a good book for frustrated supervisors.
- **"Against the Gods"** by Peter L. Bernstien. This book is an interesting analysis of business risk considerations presented in a historical context. It emphasizes that we shouldn't look just at the worst-case scenario when doing analysis. We also should consider the odds of the scenario occurring.
- **"Service America"** by Karl Albrecht and Ron Zemke. This book also was written more than 10 years ago but it continues to be a good source for how to provide great customer service.
- **"Six Thinking Hats"** by Edward DeBono. This is an excellent book that will help you improve both your creative thinking and decision-making skills.
- **"What America Does Right"** by Robert H. Waterman. Written by one of the "In Search of Excellence" authors, this book will provide you with lessons from some of the best-run American companies. It stresses the importance of organizing in a way that both motivates your employees and anticipates customer needs.
- **"If Aristotle Ran General Motors"** by Thomas V. Morris. This is an enjoyable look at mixing philosophy and business. The author shows you how to use the ideas from some of the greatest thinkers in history to increase the productivity of your marina or boatyard.
- **"Working Knowledge"** by Thomas **H.** Davenport, et al. Managing Information - not just computers has become

critical to every organization's survival. This book explains how to use your facility's knowledge to your competitive advantage.

- **"The Art and Science of Negotiation"** by Howard Raiffa. This book is an often technical and statistically driven look at negotiation designed to expand your thinking to help you find ways to negotiate the best deals for your marina or boatyard.
- **"Built to Last"** by James C. Collins and Jerry I. Porras. This book identifies similar habits of highly successful companies and emphasizes the use of goals in your business.
- **"Future Perfect"** by Stanley M. Davis. The author provides ideas to consider when preparing an organization for the future. Much emphasis is given to using speed as a competitive advantage.
- **"Corporate Culture and Performance"** by John P. Kotter and James L. Heskett. This book is an interesting look at how organizational culture impacts your results. It explains why stockholders, employees and customers should be treated equally.

If you would like a copy of my previous column's list of books or would like to make a recommendation for the next list, please drop me a note. I'll be happy to read your suggestions and compile another list for a future column.

Chapter 44
LET MEETINGS BE A TOOL FOR GOOD COMMUNICATION
July 1999

Despite almost universal agreement by boatyard and marina managers about the importance of communication, most managers struggle with the concept of holding regularly scheduled meetings. They want to be effective communicators, but they don't want to waste their employees' time.

Meetings at your boatyard or marina are essential to keep information flowing. If you're not giving the correct information to your employees, they will speculate and incorrect information will proliferate.

Meetings, if well run, also tell employees that you believe they are important to the smooth functioning of your facility's operations. Meetings are a time to share your facility's corporate objectives and vision, as well as your own. They also give employees a chance to be heard by their teammates.

Below are some tips to help you hold efficient, useful meetings at your boatyard or marina:

- **Give proper notice.** Let employees know in advance the purpose of the meeting and how long it will last.
- **Start on time.** Staying on schedule shows respect and sends the message that deadlines and commitments are important,

a philosophy that should influence employee's service to customers.

- **Have an agenda.** Though on occasion you may want to allow your employees to speak their minds, an agenda makes it easier to keep focused.
- **Have an objective.** Announce what you want to accomplish when you give notice of the meeting. Discuss it at the beginning of the meeting to remind everyone of its purpose and say it again at the end of the meeting to determine if it was accomplished.
- **Document the meeting.** Have someone take notes during the meeting to help you remember what was discussed and decided.

   Some marina and boatyard managers distribute notes from a meeting to all who attended. The notes give meeting participants a way to document progress and a starting point for planning the next meeting's agenda.
- **Assign tasks, responsibilities and deadlines.** To complete specific tasks, determine exactly what needs to be done, who has the responsibility for it and when it needs to be finished.

   For example, if you establish a new training requirement for marina service personnel, develop a program through which employees can receive the training. Assign a person the task of informing the staff members who needs to meet the new requirement and set a deadline for when the training should be completed.
- **Follow up.** Do not assume everything will get done just because it has been assigned.

The above ideas can help you run better meetings. Use them effectively to help increase your communication, productivity and profits.

For information on a related topic - how to hold effective weekly staff meetings - feel free to write and request a column I wrote a few years ago. I would be happy to send you a copy.

Chapter 45
OF "CHEESE" AND CHANGE-
A PARABLE FOR OUR INDUSTRY
January 2000

There's a great new book by Spencer Johnson, author of the "One Minute Manager," called "Who Moved My Cheese?" It's a simple parable about two mice and two "little people" who live in a maze, but it does an outstanding job of addressing concepts and difficulties related to change.

In a nutshell, the characters awaken one morning to find the thing they need most - their cheese - has been moved. The parable goes on to explore how each of the characters reacts to this change.

As I turned the pages, I couldn't help but think of our industry which, along with most others, is seeing its cheese continually moved.

I hate to think of myself as an old-timer while still in my 30's but the reality is I've seen a lot of change in this industry these past 16 years. And, it keeps coming. The result: companies that keep looking in the same old place for their cheese will be hurt substantially.

I remember a specific 98-foot boat coming into our boatyard 15 years ago and clearing out the offices. Everyone rushed out to see this behemoth. Now, in season, we may have a half-dozen boats over 150 feet on any given day. Our industry has been significantly affected by the increasing size of boats.

It's interesting to see how we're reacting to this change. Boatbuilders have tooled up and built sheds to handle the demand for these bigger boats, marinas are upgrading, boatyards are retooling their operations and suppliers are either growing to handle the change or fading away.

Some are spending millions to reposition themselves. At Rybovich we are nearing the end of a nearly $9 million capital investment program to adapt to this market change. We've reconfigured our service yard, bought more property and a new 300-ton lift, installed state of-the-art docks, upgraded our upland facilities, reorganized and upgraded our staff, launched a Web site and started selling some of our products through it. All these changes have been undertaken to keep pace with the changing environment. We're chasing the cheese.

The bigger boats are a reality and will be for decades to come. But, interestingly, some owners already are beginning to talk about going back to smaller, easier to handle, less costly yachts. We've not heard a lot of this yet, but enough to take note. A trend in the making? Something we should watch, anyway.

The international influence on our industry also seems to have mushroomed. Able to communicate instantly from anywhere, Americans think nothing of going to Europe to have a boat built or repaired. During each of the past two years, I have visited many European marine businesses and it has amazed me to see that the names in the full order books of many European boat builders were mostly those of people from the United States. In addition, the increasing popularity of services like the Dock Express is making the marine world smaller and accelerating the trend toward internationalism.

As the world continues to shrink, many others in our industry are spending time overseas, and we find we are frequently dealing with peers from other countries. We are learning from one another and my experience is that the cooperation has been exemplary. Now there is enough work for everyone, but odds are that one-day the orders will slow down. Hopefully we will continue to work together. Our biggest competitors are not the other boating businesses but those outside our industry who are trying to capture the attention of our customers.

Recently, I was speaking on the topic of "Who Moved My Cheese?" at a meeting of the American Boat Builders and Repairers Association in Annapolis, MD. We were discussing the moving cheese in our industry and there were differing opinions of where the cheese was going. Some mentioned the changing boat sizes and the internationalization I have discussed here. Others brought up the changing labor market, and some mentioned the evolving environmental and technological environments. Despite the differing perspectives, there was one thing on which all 100 attendees agreed: we absolutely will be doing business differently 10 years from now than we are today.

We know for certain the cheese will continue to move. We can either keep up with it or spend our time complaining about how unfair it is. Those who choose to spend their time complaining will be left behind; those who keep up with the changes will benefit greatly.

Chapter 46
INFORMATION AGE SPAWNS THE "KNOWLEDGE MANAGER"
February 2000

Knowledge management refers to how organizations manage what they know.

Today, astute managers are beginning to focus on knowledge management as one of their top priorities. Many of them are trying to use what their companies know to their competitive advantage.

Don't worry - if this is the first time you have heard the term knowledge manager, it won't be the last. The concept of managing what you know has become much more popular as managers begin to realize that information may be their most valuable asset.

This idea is so important that today some large companies are appointing a chief knowledge officer (CKO) to manage the process. In the marine industry, most of us would agree that this idea is important to our business.

In a recent book, "Working Knowledge," the authors give examples of companies that had accomplished something great but later couldn't remember what they did or no longer had the people with them who had facilitated the accomplishment. The most interesting and glaring example related to the Ford Motor Co. and the development of the Taurus. Apparently, Ford failed to document what it had done so successfully with the Taurus, losing that information forever.

The key to successful knowledge management is organizing your company's information so it can be accessed and used to your advantage. Though your Management Information Service department may have a role to play in this process, it's not just a MIS function. Most of this information is in peoples' heads. Also, it is very important to understand that knowledge management is not just a matter of documenting information but, more importantly, a matter of spreading it.

You would probably be surprised at how much information is in your employees' heads. Information such as company history, customer details, employee motivators, competitive intelligence, product information and "lessons learned" are all examples. This information should be proliferated throughout your organization. This is especially important when you consider that a valuable portion of each manager's day is spent in search of specific knowledge.

Can you imagine how much more effective your company would be if much of the information held by individuals was spread throughout the organization?

Here are some specific ideas to help you with knowledge management at your company:

- **Make it a priority.** Determine that spreading information throughout your company will be one of your top priorities. In your employee communications, encourage the sharing of information.
- **Document your history.** This may seem needless to you but it is amazing how often history repeats itself. Have someone talk to the "old-timers" and prepare a history of your company.
- **Let people "small talk."** Many managers are so controlling they hate to see their employees enjoying small talk. Keep in mind that these may be times when many of their work-related problems are being solved.
- **Earn your employees' trust.** Effective knowledge management

requires trust. If your employees don't trust you, they will hoard information as a way to ensure job security. Even if they are secure in their jobs, lack of trust causes employees to fear the consequences of sharing information. Try to manage in a way that employees don't get in trouble for constructively sharing information or opinions.

- **Use smart people.** You probably have smart people working for you. Don't be so controlling that you keep them too busy to use their brains and knowledge. Give them time to think and let them be creative.

- **Have regular staff meetings.** Staff meetings provide an arena for discussion of what is happening at your company. End every staff meeting by going around the table and giving each employee an opportunity to share his or her thoughts.

- **Have an open-door policy.** Encourage open communication at all levels of your organization.

- **Use training and teamwork.** Both are effective tools to use when developing your organization's knowledge management. (Drop me a note and I will be happy to send you previous columns I have written on both of these topics.)

- **Have an employee newsletter.** They are inexpensive, easy to create and they are a great way of spreading knowledge. Employees enjoy reading them.

As you do the above, be sure the steps you take tum organizational knowledge into organization wisdom. Then use this new wisdom to make proactive decisions, which create actions that improve not only your personal effectiveness but also your company's results.

Chapter 47
THE GOLDEN RULE APPLIES TO YOUR EMPLOYEES, TOO
March 2000

If there is one question I hear more than any other from managers it has to be, "How do I motivate my employees?"

Many managers struggle to find a formula that works. In fact, instead of motivating their staff, their efforts sometimes backfire. If you are searching for answers in this area, you are not alone.

Recently, while reading "What America Does Right," a book by Robert Waterman, I came across as clear a summary of the factors that motivate employees as I have ever read. Basically, Waterman says, employees have several needs that must be met.

These include:

- the need to feel in control
- the need for lifelong learning
- the need for recognition

I think we can learn something by focusing on each of these needs.

As managers, it is sometimes hard for us to give up control. We are people, too, and we also have a need to feel in control. In fact, overcoming your own need to control the people who work for you may be the toughest challenge you face. However, the sooner you learn to trust your employees, the sooner your results will improve.

The second need - giving employees something to believe in - requires a mission statement. If your company doesn't have one, write one. If you need help, contact me and I will send you some of my previous writings on how to create a mission statement. In either case, a mission statement can serve as the fundamental direction for your company. Employees need to feel their specific jobs are important. Some managers are hesitant to let their people feel important. They fear they will become difficult to manage. This happens occasionally, but most of the time people respond favorably. In fact, one good way to develop loyalty from your team is to let them know they are important to you. Of course, you must be sincere.

Your employees' need for challenge can be a real test of your managerial abilities. It is one that requires you to periodically review their objectives to ensure they have enough challenges to keep them interested. At the very least, you should be doing this annually as part of each employee's formal performance evaluation.

An employee's need for lifelong learning is one that, if met, not only keeps the individual motivated but also keeps your company productive and profitable.

Every company, no matter how small, can offer its people training.

Many boating industry trade associations (ABYC, IMI, ABBRA) and trade shows (IBEX) offer educational programs specific to the marine industry. Check out the community college, tech school or adult-education programs in your area. Traveling seminars scheduled in your town or nearby can also be a good source of inexpensive training.

There are many different ways to meet this important need for lifelong learning. But the crucial thing is that you are focused on the continual improvement of both you and your team.

The final need, according to Waterman, is the need for recognition.

I hope your company celebrates its accomplishments. Be sure your team is getting the recognition it deserves.

One caveat in the area of recognition: most employees prefer and appreciate public recognition, but some don't. You'll find some are more comfortable with private recognition. Sometimes you may be able to accomplish just as much with a private comment about how much your employee's extra efforts mean to you. But regardless of whether it is private or public, be sure you are giving recognition when it is deserved.

I hope this clarifies how you motivate employees. There is one other motivational strategy that is almost fail-proof. Our employees are just like us. Whenever in doubt, treat your employees as you would want to be treated if you were in their situation. It always works.

Chapter 48
IS YOUR MANAGEMENT STYLE CUTTING INTO YOUR PROFITS?
April 2000

Is your management style frustrating your key employees? Worse yet, are you managing them in a way that is hurting your company's results?

Many managers don't realize how frustrating they can be to work for. Some don't care; they figure, "I'm the boss and things should be done my way," or, "I have the right to be involved in any matter I choose." Technically, of course, they are correct. But they are hurting both themselves and their companies in the long run.

There are two extreme examples of poor management style. The first is the micromanager. The micromanager feels he or she has to be involved in everything. Usually, an employee who works for a micromanager steps back and lets the boss assume all the responsibility and accountability. The organization evolves to the point that this manager's superstars leave and all that's left are people who are basically robots - happy to carry out the tasks assigned to them.

The second type of manager is even more dangerous to his or her organization. This manager assigns responsibility but not authority. This type of manager won't let go completely and will interfere just enough to unmotivate the employees. Unlike the micromanager, whom employees eventually accept and adapt to, this manager is like someone continually picking at an open wound. Although the boss is unlikely to realize it, the employees feel they are being undermined. Worse, they feel their judgment is not trusted. It can significantly hamper the results of the organization.

As a manager, you should look closely in the mirror and consider if either of these management styles reflects your way of operating. If they do, you have a major problem. First of all, your own anxiety level must be high, because it is very frustrating to manage in this fashion. Second, while your employees may not be direct enough to tell you (they need their jobs) they are operating at far less than their true potential. All this adds up to less than optimal results for your company. Putting it more directly, your management style may be costing your company a lot of money.

You may be thinking, "I can't help it; I am what I am." Don't give in to this line of thought. There are several things you can do:

- **Relax** - Don't let yourself get trapped into thinking you are the ultimate source of knowledge and wisdom. If you don't have people you trust to handle things, then you have made some bad hiring decisions. Actually, most people will do a much better job than you expect if you will just get out of their way.
- **Relinquish control** - Unfortunately, most managers are control freaks. Those who are most effective are those who are able to let go. Let people do their jobs. Don't interfere. This is tough and it truly takes a tremendous amount of self-confidence. We all have an innate desire to be in control, but by relinquishing it, we benefit in the long run.
- **Build up your employees**- Many times as managers, we don't realize the importance of our words. It is so easy to make subtle little comments that tear down and unmotivate your employees. Not only is this frustrating to your employees, but in the long run it is you and your organization that pays for it. Building up your employees takes a lot of positive reinforcement, but it

is more than that. It is a sincere effort on your part to make your people feel important. This is so easy to do, but many managers still struggle with it. Bottom line: make people feel important; in the long run they will be incredibly loyal and it will pay off for you in a big way.

- **Develop your employees** -Train, train, train. Recently, I was speaking at IBEX on employee-related issues, and we discussed the importance of this management tool. You must be continually developing your staff. Remember, as Zig Ziglar says, "It is better to train your employees and lose them than not train them and keep them!"

All these issues are important parts of management and, even though I have hesitated to use the word thus far in this column, it is basically just effective delegation. If you are not delegating or you are delegating ineffectively, you most certainly are getting less than optimal results.

I have written frequently over the years on these issues. If you would like me to send you more information on this topic, drop me a note and I will be happy to do it.

Try the above starting today. However, a word of caution: when you try to change your management style, you may be viewed by your team with some degree of skepticism and you may even hear some comments about your changes. Don't let this discourage you. In the long run these principles will work for you. Stick with them, even if they are a little awkward at first, and reap the rewards over the years.

Chapter 49
ABILITY TO FOCUS HELPS BUILD
PROFITS, EFFICIENCY
May 2000

Focus is an important ingredient of successful management. It is almost impossible to accomplish your objective without the ability to keep yourself and your team properly focused. In fact, I've come to believe this may be one of the successful manager's most important attributes.

Think for a moment of someone in the boating industry who is successful. You'll probably agree that one of that person's attributes is the ability to stay focused. This skill allows such people to be extremely effective at their jobs, which makes them extremely valuable managers for their companies.

How do you know if you are focused as a manager? Some signs include the ability to accomplish objectives quickly, the ability to manage time effectively and, most importantly, the ability to get positive results.

A sure sign of an unfocused manager is frequent procrastination. There is continual emphasis on how busy this individual is-not on the results he or she is getting. You know the type - always seems to be in frenzy but doesn't seem to accomplish very much. The unfocused manager also tends to be the type who picks on details instead of making a decision.

Regardless of your current level of effectiveness, even slight improvements in your ability to focus can have a positive impact - not only on your personal productivity but also on the profitability of your business.

Some things you can do to help improve your ability to focus:

- **Know what is important.** Your company should have both a mission statement and a strategic plan. You should have a personal mission statement. If you want some help with these, drop me a note. I would be happy to email you copies of my previous writings on how to prepare these documents. Once you have prepared these statements, you should significantly reduce the amount of time you spend on activities that do not align with them.

- **Concentrate on the present and future; don't dwell on the past.** If you find that several times a day you are focusing on something that irritates you from the past or someone who did you wrong, get over it. Though you may not realize it, your preoccupation with history is having a detrimental effect on your current effectiveness.

- **Stay within your area of control.** Don't waste your energy trying to change the unchangeable. Many aspects of both your environment and the people around you are nearly impossible to change. If you waste energy on these issues, it reduces your effectiveness in the other areas that you can control. If you need more help in this area, pick up "Seven Habits for Highly Effective People" by Steven Covey and read Habit No. 1.

- **Be results-oriented.** Many managers get so tied up in the day-to-day activities they completely forget about what they are trying to accomplish. Focus on results. Whenever you go into a meeting or start a new task ask yourself, "What am I trying to accomplish here?" If you cannot think of what the result of your task is, you should probably be doing something else.

- **Be ethical.** It is difficult to stay focused if you are frequently trying to manipulate people or are not always aboveboard. Part of being ethical is related to focusing on the long-term consequences of your actions. It is also hard to properly focus on the tasks at hand if your conscience is nagging at you.
- **Take care of yourself.** It is significantly easier to stay focused if you are looking after your health. Be sure to take your vitamins and exercise. Eat right. Manage your stress through meditation, breathing exercises or other relaxation techniques. And, last but not least, get plenty of rest and allow enough time to have fun. All these things will have a positive impact on your ability to focus.

It can be hard to improve your focus but with a little effort it can be done. Focus is very hard to measure but if you try the above steps you will see improvement. Most importantly, you will find that as your ability to focus improves so will your effectiveness and profits.

Chapter 50
KEEP YOUR EMPLOYEES - TREAT THEM
LIKE VOLUNTEERS
June 2000

Most managers in our industry agree the No. 1 problem they face to-day is finding and keeping good employees. In fact, most managers in any industry will tell you that.

Recently, I spoke to an audience of nearly 100 marine industry managers at the International Boatbuilders' Exhibit & Conference, of-fering some suggestions on how to deal with this problem.

It was interesting to hear the marine companies in the Northeast talk about advertising in Florida for workers while the Florida compa-nies are advertising in the Northeast. The fact is that no one is exempt from the problem, but some managers in our industry have to be made aware of that. Many of them think their peers in another geographic area have an abundant supply of good labor and just needs to be iden-tified and tapped into. I am afraid this is not the case; we all are strug-gling to find - and keep good employees.

Since there is not an abundant supply of qualified people looking for jobs, we had better be doing a pretty good job of keeping the good employees we already have. I know this is hard. It seems there always are other companies trying to steal your best and brightest people, and many of us have seen good employees leave to take "an offer I couldn't refuse." No company is exempt.

In today's economy, there are lots of jobs available to those who are antsy or, for one reason or another, want to make a change.

In addition, today's knowledge worker maintains his or her own source of portable capital - the education and experience that make that individual more attractive to a prospective employer and, at the same time, make it easier to move on to another job. This makes it all the more imperative that we retain those people who are the most valuable assets of our businesses.

In his recent book, *Management Challenges for the 21st Century*, the management guru Peter Drucker tackles this problem and offers what is a simple, yet profound solution (I guess that's why he is a management guru!). Drucker says if we want to keep our best employees, we need to treat them not as employees, but as volunteers.

Hmmmm. Sounds like a great idea, but how do you treat volunteers?

I have the privilege of sitting on the boards of seven nonprofit organizations (four of which are marine industry-related) - all of which rely on volunteers to help them carry out their missions.

One of these organizations has more than 500 volunteers. It has an excellent reputation of maintaining a good rapport with those volunteers, and has managed to keep them coming back - eager and motivated. After reading Drucker's comments, I called the CEO of this organization and asked him his secret. This is what he told me, and I believe it's something we all can apply to our own dealings with our employees:

- **Give them a purpose** - Every company, whether it relies on paid employees or volunteers, needs to provide a mission. Creating a mission statement is an obvious start. Using goals and objectives is another way to give your employees a greater sense of purpose.
- **Keep them informed** - Everyone likes to know what is going on. At our company, we use employee newsletters, payroll

stuffers, payroll stub notices, management meetings and staff meetings in an effort to keep everyone abreast of what is going on. We also share financial information with our managers with the intention that those managers update their employees on the company's financial results during their departmental staff meetings.

- **Give lots of reinforcement and thanks** - People appreciate knowing that you recognize their efforts when they do a good job.
- **Hold appreciation events** - These can take a variety of forms, large or small. We have held all types of employee activities at our company, including subsidized professional ballgames, company picnics, after-work parties, holiday parties and, once a year, a big company extravaganza to which each employee is invited to bring a guest and to which we invite our customers and vendors. We also have given employees boat show tickets as well as tickets to a popular local festival, SunFest.
- **Keep them challenged** - No one likes to be bored. Give people tasks and objectives that not only challenge them to perform their best but also keep them motivated.

Again, simple yet profound. All these are things we can do immediately to help keep our best employees.

One of our managers, Al Genduso, once told me the definition of insanity is doing the same thing over and over and expecting a different result. Don't keep treating your employees the same old ways and expect them to react differently. All of us, including me, can learn from these recommendations.

Try them and see if this approach doesn't make your employees happier and, at the same time, save you large amounts of time, aggravation and money.

Chapter 51
MANAGE YOUR TIME BETTER AND QUIT "PUTTING OUT FIRES"
July 2000

Twice recently I have had the opportunity to speak at conferences put on by the International Marina Institute, one in Brussels, Belgium and the other in Seattle. As always, I was impressed by the fine job Paul Dodson and his team at IMI are doing developing people in our industry - both in the United States and internationally.

These two conferences attracted many managers, representing marine businesses from all over the world, and I couldn't help but focus on how similar our problems are. We all struggle with the same employee and customer issues, no matter where in the world we are. However, employee and customer matters are not the only areas in which I hear managers in our industry asking for help.

One of the most common complaints from managers has to do with their inability to manage their time. It seems like many in our industry spend a fair amount of time "putting out fires." They don't do what is important because they are so focused on handling the little things that consume their days.

In a recent talk at the International Boatbuilder's Exhibition and Conference on time management, I gave the approximately 100 managers in the room a tool they could use to rate themselves in time-management skills. After taking the test, almost all agreed they could use help.

If you are among the majority - those managers who recognize they can use some help with their time management - don't worry. Actually, there are some very simple things you can do.

Here are some of them:

- **Know what is important** - Have a personal mission for your life and a strategic plan for your business. Each of these is easy to create and an absolute must if you want to control your time. It takes more than instinct to know what is important. You must have both of these plans thoroughly thought out and then committed to writing. Once you have them, avoid activities that don't help advance your mission or business plan.

- **Delegate** - Don't be a control freak. Trust those who work for you. This is hard for many of us but it is imperative if you are going to have any sense of control over your time. Train the people around you and then trust them to do what you have trained them to do. Most managers are deluding themselves when they think they have to be involved in everything in order for things to turn out right. You don't have a lock on all knowledge and experience just by virtue of your position. In fact (now hold on), there are some things your employees may even be able to do better than you. It is the smart manager that relies on the combined knowledge and experience of all those around him, not just himself.

- **Focus on the things within your control** - Many managers waste a tremendous amount of time worrying about things over which they have no control. If you do this, you are not managing your time. But if you discipline yourself to focus only on areas you can control, you can significantly expand your sphere of influence.

- **Focus on results** - This may be the single most important key to being an effective manager. Focus on what you are trying to accomplish and not the process by which you are trying to accomplish it. Don't get buried in the details when it is not necessary. In other words, be goal-oriented.
- **Keep a to-do list** - One thing I know for certain: if you do not have a to-do list, you most assuredly do have a time management problem. In addition to your master to-do list, keep a daily "hot list" of the things you want to accomplish each day. This "hot list" should be completed each night before you leave. When you come in the next morning focus immediately on this list.
- **Get organized** - Force yourself to do it. Organize your desk and throw out unnecessary papers. Keep a follow-up file for each month so you can put the papers related to that month in it. Then just pull them out at the beginning of that month. Everything you need will be right there at the right time and you will not have had all those papers lying around in the meantime. Don't go home until your work area is clean and organized, with the next day's "hot list" lying in the middle of your desk.

Have you ever worked with someone who did not seem to work that hard but still got everything done? Someone who always seemed to make everything look easy? Odds are that person uses the tools described above to manage his or her day and you can, too. These are all simple tools that you can implement immediately. They can bring dramatic improvement - not only in your effectiveness on the job but in your life in general.

Chapter 52
CAPITAL BUDGET TIME MEANS TOUGH DECISIONS AWAIT YOU
August 2000

Do you often find yourself perplexed when trying to decide whether to make a capital purchase? You want to make the right decisions, but there are so many factors to consider. Or maybe you're not even sure what needs to be considered. How do you choose between conflicting priorities?

Determining which assets to purchase for your company is commonly called capital budgeting decisions. These can be some of the toughest and most frustrating decisions you face as a manager.

In the most general terms, there are two types of capital purchases.

Replacement capital purchases are those you need to stay in operation. Most of the time these purchases provide for the replacement or improvement of existing assets. Many times they are necessary just to stay in business.

The second type is the improvement purchase. This generally involves something that will increase your profitability. These are the purchases with which we have the most difficulty because they are discretionary- we don't need them to continue operating.

When managing capital purchases, many companies will prepare a wish list - anything that would be helpful to the business they prioritize, with replacement purchases at the top of the list.

When projects seem to be near equal in priority, there are some basic analytical tools you can use to help decide what is most important. To use these tools, you must prepare basic projections of cash flow and income that an investment will provide. And you must be able to accurately forecast the project cost.

- **Payback method.** The payback method calculates the expected length of time it will take for the positive cash flows of an investment to pay back its initial cost. This is the oldest, easiest and probably the most widely used capital budgeting technique.

    Under this method, you project annual cash flows from the investment and compare them with the original investment cost. By doing this you can determine how long it will take for the investment to pay for itself.

- **Accounting rate of return.** The accounting rate of return method compares the income provided for a new investment with the initial cost of that investment.

    Calculating this is easy. First, you must project the annual income provided by the investment over its life. Then, divide the initial investment cost into this projection. The result provides you with a percentage that is the accounting rate of return.

    By itself, the accounting rate of return may not be very meaningful. But it can be a very useful tool when trying to compare two distinct capital investments.

- **Internal rate of return.** The internal rate of return is a significantly more complicated calculation that takes into consideration both cash flows and their timing. It calculates the rate of return that causes the present value of future cash flows to exactly equal the initial cost of the project.

- **Discounted cash flows (net present value).** Discounted cash flow is the most widely accepted capital budgeting technique because it considers both cash flows (vs net income) provided by the project and the time value of your company's money. Many people have anxiety attacks when they hear phrases like discounted cash flow or net present value, but it really is not that complicated to calculate.

To use this method you must do the following:

- Select a reasonable return rate, one that you would consider appropriate in your business environment (your accountant can help).
- Estimate the annual cash flows provided by the project over its estimated life.
- Use the present value tables to find the discount rate that applies to the return rate you have chosen for each applicable year of the investment's life.
- Multiply the discount rate to each year's projected cash flow to calculate each year's discounted cash flow.
- Add each year's discounted cash flow together to determine the discounted cash flow of the entire investment.

If, after going through the above steps the total discounted cash flow over the life of the investment is greater than the initial investment cost, you have a worthwhile capital project.

If you are not an accountant these ideas can be hard to grasp. If you would like to learn more about these tools I would recommend the book "Making Capital Budgeting Decisions" by Hazel Johnson.

These are all tools you can use when trying to make capital budgeting decisions for your marine business. Though they can appear intimidating, they are really not that hard once you begin using them. Try them and see if they don't help you make sense of what can be a very confusing process.

Chapter 53
HOW VALUABLE IS TRAINING? THINK ABOUT A 33-1 RETURN
September 2000

Most managers today would agree that training their employees is one of the best investments they can make. Motorola, in fact, has determined that it gets $33 back for every dollar it invests in its training program. You don't have to be a CPA to identify that as a great investment.

Companies all over America are recognizing the utility of investing in their people. In fact, I have seen estimates that U.S. businesses spend $60 billion a year on training. That's a lot of money.

Companies like McDonald's and General Motors Corp. believe so strongly in training that they have gone to the time and expense of developing in-house universities. Intel and Anderson Consulting, among others, require their employees to commit two weeks a year exclusively to training.

How is your company doing in this regard? Does it have a training program? If you are not developing your employees you may soon find yourself at a distinct disadvantage. Employee training is not just a nice thing to do; it's a necessity if you want to remain competitive in an ever-improving world. Your company's very survival may depend on it. Your organization is no better than its people.

If training is so important, why do so many companies in our industry not do it? Interestingly enough, the most frequent answer I hear is that managers are afraid that if they invest in an employee the employee will leave them for a better job elsewhere - worst-case scenario, with a competitor.

I have to say that I have only in very isolated instances seen their fear actually realized. In most cases employees feel a heightened sense of loyalty to employers who are willing to invest in them. But, regardless, the best response to this is something I heard Zig Ziglar say several years ago: "The only thing worse than training employees and losing them is not training employees and keeping them." Think about that for a minute.

I believe our industry does a good job of offering training opportunities. Boating Week, which is fast approaching, is loaded with them. The International Boatbuilders' Exhibition and Conference also is a great source. We send many of our employees to this conference each year.

Paul Dodson at the International Marina Institute offers great programs for those in the marina business (and for some who aren't). Skip Moyer and his team at the American Boat and Yacht Council and Pat Keams at the American Boat Builders and Repairers Association both put on great training programs that have been a big help - both to their members and others. Many others, including manufacturers and dealers, also offer valuable training opportunities.

Every company in our industry should be taking advantage of these programs. They are a great way to develop your employees, with industry-specific speakers and topics.

Besides the industry conferences, there are many other ways to accomplish employee training:

- **Develop an in-house program.** This probably is easier than you think. Have people in your company conduct training sessions within their areas of expertise. One person needs to be responsible for scheduling and details, but you probably have a great deal of expertise within the organization.

- **Use vendors.** Vendors or manufacturers often will jump at the opportunity to come and provide free training to your employees. You tell them the time and place and they'll be thrilled to present information regarding the use of their products.

- **Rent training videos.** There are lots of companies offering them, and most are both entertaining and educational. They are an easy way to provide training to a group. Just remember to follow up with a meaningful discussion on the topic presented.

- **Use traveling seminars.** They come within reach of almost every town, and they offer a multitude of topics. Overall, I have found these to be very good. Usually, they are one-day affairs and are not expensive. Employees love them and almost always come back energized.

- **Start a training library.** Good books, tapes and videos are available. You can buy them and make them available to your employees. We have a number of these items at our company and we keep them in our training room - available for our employees to use.

All these are things I have done and I know they work. I'm sure they can work for you too.

There is one other thing to think about in the current business environment that has us all looking harder than ever to find and keep good employees. Training is a great employee benefit that will help you keep your best people. Let me re-emphasize: employees appreciate companies that are willing to invest in them. And, it helps your company improve its competitive edge.

Chapter 54
GET FEEDBACK, SET GOALS IN EMPLOYEE EVALUATIONS.
October 2000

You've probably heard it said that feedback "is the breakfast of champions."

One of a manager's best tools for giving employees that all-important feedback is through the annual performance evaluation.

Unfortunately, the annual review process is something that many managers and employees tread. In fact, the manager often has significantly more anxiety about the process than the employee being reviewed. Part of the reason is that many managers feel uncomfortable about the interpersonal nature of the evaluation, but there also are large numbers of managers who are just unsure about the process. This is unfortunate because how you 1andle performance evaluations can have a big impact on your team's results.

The most important thing to remember about the process is its purpose. Most managers think the objective of any evaluation is to correct past behavior, but this is completely incorrect. The focus, instead, should be on the future. This is done by setting goals with the employee for the next review period.

Don't misunderstand - past behavior should be discussed. However, it is only used to set up a discussion about the employee's goals for the next review period. The best managers deal with problems as they arise, dealing with them on a daily basis instead of saving them for the evaluation. In fact, if you have the right kind of rapport and communication with your employees there will be no negative surprises during the evaluation.

Basically, the annual performance evaluation is a three-part process. The first is the pre evaluation meeting, the second is completing the form and the third is the actual formal evaluation.

The pre-evaluation meeting is an opportunity for you and your employee to meet prior to the formal evaluation. At this point the form hasn't been completed. This meeting is designed to let you and your employee "catch up." Personally, I find this the most meaningful time in the evaluation process.

Some things to remember related to the pre-evaluation meeting are as follows:

- **Do it on time.** It is not fair to employees to make them wait for their annual evaluation. Doing it on time emphasizes its importance.
- **Keep it informal.** This meeting should be like a "chat" among friends.
- **Use a questionnaire.** I have a list of discussion points that I go through with my employees during these meetings. Mine has 17 points on it - among them, how can we operate as a better team? Are you treated fairly? How can we better serve our customers? Are you happy working here?
- **Get feedback from the employee.** During the pre-evaluation meeting the employee should do most of the talking. A very important question to ask at the pre-evaluation meeting is what the employee thinks his or her goals should be for the next review period.
- **Be a good listener.** Don't just go through the motions. Pay

attention to the employee and listen carefully to what he or she is saying.

Now that you've had the pre-evaluation meeting, it's time to complete the evaluation form. When you begin, keep these three points in mind.

- **Have an objective.** Focus on what you want the evaluation process to accomplish.
- **Choose your words carefully.** Read what you have written as if you were the employee.
- **Stay objective.** This is imperative. As manager, you must not in any way allow your personal biases to affect an evaluation. Whether you and the employee are "friends" does not matter.

After completing the form comes the tough part - the formal meeting with the employee. Some things to keep in mind as you meet.

- **Maintain your rapport.** Start the evaluation with some friendly discussion and mix small talk throughout the meeting. Try to keep the employee comfortable.
- **Avoid arguments.** Even if there is disagreement, don't let it get heated.
- **Focus on the future.** The future of the company and the employee's role in it should be the area of emphasis.
- **Be direct, but diplomatic.** Deal with problems directly, but within the framework of setting goals. Focus on behavior and never get personal.
- **Outline specific goals.** This is the most important part of the evaluation. Make sure the employee leaves the meeting with a clear understanding of what his or her goals are for the next review period.

- **End on a positive note.** No employee should leave the evaluation feeling demoralized.

Performance evaluations are not always easy, but they are important. How well you 1andle them can have a big impact on the dynamics of your team, the team's effectiveness, and ultimately your profitability.

Chapter 55
SAVING A MIFFED CUSTOMER:
I CALL IT "FUMBLE RECOVERY"
November 2000

Recently, I came very close to switching the bank our company does business with.

After a couple of mergers and seeing a turnstile of contacts, I was getting really frustrated with both the individuals and the organization at our bank. In fact, I was just a pen stroke away from making a change. I had held several meetings with potential new banks and we were in the final stage of discussions with the one we had settled on to take over our business.

Then came the call. A new contact with our current bank, Linda, called to say she wanted to come by and meet me and introduce herself and her boss, Gerry. I almost turned them down. I'd been here before - another new person, another meeting with someone I would never see again. I wasn't sure the meeting was worth my time, especially since I had gone through the process of checking out the other banks and was so close to making a change. Oh well, I thought, I'll give them 30 minutes.

Well, that 30 minutes turned into nearly three hours as I unloaded on them the litany of problems I had experienced. I kept talking to them because as we went along I was beginning to sense that they were genuinely interested in what I was saying. Could these two be different?

To my pleasant surprise they were different - very different. They took a genuine interest in our company and ended up putting together a new package for us that included a complete refinancing among other things. They kept their customer and completely blew away my grim expectations.

We all have customers from time to time that we risk losing. Many times we actually do lose the customer. However, I don't believe that we have to.

There are some great lessons from my encounter with Gerry and Linda which we all can apply to our marine businesses:

- **Stay in contact with your customers.** The reason Gerry and Linda were able to retain our company's business is that they invested the time to come and see me. I'm sure they had lots of other demands on their time, but they took the time to visit and didn't rush away when it appeared I was upset or when it became obvious that the meeting would go way over schedule.

    Many managers will never know when one of their customers is upset because they don't stay in close contact. It is imperative that we as managers maintain that contact.

- **Be a good listener.** Sometimes we need to just sit still and carefully listen to our customers. This can be more difficult than it appears. Our first inclination is to be defensive - or at least to get our side of the story out. The reality is, our side of the story doesn't matter.

    Gerry and Linda listened carefully as I vented about the same problems repeatedly. They didn't get defensive and they rapidly conceded that they could see my perspective. Effective listening is incredibly disarming. Remember, the more you talk when a customer is venting the less likely you are to salvage the relationship. The customer will make it obvious when he or she is ready to hear whatever response you may have.

- **Find out what the customer wants.** It may not be obvious at first, and the customer may not even be sure of what he or she wants. A good way to find out is to ask an open ended question along the lines of, "How can I make this right for you?"
- **Respond quickly.** I knew Gerry and Linda were different when they got back to me with their proposal within 24 hours. In this day and age of e-mail and other speedy information exchanges, people expect prompt responses. Don't delay; get back to the customer immediately with your proposed resolution of their problem.
- **Do what you say you will do.** You will make the situation with your customer even worse if you commit to fixing the problem and then don't keep your word. Remember, the key to customer satisfaction is to exceed the customer's expectations; therefore whatever you commit to the customer, go one step further.
- **Follow up.** Stay in touch with the customer after the problem is resolved.

Look at every customer complaint as an opportunity to develop a customer for life. Many times your best customers will be those with whom you have had a problem you were able to resolve. You know you managed to salvage the relationship. They know you care based on how you handled their problem.

Over the years I have called the above process "fumble recovery." Gerry and Linda did a great job of recovering a fumble by their bank and you, too, can do the same for your marine business.

Customers are hard enough to find. We need to do everything we can to keep the ones we have.

Chapter 56
KNOWING ISN'T ENOUGH - YOU NEED THE DO PART, TOO
December 2000

Not long ago, after speaking at a marine industry conference in the Chesapeake Bay area, I was approached by one of our well-respected colleagues - a man I know from years of mutual involvement in these types of events. As he approached, I could tell he was frustrated, so I listened carefully as he shared his thoughts.

He has heard me speak many times over the years, he said, and has always left "fired up"- eager to go home and change his habits. The problem is that while he knows exactly what he should be doing when he gets back, he has a heck of a time actually doing it.

I'm afraid a lot of us have this same problem. Businesses in the United States spend tens of billions of dollars a year for expertise we don't apply. We spend billions on training, billions on consultants and billions more hiring MBA's and CPA's for our staff. We get to know what we should be doing but we still don't do it.

The first time I fully appreciated this concept was when I invited a guest speaker to share this expertise with students in a management course I was teaching at our local college. The speaker was a consultant named Don Beveridge. Mr. Beveridge told the students that night that the problem he encounters with most managers is not a deficiency of knowledge but a deficiency of action. They know what to do - they just don't do it!

These managers are not lazy or irresponsible. Most of the time they are just caught up in work habits that undermine what they really are trying to accomplish.

I have just finished reading a recently published book that addresses this problem head-on. It is entitled "The Knowing-Doing Gap," and was written by Jeffrey Pfeffer and Robert Sutton.

The authors document several causes for this gap, including:

- Letting talk substitute for action
- Letting memory substitute for fresh thinking
- Letting fear prevent acting
- Letting measurement obstruct judgment
- Letting internal competition turn friends into enemies

The causes of the knowing-doing gap make for interesting reading, but most managers are more concerned about what they can do to overcome the problem. Some of the book's solutions, mixed in with some of my own are as follows:

- **Think why before you think how.** Principles are more important than procedures. Is what you are doing in line with your company's mission?
- **Be results-oriented.** Many managers get so tied up in the process that they lose sight of the end result. Being results oriented is one of a manager's most important attributes. Funny thing, but you can easily pick out results-oriented managers because they're the ones who make everything look easy. They just get things done - no mess or fuss.
- **Actions are more important than plans.** Don't get me wrong; planning is important. But if you spend all of your time

planning and have none left for doing, you're going to have real problems in the long run. Do your planning, then roll up your sleeves and dig in.

- **Forgive mistakes.** Many employees are paralyzed by the fear of making a mistake. This is tragic because an employee who won't make a mistake probably won't do anything remarkable, either. If you have to choose, it is better to criticize someone for not doing anything than for making an honest mistake. Try to drive fear out of your organization. If employees fear losing their jobs or getting yelled at over a bad decision, they are likely to make no decision at all.

- **Focus competition outside of your company.** Our external competition is fierce enough; we don't have to foster it internally. Focus, instead, on teamwork. Develop management incentive plans that enhance teamwork, not destroy it.

- **Manage your time effectively.** There are plenty of tools and techniques you can use to effectively manage your time. Drop me an e-mail and I'll be happy to send you copies of my previous writings on time management. Improving your ability to manage your time is one of the most liberating things you can do.

- **Get some help.** Find some instructional books or tapes. The Pfeffer/Sutton book would be a great place to start.

Don't become one of the many managers who knows all the right answers but doesn't actually do anything right. Step out, take some action and avoid the paralysis that incapacitates so many managers. Not only will your new "doing" mentality help your company's profits but you'll feel much better about yourself along the way.

Chapter 57
A LEADER SUPPLIES A VISION, A MANAGER IMPLEMENTS IT
January 2001

What is the difference between a manager and a leader? Which are you? Is one better than the other?

These are all interesting questions, and knowing the distinction between the two terms can make you a more effective executive.

First of all, while both roles are important, there is a big difference between a manager and a leader.

A leader is someone who has the ability to create a vision for his or her company and then clearly communicates that vision to others in the organization. A leader also has the ability to organize people in a manner that facilitates them in implementing the vision. And, perhaps most importantly, a leader has the ability to motivate and inspire people to want to attain the vision.

A manager is someone who carries out the direction set by the leadership. A manager staffs the organization, sets procedures, controls activities and solves problems that come up in carrying out the plan.

Before you conclude that based on these definitions you must be the chief executive officer of your company to be a leader, consider this. A leader can be a CEO; however, many companies - unfortunately for them - have CEOs who are not leaders. A leader can also be a division department head or even a line employee. In other words, you or anyone else in your organization can be a leader.

While both leaders and managers obviously are necessary, in times of a significantly changing business environment it is more important to be a leader. A military analogy often is used when comparing leadership to management. An army, it is said, needs competent leadership at all levels. No one has yet figured out how to manage an army into battle; the troops must be led.

How do you become a leader in your organization? During the 1980s, entire forests were sacrificed in what was a proliferation of writing about leaders and how to become one. Particularly in the United States, leadership has been a hot business topic. However, despite all this writing, people still struggle with how they can become leaders in their organizations.

Do you want to become a leader? Here are some attributes you can use to determine if you are a leader, or work toward developing if you want to become one:

- **Leaders see the big picture.** It is almost impossible to be a leader without conceptual skills. You have to be able to see how changes are impacting or could impact your entire organization and not just one aspect of it.
- **Leaders create the mission.** Another key attribute of a leader is the ability to be visionary. A leader sets broad objectives for his or her organization and documents those objectives in a mission statement.
- **Leaders do the right things.** You probably have heard the phrase that while it is important to do things right, it is far more important to do the right things. Leaders are focused on making sure the right things are being done and less worried about the details of how they are being done. Leaders let managers worry about the details.

- **Leaders are results-oriented.** I've written before that probably the most important thing you can do to be effective in your job is to develop a "results" mindset. Focus on results, not process.
- **Leaders are good communicators.** Leaders not only say the right things but also know how to say them. As a leader nonverbal communication is more important than the actual words spoken. Leaders have a "presence" about them that exudes confidence.
- **Leaders care about people.** Being a "people person" is important, but a leader actually cares about people.
- **Leaders are generally democratic.** Sometimes situations dictate that a leader must be autocratic, but generally leaders ask for input and get the buy-in of those who work around them.
- **Leaders don't micromanage.** Leaders help employees set their goals and then back off to let them do their jobs.
- **Leaders are agents of change.** Leaders are good at identifying and supporting necessary changes in their organizations.
- **Leaders inspire.** This may be the most important leadership attribute. Leaders encourage their employees to new heights. Leaders use positive reinforcement to encourage and motivate. People are willing to go the extra mile for leaders.

Based on these criteria, are you functioning as a leader in your organization? If not, try working on these items. If you need help there are plenty of books available in each of the above areas.

Being a good manager is important, but managers do not run the most effective companies - leaders run them.

Chapter 58
GIVE STAFFERS AUTONOMY, THEY'LL
GIVE YOU RESULTS
February 2001

My daughters, Erin and Amanda, are now 10 and 9 years old, respectively. As much as I hate to see it happen, I have read enough parenting books to know they have reached the age at which they need a little independence.

Actually, Erin and Amanda are not exceptions - almost all people start looking for some independence at their age. While most good parents recognize this natural state of development and adapt to it, many bosses act like independence is an unknown concept.

Did you know that the more independence you give your employees to do their jobs, the better they will do them? Or that letting employees personally take responsibility for getting the results you want will help them do it?

We can argue about why, but the fact remains that when you leave employees alone they almost always will get better results than when they are closely supervised.

As bosses, we have a tendency to want to micromanage. Basically, micromanagement is interfering in our employees' work in a way that really does not make a substantive difference in the result. For example, micromanagement is asking an employee to change the way he or she is performing a task, even when the end result would be basically the same as if it had been done your way. And it drives employees crazy.

If you are a micromanager, try to loosen up. Your employees will be happier, more motivated, get better results and want to stay with you longer.

Here are some ideas to help you do this:

- **Don't think you're God.** Of course, this is an exaggeration for emphasis, but keep in mind that most of your employees also have the experience, education and intellect necessary to make good decisions. Just because we are bosses does not give us a monopoly on all the insight and judgment needed to run our businesses effectively.
- **Give employees the benefit of the doubt.** Almost all employees want to be affiliated with a successful company. They want what is best for the organization they are a part of, and almost always will do their best to make the right decisions when given the chance.
- **Hire good people.** It is a lot easier to avoid micromanaging if you pay the right amount of attention to the hiring process. When you hire someone you usually are making a multi-year, six-figure commitment. Be sure your hiring decision gets at least as much attention and scrutiny as a capital purchasing decision of the same amount. Get good people around you and the rest of this becomes easy.
- **Set goals.** Avoiding micromanaging does not mean you avoid giving any direction. In fact, as a manager it is imperative that you set the course. However, most of this direction should be through the mutual setting of objectives. Your role as a manager is to be very involved in helping set the objectives. Then you sit back and let your employee carry them out.
- **Monitor** results. Another important role you have as a manager

is to have an effective method of monitoring the results. This should determine whether you achieve the objective you and the employee have set. Results will almost always improve once you start measuring them.

- **Resist the temptation to fine-tune or "tweak."** If an employee brings you an idea that is basically what you want, resist the temptation to fine-tune. The results you will get by letting the employee carry out his or her plan is many multiples of the results you will get when the employee carries out the plan after you have modified it.

- **Don't disguise micromanaging as communication.** Communication with employees is critical. When you get to the bottom of almost any management problem, it generally is a communication problem. However, your communication with your employees should be primarily focused on the mutual setting of goals, getting input on critical decisions and keeping them updated regarding important company matters.

One key principle to remember when implementing these practices is to delegate authority as well as accountability. Both are important. You must give employees the authority they need to carry out their jobs but you must also hold them accountable for the results. Some employees, when they realize they are now being held accountable for what they do, may even long for the old days when you micromanaged. However, I believe most will love the challenge and do a great job.

Do you want your employees to function at 100 percent motivation? Do you want to keep your best people? Do you want to manage your team in a manner that optimizes your company's financial results? Of course, the answer to all of these questions is yes. Then try giving your employees space to do their jobs and see if it doesn't result in both happier, more motivated employees and also better results for your organization.

Chapter 59
SOME PERSONALITY TRAITS YOU JUST CANNOT CHANGE
March 2001

I've been following the race to map the human genome and I find myself amazed at what science is learning about our neurobiological makeup. Discoveries in biotechnology over the next few years are going to transform our lives in ways we can't even imagine today.

So, how do these discoveries affect us as we try to lead our marine businesses?

Actually, I'm not sure. I find it interesting that I have not read anything or heard even one discussion on that subject. Nevertheless, I am sure the new knowledge eventually will impact management thinking and I am even more certain it will be controversial.

Fact is, even though many of us may find it counter-intuitive, we are learning that our neurobiology impacts our behavior significantly more than we realized. If a person's biological composition affects his or her personality, compulsiveness, inclination toward depression, or even criminal conduct (it's been used by attorneys as a defense), then certainly it must impact behavior on the job.

Can a leopard change its spots? Managers, philosophers and sociologists have been debating that point for years. If you've been managing people for any time at all you, too, have probably faced a situation in which you had to decide whether an employee was going to be able to change an unsatisfactory behavior pattern or whether you were going to be forced to make an unpleasant personnel change.

Some facets of an employee's temperament can have a direct impact on job performance. Among them are degrees of assertiveness, leadership ability, results orientation, social ability, analytical attributes, sense of urgency, detail orientation, degree of subjectivity in decision making, energy level and attitude toward risk.

Every job in your company requires some mix of these attributes. One job may call for leadership and a sense of urgency while another demands an orientation toward detail Your job as a manager is to put the right people in the right jobs.

At our company, we use an organizational tool called the "Predictive Index" that helps u identify the relevant aspects of each potential employee's temperament. This is an incredibly accurate tool that has helped us immensely in steering the right people toward the right jobs. Without a tool like this, it can be very difficult to determine a prospective employee's personality profile during the interview process.

Identifying the temperament of prospective employees can be very helpful, but what about current employees? What if you have someone who is definitely a wrong fit for his or her job? Dealing with this can be extremely difficult - in fact, it's the toughest management issue, by far, we have dealt with at our company.

It's especially difficult if you want to be fair and treat people with respect. You want to give the employee every chance to make the behavior modifications necessary before you have to make a change.

Despite every effort to be fair, my experience has been that some personal attributes are very difficult to change. For instance, if you need an employee to be assertive in his or her job, it is nearly impossible to take a timid, nonassertive employee and make that person assertive. The same thing applies to detail orientation and almost all the rest of the attributes listed earlier.

Some managers make the mistake of thinking that employees who don't fit the job are lazy or stupid. This is blatantly unfair. I like to think I am both smart and hard-working but can think of many jobs in which I would be a horrible fit.

Sometimes, for the sake of the organization, you must be willing to make a change, even one that necessitates replacing the employee. It is unfair to the organization as a whole and to the other employees to limp along with someone who doesn't fit in his or her position.

Many times we don't want to make changes because we are concerned about the feeling of the employee. That's nice, but you have to realize most employees who find themselves in bad-fit jobs are miserable. I've seen cases where making a change liberated the employee. They were actually relieved when the change came.

I have been preaching training for years now, so how does that fit into this discussion? believe before you make a change you must offer the employee training, to learn how to make the changes they need for the jobs. If it is knowledge they need, that is easy training Personality modifications are much more difficult. However, many times small changes resulting from training can result in disproportionately positive results, so you have to give training a chance.

People issues are tough but, as managers, we must deal with them if we are to do our job well. When you get the right people in the right jobs, not only does your job become much easier, but you will also see your company results improve dramatically.

Chapter 60
SOME BOAT SHOW EXHIBITORS MUST HAVE MONEY TO BURN
April 2001

What would you say about a business that, in an effort to meet prospective customers, spends thousands of dollars - tens of thousands of dollars in many cases - and then ignores those prospects when they arrive?

Is this a company that doesn't really need new business? A business that has money to burn?

Spending a ton of money to attract potential new customers and then ignoring them would be stupid, you say. A complete waste of money.

Well, unfortunately, that's exactly what many in our industry do each time they exhibit at a boat show.

I've always thought it unsettling how so many exhibitors ignore potential customers who walk into their display areas at boat shows. But what I saw at the recent Southern California and Miami boat shows took my disbelief to a new extreme. I made a game out of watching prospects walk into booths - only to be ignored.

I thought maybe it was just me. But, soon after these shows were over I asked others about the reception they got when they walked into exhibitor booth display areas. Almost everyone gave the same response - "I was ignored."

I also found it interesting to ask what the exhibitors were doing during most of the time they were ignoring their prospects. Some said the exhibitors were talking on their cell phones, but almost all of them replied that the exhibitors were too busy talking among themselves to address a prospect walking to their display area.

Employees talking among themselves while ignoring the prospects is just plain dumb but, unfortunately, it happens all the time. I have attended boat shows in Asia, Europe and throughout the United States, and I see it in show after show.

Now, I admit that I enjoy the social aspects of boat shows. They're an opportunity to meet old friends and renew acquaintances. In many cases, it's the only chance during the year to meet some of these industry friends. But even talking to old industry friends is dumb if you do it while prospects are visiting your display area.

I hate to run the risk of overgeneralizing and upsetting people in our industry, because there are some companies that do a great job of handling their sales prospects at boat shows. Nevertheless, I cannot begin to imagine how much money we, as· an industry, have lost over the years because of this problem.

The sad part is that the solution is so simple. It's easy to make prospects feel welcome in your booth. Here are some simple things you can do to make your prospects feel like valued guests at the next boat show:

- **Greet people immediately.** Get off the phone. Leave your fellow employees or those old industry friends. Do whatever else it takes to give your prospect a warm greeting as soon as he or she walks into your booth. Make the prospect feel important.
- **Smile.** Project a positive persona even if you are having a bad day. You want the prospect to have a good feeling about you and your company. Smiling is one of the easiest things you can do to make a visitor to your booth feel good.
- **Ask people their names and then use them.** People love to be addressed by name. Don't overdo it but you almost certainly

can find a few legitimate opportunities to use a prospective customer's name during his or her visit to your booth.

- **Give people your undivided attention.** Be a good listener. Don't talk to the employees when a prospect is in your booth, even if that prospect says he or she is just looking and dismisses you. Turn your cell phone off.
- **Say goodbye nicely.** Even if the prospect doesn't buy anything during the visit, you still want him or her to leave with a good feeling. Many exhibitors ignore a potential customer as soon as they realize there is not going to be an immediate purchase. Say things like, "Enjoy the show," and "Have a nice day," as the prospect leaves.
- **Don't prejudge.** Treat everyone who enters your booth as if they have the potential to be your biggest customer. In actuality, they do.
- **Have candy in your booth.** This is a nice touch. Even though most prospects won't take it, it still makes them feel welcome.

Your company is paying big bucks to be in a boat show and it is important to get a good return on that investment. In order to get a good return we must treat everyone like gold. It is the best chance we have to make sure some of the gold eventually flows our way.

Chapter 61
HAVE A GLOBAL MINDSET? NO?
YOU'D BETTER GET ONE
May 2001

I'll never forget my first international trip. My wife, Leigh, was an employee for Eastern Airlines and we were flying "standby" from New York to London.

Just before takeoff time, the gate attendant called our names. He had both good and bad news. The good news: there were two seats left on the plane; the bad: one was in first class and the other was in the middle of a five-seat section of coach.

Being the gentleman that I try to be, I told Leigh to take the first-class seat; I would fly coach. Little did I know that I would be spending the night between two people who were, shall I politely say, bigger than their seats. About halfway into the trip - sometime around 2:00 am - I was getting pretty miserable, so I decided to climb over two sleeping passengers and find my wife.

My first problem was getting into first class to see her.

The flight attendant, who seemed to have been trained by the Gestapo, treated me as if I were trying to get into the pilot's area and grab the controls. Clearly, in her view, I didn't look worthy of entering the first-class section.

Eventually, I was able to convince the flight attendant to let me see my wife.

This turned out to not be a great idea. Leigh, you see, was stretched out in an oversized seat with a foot-rest, wearing slippers given to her by the airline with a half-eaten shrimp cocktail on her tray. Not quite the experience I was having back in coach.

Despite my miserable night on that plane we ended up getting to London just fine and had a wonderful vacation. Since that trip, I have had the opportunity to visit over 20 countries and have learned to love international traveling.

Odds are that many of you reading this column have also had some international experience. And you certainly have done some international business. Today there is virtually nothing you can buy that does not have an international element. It is not just a cliche - the world IS getting smaller and it is called globalization.

All of our business is going to be affected by globalization, so if you haven't started to develop a global mindset, you better get to work on it.

It is amazing the extent to which globalization has impacted our company, Rybovich, in the past five years. We now regularly travel internationally to bid on jobs and attend boat shows. Our customer list reads like an international Who's Who. We bid against competitors all over the world. We have visited with and discussed alliances with other marine businesses in Europe. We purchase from suppliers and send supplies to customers at all four corners of the earth. We worry about international exchange rates and how they affect our ability to compete. We have been investigating the feasibility of international recruiting.

You probably agree that developing a global mindset is important but you may wonder how to do it. The first thing to remember is that it doesn't require you to deal with international issues every day. It does mean that you have an international perspective. So, how do you get that perspective? Here are some ideas that can help:

- **Do some international traveling** - Take your next vacation out of the country. It is probably less expensive than you think.

I have flown to Paris for $250 and Zurich for $350 in the past couple of years. You can too if you plan ahead. There is no faster way to get a global mindset than to get yourself out of the country.

- **Visit marine businesses abroad** - My experience has been that our peers in other countries are very gracious - delighted to meet with Americans. The United States still is highly respected around, and you'll find most foreign business people are thrilled to spend some time with you. You can learn from one another.

- **Expand your knowledge** - I recently completed an international management course and an international marketing course. Your local college probably has similar programs. Go to Amazon.com or your local bookstore and get some reading material on international business. Seek out the international columns in business periodicals. Bear in mind that there are many types of international knowledge you can pick up - management, marketing, economic, political, cultural, historic, and geographic. If you are like me you will find it all very fascinating.

- **Avoid the "not invented here" syndrome** - This mentality can be the death of a manager. I have always been amazed at how much I have learned when I have allowed myself to be exposed to other ways of thinking. Why some managers think they have the corner on knowledge is beyond me. The more you expose yourself to different ways of doing things, the smarter you become. I think it is a negative trait of many American managers to believe that the American way is the only way - or even the best way. Believe me, there is a lot we can learn.

You have probably heard the phrase "think globally, act locally." As the inevitable process of globalization increasingly impacts all of our businesses, we had better be in a position to deal with it. We must all develop a global mindset. The consequences of those who don't will be dramatic. By starting today, you will be protecting both your company and your career.

Chapter 62
A STRATEGIC PLAN WILL SERVE AS YOUR BUSINESS ROADMAP
June 2001

Would you start to build a new house without first consulting an architect? Go on a long car trip without looking at a map? Of course not.

But, you might be doing something just as foolhardy if you are trying to run your marine business without a sound strategic plan.

Almost anything we do in life goes a little smoother if we take the time upfront to do some planning. More importantly, we are more likely to accomplish the right things in our marine businesses if we have a good plan.

I heard someone say once that while it is important we do things right, it is much more important we do the right things. That's what a strategic plan can do for your company - help you identify the right things to do.

The development and use of a strategic plan is certainly not a new concept. Almost every manager I speak with agrees it can have a direct and positive impact on a company's effectiveness and profitability. They agree it can provide the vision and goals every company needs. That of course begs the question: why do so few companies in the marine industry have one?

The reason, despite the obvious benefits, is the widespread belief that the process of developing such a plan is onerous, time-consuming and basically just a lot of work.

Truth be told, many managers have no idea how to go about preparing one. Many other managers get started but quit frustrated along the way.

Actually, preparing a strategic plan is easy if you follow the right steps. Here's how to go about it:

- **Understand the purpose of your plan** - Believe it or not, you can predict the future for your business. Your company's future results are a direct outgrowth of the decisions you make today. That gets us to the main purpose of a strategic plan: to improve your company's future results by giving you a framework for making smart decisions now. Ideally, your strategic plan should tell you specifically what you could do today to have better results down the road.

- **Conduct a situation analysis** - A situation analysis is a description of your company as it operates in its current environment. Much of this information you will know intuitively, but you should still go through the exercise of documenting it. It will force you to think about your business in ways you might not otherwise consider. A situation analysis includes a summary of your market, an assessment of the competition, a charting of your organization and a review of your financial results. A completed situation analysis should give even a stranger to the business a good overview of your operation.

- **Prepare a SWOT analysis** - A SWOT analysis is a summary of your company's strengths (s), weaknesses (w), opportunities (o), and threats (t). I have found the best way to undertake such an analysis to list the top five strengths and weaknesses of each major segment of your operation. Then do the same for the business as a whole. Next list the opportunities and threats related to each of these strengths and weaknesses The more detailed this examination, the better. And don't go it alone. Have a meeting with some of your key employees and get their input. It is important that a SWOT analysis not reflect the thinking of just one individual.

- **Prepare a plan of action** - This is the most important step, and also the point at which the process shifts from being a science to an art. In order to prepare your plan of action, you draw on all of the information you have developed in the previous steps. Use it to select 10 key areas that most deserve your attention. These should be "big picture issues that can have a significant impact on your business. For each of these ten areas identify the specific steps you must take to accomplish your goals. This plan of action now becomes your road map - the document that directs your travel to your desired destination.
- **Prepare an executive summary** - The executive summary is a concise version of your plan that appears at the beginning and sums up what is to follow. It should emphasize the 10 primary areas on which you have decided to focus.

After you have completed all these steps, collate your plan into a professional-looking binder with tabs for each section outlined above. This will make it easier to refer to in the future, and give your plan the appearance of importance it deserves.

One thing to bear in mind: creating your strategic plan is not an end, it is a beginning. A strategic plan is a good way of controlling your future but it's not going to control anything if you don't implement it.

After putting in all the effort to develop it, don't let your strategic plan just gather dust on a shelf. Put it to work for you. It's important to know what to do, but it's even more important to do it.

Chapter 63
STAYING AHEAD OF "ENTROPY" MEANS STEADILY IMPROVING
July 2001

Recently, while listening to an audiotape series called "The Great Principles of Science," I learned a new word.

Apparently, I had not been as focused as I might have been in my high school and college science courses because I was certain I had never heard anyone use the word entropy before.

If you are like me, and cannot remember every detail surrounding the Second Law of Thermodynamics, you too, may have forgotten about entropy. In a nutshell, the concept is quite simple: all systems in our universe tend to become more disordered with time.

Because of the way my mind works, I immediately tried to make an association between entropy as a principle of science and entropy in the world of everyday management. As managers, are we, and the systems we create, exempt from this scientific law? The more I thought about it the more I realized that we weren't.

Actually, I came to recognize that entropy can be a very dangerous - even deadly - force in our marine businesses. In extreme circumstances (if we are really complacent), it can put us out of business.

Any segment or aspect of your business that does not get your constant attention carries the risk of deteriorating. Not only do you need to stay continuously focused on all aspects of your business, but you also must regularly work at improving them. The less you focus on improving your business, the greater the likelihood that entropy is going to take its toll.

Here are some key areas to stay focused on to ensure that entropy doesn't destroy your marine business:

- **Customer Service** - This is one area in which you don't want to take anything for granted. Each Thursday morning I have a staff meeting with many of the people who report directly to me, and I make it a point to frequently emphasize our customers and customer service. Provide your employees training in this area through our marine industry trade organizations, and the conferences and teaching programs these groups make available. You also might consider those traveling seminars when one is making a stop in your region. You also should regularly survey your customers to stay in touch with their perceptions of your service or products.
- **Employee Relations** - I know it can be hard, especially if your organization is a large one like ours (180 employees,) but you must maintain a focus on trying to keep your employees motivated. Each year we do a complete review of our benefits package and try to offer as much as we possibly can. You won't keep everyone happy but you can at least try to keep yourself competitive.

    Training and development opportunities can go a long way toward retaining employees. We have a significant training budget that includes industry events such as IBEX.

    If you are like us, you are not perfect. Nonetheless, there are a great many things you can do to help keep your employees motivated and productive. One of the things we do is keep an eye open for opportunities to reward our employees. This could include tickets for boat shows or other community events.

- **Technology** - I am not one who believes you should be on the cutting edge of every technological change. Sometimes it is better to let others work their way through the initial growing pains. However, you need to stay on top of changes in technology that will affect your business, whether they are administrative or operational.
- **Marketing** - I would never claim to be a marketing expert. You are much better off getting your marketing advice from my fellow writer, Wanda Kenton Smith. However, I do know enough about marketing to know that if you keep doing the same thing over and over, and don't closely follow trends in our industry, you will get your company in trouble in a hurry.
- **Planning** - You need to stay focused on your plan for your business. If your company's Strategic Plan is just a document that you wrote a couple of years ago and left on a shelf, you are probably running your business in a very reactive mode. Be proactive. Time invested in planning almost always saves many multiples of that time that would be spent reacting.

I am sure that there are many other areas of your marine business to which you can apply 1is concept of entropy. However, the best way to avoid its deadly effects on any part of your business is to stay focused on a concept we used to hear a lot more about - continuous improvement.

The first two words of the mission statement at our company are "Continuously improve." I hope that concept is important at your company too. If we all keep improving, hopefully we'll all be able to stay ahead of entropy and its potential negative impact on our businesses.

Chapter 64
HOW TO CUT COSTS AND STAY POSITIONED FOR A RECOVERY
August 2001

I must admit that I have been more than a little distraught over the kind of talk I have been hearing at various marine industry functions. The bottom line: many companies in our industry are experiencing significant slowdowns in their businesses.

The leader of one trade organization told me his members are reporting sales figures that in some cases are 35 - 40 percent off their targets. The CEO of one company told me one of his locations has dropped from over 100 employees to just 15 in the past few months. I hear similar tales from many others.

The economic slowdown has hit certain pockets of the industry in a big way, and the managers at those companies most affected are looking for ways to deal with it. In times like these there aren't many executives who aren't reviewing their cost structure.

If you find that you, too, are looking closely at your company's expenses, here are some ideas that can help you:

- **Use a "zero-based" approach** - Examine each cost from the perspective of whether you need to spend the money at all. Many times managers don't closely scrutinize some of their costs because they are virtually the same, year after year. It's a "that's the way we've always done it" mentality. Look at each cost and ask yourself, "What would happen if I didn't spend this money at all?" Many times the negative impact of not spending that money won't be as damaging to your business as you might have thought.

- **Prepare good projections** - It is imperative that you have good projections of your company's financial results at various levels of sales volume. These projections will help you identify the targeted cost reductions you will have to make at various sales levels to remain viable.

- **Review your fixed costs** - Fixed costs are those that stay the same regardless of your sales volume. Variable costs are those that fluctuate (usually directly) with your sales levels.

  When it comes to cutting costs, most people tend to focus primarily on variable expenditure. This is a natural approach because variable costs are usually the easiest to cut. However, if you really want to make an impact on your companies cost structure, look closely at your fixed costs.

- **Get good information** - If your accounting system does not provide you with solid, reliable information about your costs, you could have a big problem. You need timely and accurate data to make the right decisions. Your accounting system should provide you with a listing of all of your organization's costs - in total and by department. There should be an itemized breakdown of each of those costs. You should have complete and detailed financial statements for each month by the 10th of the following month. If you're not getting this information from whoever does your accounting, insist on it.

- **Be imaginative** - Look for other ways of accomplishing what you are doing now, but in less expensive ways. Get "out of the box." Break those old paradigms. When times are really tough you'd better figure out how to get creative.

- **Kill the "sacred cows"** - Look everywhere for cost reductions and be prepared to deal with whatever you find. You must be willing to initiate cost savings no matter where in the organization you find them.
- **Get employee input** - Most of the time, cost-cutting affects your employees directly. Don't hesitate to ask for their opinions. Often you'll find you're getting ideas from them that you had not considered. If you're the boss, it ultimately is your responsibility to decide what needs to be done, but employees can be a great source of ideas in this or any other area of your business.
- **Stay focused on costs** - Don't let up on the cost management area of your business. Don't think that because you have reviewed your costs once for potential savings your work is done. Keep reviewing your expenditures regularly to look for areas of savings.

One caveat - while it is certainly a good idea for you to take these steps to review your cost structure, it is also important to realize that only rarely is it possible to cost-cut your business back to profitability. As you reduce expenses, you are also reducing your ability to make money. You want to reduce unnecessary costs but you don't want to eliminate the possibility of being able to get out of the slowdown. In other words - cut fat, not muscle.

That may sound like a case of stating the obvious, but oftentimes there is a fine balance between the two.

Most importantly, your company must live within its means. If you want to survive long enough to enjoy the eventual recovery, you had better be looking closely at your cost structure today.

Chapter 65
ESSENTIALS OF LEADERSHIP: VISION, TALENT AND FOCUS
September 2001

Have you ever known someone who seemed to be a natural leader? Have you wondered why some managers are highly successful while other managers in comparable situations seem to fail - or, why some appear to have a golden touch while others struggle?

I have considered these questions many times and I think I finally understand. Successful managers have three attributes their unsuccessful counterparts don't: vision, talent and focus.

If you are taking the time to read this column, odds are that you aspire to be a successful leader. So, what can you do to develop these three attributes? Here are some ideas that might help:

Vision

The Proverbs say that where there is no vision, the people perish.

Vision is the ability to think big - I mean really big - and not be constrained by paradigms that limit most people.

In the past couple of years I have seen two organizations with which I am involved totally transformed by new leaders, each with a big vision. Both of these leaders' new visions brought into play forces that re-energized their respective organizations.

Funny thing is that the leaders they replaced were also perceived to be visionary, but they weren't. Both organizations were dismayed to lose their original leaders but both now are thriving - eagerly responding to a leader with a big vision.

If you can catch a big vision, you can transform your organization, too.

The tough part is that some managers have vision and some don't. To some it comes naturally while others seem to be able to attain it. However, even if it doesn't come naturally, you should still try. A vision for your marine business may be one of the most important things you can have.

If you want to catch one you must first break out of your old paradigms. Forget about the way it used to be done and all the reasons you can't do it.

Think big! Imagine what you could do with no constraints. Dream.

Talent

Once you have your vision you need the talent to carry it out.

Perhaps the most important skill is the ability to communicate. When you get to the bottom of any management problem it almost always is a communication problem. Also, important as vision is, it is almost useless if you can't communicate it. Luckily communication is a talent that can be learned. There is an abundance of books and classes- many of them very good - on improving your communication skills.

You can become more talented in almost every area of management. The key is to stay focused on improvement. Keep learning. Go to industry conferences that offer training Look for distance learning opportunities. Read management books and periodicals; listen to management books on tape. Don't ever settle for your current level of knowledge Participate in traveling seminars that come to your city. There are many opportunities to become more talented.

Any manager who thinks he or she knows everything there is to know about the job headed for a fall. Don't let yourself be drawn into that trap. Keep improving no matter how comfortable you are with your current performance.

Focus

I believe one of the biggest problems managers have is the inability to focus. Successful managers can hone in on the issues they are confronting. Their less successful colleague it seems, are far too easily distracted.

A prerequisite to the ability to focus is the ability to identify what is important. That means having goals, a mission statement and a strategic plan. It also requires being oriented toward results and focusing on the present and future, not the past.

There are more specific steps you can take to help improve your focus and I have written an entire column on this topic. Drop me an email and I will be happy to send you a copy.

Successful managers in the marine industry (or any other industry for that matter) rise to the top because they have clearly identified attributes less successful managers lack. I have listed some of those attributes. It is important to work hard but it is equally important to develop the characteristics you need to be successful - vision, talent and focus.

Everything rises or falls on leadership. If an organization does well over the long run, it's usually because it has effective leadership. Effective leadership - and more importantly the right leader - can make an enormous difference in your marine company's performance.

Chapter 66
COLUMN ON LEADERSHIP HIT HOME FOR READERS
October 2001

I've been writing these monthly management columns for nearly six and a half years, but I have never had a reaction anything like the response I had to last month's column.

Usually I receive a handful of emails each month making some type of comment, usually complimentary. However, as I write this - three days after people in our industry started receiving the September Soundings Trade Only - I have already received a couple of dozen responses to that column ("Essentials of Leadership: Vision, Talent and Focus.") Considering it has only been three days, I expect I will receive many more. My computer continues to beep regularly with the sound of new emails arriving.

To give you some perspective, these are some actual quotes from emails I received:

- "I am very much interested in this topic."
- "I agree with you wholeheartedly."
- "Vision, talent and focus seem to be lacking in my own life, to be sure. Most of my time, if I were to be truthful, is spent trying to "make things happen," with no real plan. I intend to rethink my approach after reading your article."

- "Your view is well taken; we too often overlook why our efforts seem to take no firm shape, and eventually fizzle. Why do those we try to communicate with seem to not hear? To where do our goals disappear?"

- "Great article; keep up the good work. Focus is the toughest of all."

- "It was inspiring. I'd love to have a dialog with those two people you were referring to as having the "vision, talent and focus," to hear their experience first hand. The "focus" is the hardest thing. Your writing always makes me think, but this time it was really close to home."

- "I'm trying to break out of my established role but as I try to buck the system a little, I find myself getting off track and am having trouble maintaining the focus that I need."

- I just wanted to drop you a note to express my appreciation for the article you wrote on leadership in the Soundings September 2001 edition. I thought it was fantastic and I made copies for each of the members of my group."

- "I have been involved in my family's marina for the past 25 years. I have vision and communication skills but we are having difficulties getting bigger. So this article really hit home for me."

That is just a sampling.

I have to admit that I have spent a considerable amount of time over the last three days wondering why this column touched such a nerve. I've concluded it's because the managers in our industry are truly looking for help in reaching their full potential as leaders.

Over the next few months I plan to write in more detail on each of the three elements of leadership: vision, talent and focus. Each of these topics certainly deserves a column of its own.

In the meantime, if you are looking for help reaching your leadership potential, there are many organizations in our industry that I believe are doing a good job offering management development training. Some of those organizations are as follows:

- **International Marina Institute** (IMI) - Paul Dodson and his team offer excellent training opportunities for those in the marina business. Their Certified Marina Manager program is first class. They can be reached at 941-480-1212.
- **American Boat and Yacht Council (ABYC)** - Skip Moyer and his team offer great technical training courses including some certification programs. They can be reached at 410-956-1050.
- **American Boat Builders and Repairers Association (ABBRA)** - Pat Kearns coordinates several programs for boatyard managers. Maybe the most exciting is the new Boatyard Manager certification program that ABBRA is offering in conjunction with the IMI. Pat can be reached at 410-604-0060.
- **IBEX** - This is one of the best things our industry has to offer with many training courses on various tracks. Each February thousands of people from our industry travel to Ft. Lauderdale to attend the IBEX courses. The IBEX team can be reached at 573-374-6039.

Many people in our industry are looking for assistance in developing their skills as a manager and the sources I mention above are all programs that I have been involved with and can recommend to help you. Make the time to attend some of their programs; I am sure you will be glad you did.

Chapter 67
AN INSTANT 8-STEP FORMULA FOR
BETTER BUSINESS LETTERS
November 2001

Do you struggle with your writing? Does the thought of composing a letter make you cringe? If so, you are not alone.

If you receive as much correspondence as I do you know most people really have difficulty with their writing. Their letters fail to get across the messages they intend. They don't get the reader to take the action they were hoping for, and - perhaps most damaging - their poorly written letters undermine the positive images they are trying to convey for themselves and their companies.

Unfortunately, many people don't even try to improve their writing skills. They believe writing is an art - either you have a flair for it or you don't. That is just plain wrong. You can improve your writing, and you can do it immediately.

You can take a class at your local community college or even sign up for one of those one-day classes that come through many of our cities. Or you can buy a self-help book. Any of these alternatives can have a dramatic impact on your ability to communicate more effectively through your writing.

Meanwhile, here are some tips you can use immediately:

- **Write as though you were speaking** - This may be the best advice I or anyone else can give you. Just write your letter as though you were talking to whom the letter is directed. Remember: writing is communicating, just like talking, except in a different form. Stop and think: what would you say to this person if the two of you were standing together having a conversation? When you've determined what you would say, let those words form the basis of your letter.

- **Have a purpose** - Know what you want to accomplish. Many times I have finished reading a letter and found myself wondering, "What was that all about?" Remember, write with a purpose and make sure the letter conveys that purpose.

- **Get to the point** -After determining the purpose of your letter, get right to it. Don't be wordy. In many situations, you'll find it's much more effective to emphasize a letter's key elements by using bullet points, as I have done in this column.

- **Write simply** - When many people start a letter, they somehow feel the need to inject words and phrases that they would never use in conversation. Don't treat a letter as a display case for big words or high-minded phrases. "Keep it on the bottom shelf - where everyone can reach it" is a good concept to bear in mind when you approach your letter writing.

- **Don't use slang** - This may be the one exception to my recommendation that you write in a conversational style. You never want to use slang in a business letter.

- **Think of your reader's perspective** -After completing your letter try to read it back from the perspective of the individual receiving it. Try to take into account the biases of those who will be reading the letter. What you may have intended as a harmless phrase may be explosive from the reader's point of view.

- **Have someone else review it** - It is always a good suggestion to have a second set of eyes - someone to proofread your letter and offer editing suggestions. Don't feel this demeans either you or your writing ability. I do this myself, and often the proofreader will come up with some point or perspective I have overlooked. I may be frustrated with myself for having missed whatever it is, but I never regret having the proofreader look at it.

- **Ask for action** - This is also essential. If the objective is to persuade the recipient to do something, make certain it directly asks him or her to do it. Many times I have received a letter that was informational, but left me with no idea what the writer wanted from me. Or, I can figure out what the writer wants me to do but he or she never actually asks me to do it. Be specific. Make it absolutely clear to the recipient what you want done. This is especially important in those instances you are writing to a customer a letter to collect money.

I've said many times that at the bottom of almost any management problem there's a communication problem. Obviously, writing is an important part of communication. However, writing is just like everything else in life - with a little direction and some practice you can become better at it.

Try implementing some of these tips - I think you will see your management problems lessen while the image you convey improves.

Chapter 68
SEVEN SIMPLE STEPS
TO REDUCING PREMIUMS
December 2001

As you already know if you've read the page 1 story in this month's Soundings Trade Only, the insurance markets are in turmoil. A combination of a depressed stock market, huge global losses over the past few years by reinsurers, windstorm anxiety, and now the events of September 11 have affected rates to a degree that many of us have not previously experienced.

If you have not renewed your insurance policies in the past few months - brace yourself. You are probably going to be hit with a big increase, and not just in one type of coverage but across the board.

Over the years there are many steps that I have taken to try to make our company's renewals less painful and (hopefully) less expensive. Some of the things I have found helpful may benefit you with your renewal. Here are some tips:

- **Have an agent who understands your industry** - If your agent sells all kinds of insurance, including coverage for your brother-in-laws' car, you may want to look at your alternatives. You need an agent who has other clients in our field and understands Marine Operators, Longshoreman's and Jones Act coverage. If you don't have an agent in your immediate area who understands the marine market, don't worry - you can find one outside your area. While it is nice if your agent works close at hand, it is not imperative. It is more important that he or she understands your business, the industry you are in and the peculiarities of coverage for our industry.

- **Avoid a January 1 or July 1 renewal date** - Odds are that almost everyone reading this column has either of those two renewal dates. Several years ago I changed our company's renewal date from July 1 to November 1. When you get out of the January 1 and July 1 cycles your agent and underwriter have significantly more time to focus on your account.

- **Resist the temptation to file every claim** - Many people feel that if a claim exceeds the amount of their deductible, they will file. "That's why I pay for insurance so I am going to get my money's worth" they believe. Unfortunately, that perspective can cost those people more in the long run. Two of the key factors underwriters look at when they are pricing your coverage is both the frequency and cost of your prior claims; therefore, these are both factors that you want to keep in check.

- **Make sure your deductibles are high enough** - If you are going to take my advice above and not file every little claim, then make sure your deductibles reflect this philosophy. I imagine many people reading this column have $250, $500 or $1,000 deductibles, when they could very easily increase those amounts and enjoy the policy price reductions that follow.

- **Stay on top of your loss history** - Your health insurance losses should be reviewed monthly. You should also review your workers' compensation loss history every month, or at least quarterly. You should be sure to review your loss history on your other policies each year before you renew them. On more than one occasion I have found the rates I was being quoted on renewal were mistakenly high because of an error in our loss history. By reviewing this yourself you can potentially save your company a lot of money.

- **Manage your claims** - Don't think your job is over once you hand a claim over to the adjuster. Stay involved and be sure that the claim is settled as economically as possible. I am always surprised when adjusters tell me that I am unusual because I want to help them get the claim resolved. It is to your long-term advantage to help them.

- **Know your underwriters** - Most people have little or no interaction with their underwriters. I have relationships with all of ours, some of whom have become good friends. The better the relationship between the underwriter and you and your company, the better the odds are that they are going to work with you when you really need them. I tell our underwriters that I want them to make money in their dealings with us. It may sound contradictory but the more money your insurance company is making off you the lower your premiums in the long run.

Many of you, as I said earlier, will be facing renewals this month for January 1. Try using some of these techniques and see if they don't help you; I know they have helped me.

Chapter 69
"JACK" IS AN INSTANT CLASSIC, BUT THEN, IT'S JACK WELCH
January 2002

I love to read and I really enjoy learning from someone I consider a true master. So, needless to say, when I can combine these two passions I truly consider it a unique opportunity. That's exactly what happened recently.

If you're at all familiar with the world of big business, you've no doubt come across the name of Jack Welch. Mr. Welch earned himself a reputation as the best CEO in the world during his 20 years at the helm of General Electric. It's a reputation that is well deserved. The impact he and the team he put together had on GE's results and stock price during his tenure was nothing less than phenomenal.

Luckily for us, Mr. Welch took the time before he retired to write a biography - one that seems certain to become a true business classic. The title is "Jack - Straight From the Gut," and if you are a CEO or upper-level manager in your company, I cannot overemphasize the importance of reading this book. It is excellent.

It would be impossible for me to summarize the book in this column but I would like to share some of the points Mr. Welch makes that had an impact on me.

- **Find excellent people and let them do their jobs.** Finding good people to join your team and then getting the right people in the right jobs has to be one of the critical elements of successful management. The tough part is to back off and let these people do what you have hired them to do; however, it is imperative if you want to maximize your company's results.

- **Develop and train people as much as possible.** Continuous improvement is important to the success of any company. You must continue to develop both yourself and your employees if you want to stay competitive. Training is also a wonderful employee benefit that helps the company, too. And most employees welcome the opportunity.

- **Be good at what you do or don't do it.** This seems like common sense but it is tougher than it sounds, especially if you have parts of your business that have been producing mediocre returns for years and years. We tend to justify the existence of those areas of our businesses that we are not good at managing.

- **Get unnecessary work out of the system.** Always be on the lookout for productivity improvements. Don't keep doing things just because, "That's the way it has always been done." Use technology whenever you can to make both you and your company more productive.

- **Get employee input.** You pay for the work of your employees' hands but they usually are willing to give their brainpower free of charge if only you will ask. Unfortunately, many managers think they know it all and usually those same managers pay a big price for not asking their employees' opinions.

- **Integrity.** I can't overemphasize the importance of integrity in all aspects of our businesses. I believe integrity by itself is the right course to follow, regardless of whether it helps our businesses or not. I also am one who believes that those who maintain a high level of integrity in their dealings with others are rewarded. They benefit many times over in their businesses through improved employee, customer and vendor relations.

- **Globalization.** It is interesting that I read this book while visiting boat manufacturers, marinas, and boatyards in Australia and New Zealand. Our customers are taking their boats overseas much more often for pleasure, and sometimes using the difference in exchange rates to their advantage when they need service on their boats. Boat manufacturers now are taking a worldwide view when they look for the best places to build their boats. The world is getting much smaller and if you don't already have a global perspective, you should get one or run the risk of being left behind.

These are some of the points in Welch's book that jumped out at me. You may find other ideas that affect you in the same way. It's amazing how the creative juices flow when you are reading a book like this one.

Even if you don't normally enjoy reading. I encourage you to make an exception for this book. I guarantee you there is something in it that will help you as a manager. It will soon be held up as a classic - a book that is sure to have an extraordinary impact on managers all around the world.

Chapter 70
A GOOD LEADER GETS FOCUSED; A GREAT LEADER STAYS FOCUSED
February 2002

Last year in one of my Soundings Trade Only columns, I identified what I believe to be the three essential characteristics of an effective leader - vision, talent and focus.

Since that column appeared, I have received lots of feedback about those characteristics. Many of the comments were general in nature, but the quality that has drawn the most response by far was the third on that list - focus. Almost everyone, it seems, has trouble maintaining focus at one time or another.

The topic came up while I was teaching at an International Marina Institute Advanced Marina Manager School in Palm Beach Gardens, Florida, recently. After some discussion, the group voted on which of the three leadership characteristics they collectively struggle with the most. Not surprisingly, focus won easily.

Brad Gross, a San Francisco marina manager who was one of the students, pointed out how difficult it is to maintain your focus when you have a dynamic operation and are trying to be all things to all people. Nancy Cutka, who manages a marina in Indiana, agreed. She talked about how tough it can be to keep your focus when your mind is busy with all of the things that have to be done at once. These are both good points.

Nevertheless, as I think about the people I perceive to be successful - either professionally or personally - I find they almost always have a heightened ability to focus. These people have what I call a "laser beam focus" - they always seem to be in touch with what is important and what needs to be done.

I am sure you, too, have seen people like this. People who have this ability to focus are significantly more effective than those who do not.

In the current economic and political environment, it may be more important than ever to keep your focus. The future of your company (as well as your career) may depend on it.

Unfortunately, many people think focus is unattainable. That couldn't be further from the truth! Not only can you develop your ability to focus, but it may also be easier than you realize.

Many times we as managers have a hard time keeping our focus because we are not exactly sure what we should be focusing on. It is important that we set objectives, both for ourselves and our companies, that clearly define what is important.

Two of the tools most commonly used to establish these objectives are a mission statement and strategic plan. I strongly believe that any organization that wants to be successful (and don't they all?) must have both of these documents. If you don't have either and want help developing them, drop me an email and I will send you copies of previous columns that can help point you in the right directions.

While creating a mission statement and strategic plan are very important, these are external things. Keeping your focus is also an internal process. You must develop the habit within yourself that can help.

I have said before that the most effective people I know are all results-oriented. In fact, this may be the most important quality - not only to maintain your focus, but also to ensure success in general. Being results-oriented is a mind-set. It is refusing to let yourself get so caught up in the unimportant things that pop up every day that you lose sight of the results you are trying to achieve. It is an essential internal ingredient of keeping your focus.

Another internal ingredient is the ability to stay within your boundaries of control. Many managers spend so much time thinking about things they can't control, including things that happened in the past, that they often neglect those areas that they do have control over. Spend time on the areas you can control - matters in the here and now and under your area of responsibility - and you will find those areas will grow quickly.

One other note: I recently heard an interesting quote attributed to one of our former presidents. He said that every major mistake he had ever made was when he was short on sleep. It is a lot easier to keep your focus if you take care of yourself physically. Don't underestimate the impact lack of sleep or exercise can have on your ability to focus.

Sometimes taking care of yourself can include getting away to a training program. Another of the IMI students, Sean McKenna, a marina manager in St. Augustine, Florida, talked about how much his focus had improved just by attending the class. I think all of the students in that class would agree that, to use Sean's words, their "batteries were recharged!"

Finally, a sharpened focus is not something you are going to achieve overnight. Keep working at it and don't get discouraged if you struggle at first. And once you get your focus, don't take it for granted. Keep doing what I have suggested even after you think you have achieved a good degree of focus. In other words - keep focused on staying focused.

Chapter 71
ATTRIBUTES OF LEADERSHIP: WHAT THE LEADERS THINK
March 2002

Over the past few months, I've found myself wondering why some managers seem to succeed in everything they do, while others struggle.

Based on feedback from my September Soundings Trade Only column (the three essentials of leadership), it's clear that I'm not the only one in our industry who wonders. As I went over the responses to that column, a question arose in my mind: what do the leaders in our industry think? Could they provide some insight?

I emailed some friends who hold such leadership positions, asking them to identify the most important characteristics of an effective manager. Their individual responses impressed me; taken together they offer a gold mine of collective wisdom.

Here, with their permission, are some of their thoughts.

Paul Dodson, President and Co-Founder, International Marina Institute:

"Excellent communication (skills are) a key attribute. Through effective communication a leader will not only inspire his or her people, but also clearly and concisely convey a plan of action to reach organizational goals. It is equally important to be a good listener and to make those around you feel important."

Larry Halgren, President, Bellingham Marine:

"Work hard to see all sides of every situation before you take action. Customers are the most important part of your business; listen to them and understand their needs. Always deal with integrity."

Skip Moyer, President, American Boat and Yacht Council:

"Leaders motivate people to work with fervor and pride. They should be role models and sources of vision and direction. Attributes include honesty, integrity and, most of all, accountability."

Dennis Nixon, Dean and Professor, University of Rhode Island, and Co-Founder, International Marina Institute:

"An effective leader has goals, understands the strengths and weaknesses of his or her organization, and is committed, upbeat, energetic and willing to motivate everyone to excellence."

JJ. Marie, CEO, Zodiac North America:

"Good leaders lead from the front. They master the art of delegation without abdication. They recognize talent, they inspire and lead through vision and example."

Dennis Kissman, CEO, Marina Management Associates:

"Good leaders inspire others to achieve their highest potential. They can recognize an employee's strengths and weaknesses, capitalizing on the strengths and mentoring the weaknesses. A good leader will make the tough and sometimes unpleasant decisions."

Bill Slansky, President, National Marine Distributors Association and CEO, Land N' Sea Distributing, Inc.:

"Good leaders assemble the right teams and then get out of their way - they don't micromanage. They assess their teams in light of the organization's goals and culture. They communicate the organization's vision effectively in a manner that gets everyone to make the vision their own."

Gregg Kenney, President, Flagship Marinas:

"Good managers recognize that their success is dependent on their people. He or she will be able to select the right people, understand their strengths and weaknesses, and know the right time to praise or reprimand. The great managers must be able to communicate effectively and have integrity."

Phil Keeter, President, Marine Retailers Association of American:

"An important attribute is the ability to be a multitask manager. The ability to delegate responsibility and tasks to others and then effectively monitor them is paramount."

Pat Kearns, Executive Director, American Boat Builders and Repairers Association:

"Leaders replace "Why not?" thinking with "What if" thinking. Real leaders think big and are willing to give back to their industry."

I was impressed with their responses. Each of their perspectives was outstanding.

I found it interesting that the ability to inspire or motivate was mentioned more than any other attribute. I have believed for a long time that you cannot be an effective leader if you don't have a positive impact on the morale and demeanor of those around you. It's an unpleasant reality that if you are not providing your team with positive energy, you are not an effective leader.

Other points that got multiple mentions were the significance of assembling and understanding a team, and the importance of dealing with integrity.

These comments have certainly been a help to me in keeping what I do in perspective. You too may want to read them over again and ask what you can do to be a more effective leader.

Chapter 72
A VERY FINE LINE SEPARATES CHAMPIONS FROM THE PACK
April 2002

Although I'm not a golfer, for many years I have been keenly interested in what I consider to be a statistical quirk related to professional golf.

The quirk is this: in most years there is a disproportionate relationship between the average per-round score of PGA tour players and the amount of money they earn. The difference in the per-round stroke average between players who win millions of dollars a year, and those who earn significantly less, is usually around two strokes per round. The message is clear. Golfers who play just a little better win a lot more money.

I was reminded of this point once again during the 2002 Winter Olympics in Salt Lake City. Picabo Street, the American alpine skier, finished a disappointing 16th in the women's downhill race.

Many Americans hoping Picabo would win another gold medal after reconstructive surgery on both knees were sorely disappointed. Sixteenth place seemed like a poor performance to those who had convinced themselves another American victory was in the cards.

What was barely publicized was that Street came within 1.6 seconds of winning the gold. That's less than two seconds in a race of nearly two-minutes. Once again a small difference in performance produced a huge difference in outcome.

I believe these sports analogies carry over to the business world. Those managers who get great results may be doing things only a little differently than those who are less successful. That should come as great news to those of you who are not happy with your results. Improvement may be closer than you think. You see, if we identify a few things to do a little better and improve our management scores by just a couple of "strokes," many times we, too, can experience the disproportionately better results that come with those little improvements.

Can you identify a skill that could give you that extra edge - a skill you could develop or enhance that would dramatically improve your job performance? If that's the case, go all out to better yourself in that skill. Buy a book, attend classes or seek advice from others who do it well. Pick one area in which you want to improve, then concentrate on it with a laser-beam focus.

Perhaps it's time management. If so, you are not alone. I get calls and e-mail messages all the time from people asking for materials or help in this area.

While time management is a common source of anxiety, it's really pretty simple. Basically there are three things you can do in this area: discontinue low priority tasks; delegate; or use the right time-management tools. Of course, a "results" orientation doesn't hurt either.

Through focus and some sound advice, you can improve. This, however, is not a time management column. My point is that by focusing on any area, and learning what you need to do better in that area, you can improve.

I once heard someone say that most managers don't suffer from a deficiency in knowledge; they suffer from a deficiency in execution. Many managers know what they need to do but they just don't do it.

Some managers become paralyzed when they try to improve because they spend so much time focused on the details they miss the big picture. They are more focused on doing things right than doing the right things. Of course, it's important to do things right, but it's much more important to be doing the right things.

If you read back through this column you will see I have used the word focus several times. I have also written about this topic a couple of other times in recent months. I emphasize that word again because in polling conference participants around the world I have found that every group, without exception, identifies focus as an area in which managers can use help.

Many times improving focus can be as simple as identifying what is important to you and your company. That's where a mission statement, a strategic plan or even a personal mission can be very useful - helping you prioritize.

There are a lot of little things you can do to improve your management score by just a "stroke" or two. Look for the area in which you need to improve your score, find the help you need and watch as you, too, experience the disproportionately positive results that are generated by making those improvements.

Chapter 73
IT'S A KARMA OF BUSINESS: INTEGRITY PAYS DIVIDENDS
May 2002

Recently I had the opportunity to peruse the "code of business conduct" drawn up by a Fortune 500 company.

As I read through the document I was impressed to note the degree to which this company goes to define appropriate behavior for its people. I was particularly impressed with the organization's approach - it is not an exercise in micromanaging but is done in a manner that encourages the employees to deal with integrity in all of their actions.

I have had the opportunity to meet both the CEO and some of the board members of this company, and I know they believe in what they preach; these are not just empty words. Appropriate business conduct is important to them and the document identifies four specific groups with which the organization wants to deal fairly.

These are the groups and some of my thoughts on each.

- Customers - It is impossible to treat customers unfairly and benefit in the long run; it always catches up with you. While our company has had an occasional disagreement with a customer, the same as anyone else, I can look anyone in the eye and tell them we do our best to deal honestly with people.

Companies that treat customers right develop reputations that are worth more than you can value.

- Employees - Our companies cannot accomplish more than our team will allow us to accomplish. If we don't treat our employees fairly, we will pay for it many times over in lack of motivation and productivity. If we want our companies to perform at an optimum level, we must invest in our people.

- Shareholders - This may seem like a strange constituency to include, but we must treat our company owners fairly. In fact, the most effective company cultures are those in which customers, employees and owners are treated equally well. A business owner needs a fair risk-adjusted return on his or her investment or we will have no owners. Then we will really have a problem.

- Communities - At our company, we try hard to be good neighbors by serving on boards and helping out in other ways with community causes. We all need to be willing to give back to those around us.

When I think of integrity I can't help but think of my Dad. I was 37 when Dad passed away and I believe he was the most honest man I ever met. I never saw him do anything unethical and I have never met anyone who has remotely insinuated that Dad dealt unfairly with them. A legacy like that isn't bad for any of us.

There are two other men - both in our industry and both of whom, unfortunately, are retiring this month - who I believe also have demonstrated very high levels of professionalism and integrity. They are Paul Dodson of the International Marina Institute and Skip Moyer of the American Boat and Yacht Council.

I have worked with Paul and Skip for years now and have always been impressed. They handle themselves and represent their organizations with total professionalism. They have made our industry more professional and a better place to work.

We will miss Paul and Skip. We can only hope others will step in and fill the character voids these two will be leaving. Hopefully, we can keep them at least peripherally involved in our industry through service on boards or other means. Each has been a great example to us.

Finally, there was an interesting article in a recent issue of Scientific American magazine called "The Economics of Fair Play." In a nutshell, the article suggests that we humans are actually programmed in a way that highly values fairness and causes us to act in ways that benefit us in the long run. In other words, we know innately that treating people well and fairly has immediate benefits for them and longer-term benefits for us. This is similar to our saying, "What goes around comes around," or the Eastern concept of karma.

I don't want to get overly philosophical, but treating others fairly not only is the right thing to do, it benefits us in the long run on many levels.

Almost everyone I have met in our industry over the years has demonstrated a high degree of integrity and fairness. We are an industry made up of good people. We are losing two of those good people this month.

Skip and Paul, we will miss you.

Chapter 74
EVEN WITH A GOOD ACCOUNTANT, YOU NEED YOUR OWN SCORECARD
June 2002

Some of my friends in the accounting field are not happy with all the attention they've been getting lately.

For a long-time, certified public accountants have argued that they should be allowed to regulate themselves, that they are professional enough to set their own standards and do not need government oversight.

Needless to say, the Enron debacle is changing the perspective many people, including those in government, have of accountants and the accounting profession.

Despite the well-publicized abuses of a few, accountants still are an important part of our businesses. They are critical, in fact - enabling us to manage in a way that helps our companies survive and thrive.

Whatever the size of your company, you need good financial controls and information.

The business headlines of the past year have left many managers reconsidering what they are doing in the areas of finance and accounting. You too should periodically review those aspects of your business. Here are some thoughts to consider.

- **Hire an expert.** Your team should include someone on whom you can rely to provide information that is both useful and timely. Don't be shortsighted and try to get by with someone who is less than capable. If you don't have someone very knowledgeable helping you with the financial end of your business, it could be costing you a great deal. Many companies settle for less than they should because they don't realize that better help is available. Ask around and find out who some of your peers use; you may come across someone who can really be an important resource to you.

- **Get a basic understanding.** Even when you have an expert, you should have a basic understanding of the financial aspects of your business. Your financials serve as a scorecard. You need to understand how the score is calculated if you are going to play the game. Take an accounting course at your community college or watch for one of the many "understanding financial statements" courses that are offered.

- **Generate detailed financial reports.** You should have financial reports by division and by department. You should be able to track margins easily. Expenses should be detailed by division, department and in total.

- **Track key indicators.** Every company has certain financial indicators that are important. Identify the financial indicators that are most crucial to your organization and track them closely. Track them in a way that will help you identify good or bad trends. Examples of key indicators might be your margins, billable hours, realized rate, occupancy level, inventory turnover or collections rate. The indicators will differ for each company but the key is identifying what is important to your operation and tracking it closely.

- **Make sure your information is timely.** You should receive reports weekly tracking your most important indicators. Your financial statements should be done between the eighth and tenth of each month.

- **Have a budget.** The process of preparing your budget is as important as the budget itself. Use a "zero-sum" approach to determine your expenses. In other words, consider each expense in the light of, "What if we didn't spend that money at all?" or, "If we started fresh today, how would we do that?" Once you have a good budget, use variance analysis to identify and explain differences in your budget and actual results. Use your variance analysis to determine steps you need to take to adjust your operations.

- **Share financial information.** Give out selected financial information to your managers and employees. They're always going to be speculating, anyway, so you might as well give them an accurate picture. It will make your team more effective.

- **Manage your cash.** Most importantly, watch your cash on a daily basis. You should have a good daily cash report showing your beginning balance, all of the day's receipts, all of the day's checks and an ending cash balance. This is a fundamental control - important information for you to follow.

These are some basics that will better prepare you for the financial management of your company. Don't settle for less than you need in this information area. If you are not getting the financial information and advice you need, it is probably hurting your business more than you realize. There are a lot of good financial managers who can help you. Don't wait until it is too late or until you have wasted untold dollars settling for less than the best.

Chapter 75
CREATING A CLIMATE OF CHEER WILL
PAY OFF IN THE LONG RUN
July 2002

People should enjoy coming to work. We spend so much time getting ready for work, going to it, doing it, driving home from it and thinking about it that our jobs had better be enjoyable - or our lives will be pretty miserable.

Don't get me wrong. I don't expect employees to be bummed that the weekend is coming, but making our workplaces enjoyable can significantly improve the quality of their lives.

Not only will the employees benefit, but you can significantly improve your profits. People who enjoy their jobs are more productive and more motivated.

I was reminded of all this when I visited the United Health Care offices in Ft. Lauderdale recently and found each office section decorated in a different festive theme.

One section, for instance, was done up in a nautical theme while another was decorated as a maternity ward. One had a Hawaiian look and another was a winter wonderland. All in all, there must have been 20 different sections - each done in a different theme. And that's not all: the people in each section dressed to suit their particular theme (No, there was no beach section!)

I was really impressed by the interest these people must have in their workplace and in one another. I was also impressed that they were allowed to do it.

Many bosses would cringe at such a spectacle. They want to see noses to the grindstone all day. Of course, it's important that your employees stay focused, but I also believe they get a lot more done if they are enjoying their surroundings.

We are fortunate at our company to have two women, Mary Wilson and Josee Olsen, who fulfill this role. Our service office has been decorated for Mardi Gras (even though we're a few hundred miles from New Orleans) and turned into a celebration of spring. That's in addition to normal holiday decorating.

Mary and Josee provide an atmosphere that makes our service office fun to be in - both for the employees and our customers. And, I might add, their enthusiasm is contagious.

While decorating for special events is fun, there are other things you can do to make your workplace enjoyable:

- **Don't micromanage;** let people do their jobs. Don't sit over people or bug them. Employees who have autonomy generally enjoy coming to work.
- **Celebrate accomplishments.** When someone does something good, let everyone join the celebration.
- **Celebrate important dates.** At our company, whenever an employee has a birthday or an employment anniversary we send a reminder to the employee's supervisor and to company executives. These people then can acknowledge the employee's special day. People like to be remembered.
- **Have picnics and parties.** Not everyone will participate and it is usually a lot of work, but most people enjoy parties.
- **Sponsor activities.** We occasionally will run a trip to a pro sports event. They are great camaraderie builders.
- **Use positive reinforcement.** Tell people when they do a good

job. This is the easiest -but most underused - way to make your workplace enjoyable.

As long as people are completing their tasks, be glad if they also have time to enjoy their jobs. Of course, there are limits, and an employee's primarily reason for being in the workplace is to get the job done. However, I have never been one to criticize people for taking a few minutes to catch up after the weekend or talking about something important going on in their lives.

If you let people enjoy their jobs, your company will benefit in the long run. You '11 make more money, and you just might find yourself a little happier too.

Chapter 76
AS THE ECONOMY HEATS UP, SO WILL THE WAR FOR TALENT
August 2002

Early last year organizations looking for good employees faced a nightmare situation. Companies were struggling to find the human resources they needed to keep up with business demands.

Our company was no different. We faced this problem and responded to it by developing and implementing the Aggressive Employee Recruiting Plan that had me traveling around the country. I spent several weekends away from my family on recruiting trips.

Then, later in 2001, the job market completely reversed course. The triple whammy of a declining stock market, weak economy and then the events of September 11 resulted in hiring freezes and downsizing at many companies. Suddenly job seekers were flying in to see us.

Here in 2002, the situation is changing again. Companies are hiring and once again, good employees are in short supply.

I believe 2001 was an aberration. Although I am no futurist, I have seen enough to make me believe that over the next several years - and maybe indefinitely - the type of employee we need to effectively operate our businesses is going to be very hard to find.

How, then, can we make sure we have the talent we need?

I was discussing this problem recently with a friend, Neal Harrell, who is President of Brooks Marine Group. Fortunately for me, Neal suggested I read a book called "The War for Talent," by Ed Michaels, Helen Handfield-Jones, Beth Axelrod from McKinsey & Company (September 200 I , $27.50).

I have read countless business books over the years but I cannot remember one that had a greater impact on me than "The War for Talent." I highly recommend it. Besides corroborating most of what I have written and said over the years about the importance of having a great team, the book really broadened my perspective and re-emphasized to me the importance of acquiring and developing talent.

Lack of talent will severely limit your company's results, so you should be on a perpetual talent search.

Here are some ideas that can help:

- **Be focused on talent.** This is a mindset, not a process. It is important that you have a good human resources process, but it is exponentially more important that you have a talent mindset. If you are the CEO, you need to be spending a high percentage of your time acquiring and developing talent. If you let yourself get caught up in the day-to-day problems others should be handling, you'll be neglecting the development of your people and you'll pay a huge price in the long run.

- **Always be recruiting.** Occasionally economic downturns may make finding new employees easier over short stretches of time, but over the long haul, good people will continue to be hard to find. Never pass on a prospect who can dramatically upgrade your team, regardless of the economic or business environment at the time.

- **Don't be cheap.** Management recruiters all tell stories of companies that let a first-rate prospect getaway over a small amount of money. If you identify a dynamite talent who can really help your organization, do what it takes to hire him or her. The incremental amount you will pay that person is peanuts compared to what he or she can bring to your organization in the long run.

- **Be prepared to make tough decisions.** Organizational decisions that affect individuals negatively are always very difficult. We all struggle with these types of decisions, but in the long run we must have the fortitude to make them. Your very organizational survival is at stake. Other employees working for your company are also counting on you to make the tough choices when necessary. As difficult as it might be, you have to be willing to do what it takes to develop a top functioning team.

In a nutshell-talented people are very difficult to find; when you do come across one, do everything you can to recruit him or her to your team. After acquiring the people you need, ensure that you are making the necessary investments to continually develop them. If you settle for a mediocre team, your results will be poor. Good people will give you a huge competitive advantage.

There is a definite correlation between the level of your organization's talent and your financial results. Do what it takes to continually improve your organization and enjoy the many benefits that result from having a first-class team.

Chapter 77
ACCOUNTING/CEO SCANDALS PUT THE SPOTLIGHT ON TRUST
September 2002

Over the years I have developed a friendship with a business consultant I truly respect.

Pat Conway and I worked together many years ago at the CPA firm then known as Coopers & Lybrand. For the last 20 years, Pat has owned a consulting firm specializing primarily in organizational and people issues. I have known him as a peer, client and most importantly, as a friend.

Pat is one of those people who always has something insightful to say. He has worked with thousands of managers and companies over the years and has learned a tremendous amount from them - both from their successes and their failures. He has a front-row seat in the managerial arena.

A while ago, Pat and I were sharing some ideas related to a book we are writing together when Pat offered an observation about successful managers he has worked with over the years. I am reminded of that comment each time I read or hear about the accounting scandals and executive misrepresentations that have been so much in the news in recent months.

What Pat said is that the managers he considers successful share two attributes: consistency and trustworthiness.

Consistency

As managers, the changing environment in which we operate our business constantly buffets us. The one certain thing we have to deal with is change.

I have written and spoken in the past about change and how we, as marine managers, can successfully deal with it. One book I have previously recommended is "Who Moved My Cheese?" by Spencer Johnson. It is a compelling parable about change that suggests approaches we as managers can use to successfully guide our companies through the change.

Is it contradictory to suggest that we should remain consistent and at the same time, be willing to change? Of course not. But how, then, do we remain consistent in the face of constant change?

Consistency relates primarily to the overall values of your organization. Change may force you to modify some of the methods you use, but it rarely - if ever - will change your values.

In the past, we at our company have identified our values as providing outstanding returns to our employees, customers and stockholders. Additionally, we have held safety in the workplace and integrity in our dealings as important values in our business.

Though our business environment may change, the values we hold do not.

But consistency goes beyond values and into our day-to-day dealings with people. Nobody - your employees and customers included - wants to feel they are dealing with a different you every day. It is important that we remain consistent with the people we deal with. Employees, in particular, will be much more productive working for a boss who is consistent in his or her dealings with them.

Trustworthiness

I really cannot overemphasize the importance of being trustworthy with the people you deal with. Odds are, most of the people reading this column believe they are.

However, the people around you may not share that perception, may not consider you as trustworthy as you believe you are.

Where most managers get hung up on the trust issue is in the little things. Most of us would never think of stealing from an employee or intentionally cheating a customer.

What we might do, however, is make commitments in passing that we then forget about. Or we may make what others perceive to be commitments, when in our minds we are doing nothing more than "thinking out loud."

An employee or customer may remember for years something you have said in passing - a remark you have quickly forgotten about. Whatever it was, it may not have been important enough for you to remember. But to the customer or employee, your failure to follow through is a reflection on your very integrity. You may think that's unfair, but, sorry - that's the way it goes. Something I try to do to help me remember my commitments is to write down everything - absolutely everything. If I put it on my to-do list I know I won't forget it. You may want to try the same thing.

Another important thought related to trust is that the communication level in your organization will never rise higher than the trust level. If you are having problems communicating with your people, you may want to look at how much they trust you.

Unfortunately, today's business environment of accounting scandals and executive misrepresentations makes most people wonder whom they can trust. However, there is an upside to this. Those who have demonstrated integrity and trustworthiness over the years are more valuable than ever.

Both of these areas - consistency and trust - are important for us to focus on if we want to help our companies, and ourselves, reach our true potential.

Chapter 78
SOUND MANAGEMENT TIPS FOR A FAST-FOOD OPERATOR
October 2002

At the risk of being too general, let me say I hate going to fast-food restaurants.

It's not that I don't like the food or that I'm overly health-conscious. I hate going to fast food restaurants because a very high percentage of the time their service is terrible.

Maybe it's just me, but it seems like most fast-food restaurants - at least those in South Florida - would make great case studies in poor customer service. The employees act as though they're put out when a customer approaches the counter or pulls up to the drive through. They barely know how to work the cash register, and they frequently get the order mixed up. All of this incompetence results in an experience that's anything but "fast" and if you are impatient like me, it can be very frustrating.

Because I firmly believe everything rises and falls on leadership, my first inclination is to blame the owners of these franchises for not properly training their employees. The problem with this theory is that the employees turn over so quickly they are usually gone before any real substantive training can be completed. Come back to any fast-food outlet a few weeks after any visit and you'll almost always find a new crew.

Now that I've vented my frustration with South Florida fast-food restaurants in general, let me say there is one that stands out like a shining city on a hill. It is a particular Wendy's not far from my office.

Jim Bronstien, our company President, and I eat at this Wendy's two or three times a month. The service is always fast and courteous, and the crew always gets the order right. Everyone in the store is friendly and they act as though they really appreciate our business. And the same people have been serving us there for years.

I have seen evidence many times over the years that this restaurant is exceptionally well managed, but it wasn't until recently that I took the time to meet the owner. His name is Robert Morden. I have seen Robert working here for years, but I had never made it a point to talk with him. Finally, in an effort to learn the secret of his success, I introduced myself.

I asked him how he was able to run such a smartly functioning operation when all the other fast-food outlets in our area seem to be so mismanaged. His response was fascinating.

I realize that virtually everyone reading this column is involved in the marine business; however, I hope you won't stop reading. Regardless of our business or industry, I believe there's a lot to learn from what Robert shared with me. Here is some of what he had to say.

- **"The customer is not the enemy."** That was Robert's very first response when I asked him why his restaurant stood out from the competition. He says he emphasizes over and over with this staff that the customer is important, and he's absolutely convinced it pays off. You can't leave his place without one of the employees wishing you a great day. Talking with Robert served to reinforce in my mind the value of continually impressing upon employees the need to exceed a customer's expectations.
- **He is focused.** While we were talking. Robert was quoting me figures on the length of time it takes to get through his

drive-through compared with those of his competitors. This impressed me on two levels. Not only was he aware of the objectives and results at his store, but he had invested the effort to learn those of his competitors.

- **He is always there.** I don't remember ever being in that restaurant when Robert wasn't there. He is committed to doing what it takes to be successful.

- **He surrounds himself with good people.** During our conversation, he called over Suzie, the co-owner and manager. Before Robert bought the restaurant, he insisted that Suzie join him to run it. Otherwise, he wasn't going to go through with it. When she agreed, he gave her a share of the ownership and now gives her all the credit for the results. It reminded me that we need to not only develop those around us, but also give them all the credit when things go well.

- **He pays a little more.** Robert hires good people, motivates them and keeps them - in part because he pays them slightly above the market rate. Business owners should take their best people out of the job market by paying them a little more than they are worth. Your best people are almost always worth a market premium to keep them at your company.

Even though we aren't serving fast food, these are powerful principles that can help all of us manage our businesses better. And when we manage our businesses better, the profits are sure to follow.

Chapter 79
YOUR MOST VALUABLE ASSET?
IT COULD BE YOUR BRAND
November 2002

If I were to ask you to identify your company's most valuable asset, how would you respond? Think for a moment.

Most managers would answer this question by naming a tangible asset such as property or machinery, or maybe even a people asset- the employees or customers. Most would also agree that whatever it is, it should be carefully cultivated.

What many don't realize, however, is that their most valuable asset may be their brand.

According to the American Management Association, a brand is a name, term, sign or symbol (or combination thereof) that differentiates your product. For many of us it is our company name. In the broader sense, it is the company's goodwill.

Your company's brand is not listed on your balance sheet, but it may be worth more than you think. In today's knowledge-based economy, an intangible asset such as "brand" can regularly provide more value to a company than tangible assets.

For many, in fact, the brand may be their most valuable asset. Companies perceived to have a good brand name are consistently valued at a premium over similar companies without brand recognition.

Many times brands by themselves are bought and sold for considerable amounts of money.

Many of you reading this are employed by companies that depend on a brand name for a least some portion of their revenues and profits. Those of you who don't rely on a brand should be developing one. Even if you're a one-person operation, you should come up with a brand that will be closely tied to your reputation.

Now that we have established the importance of brands, here are some things you should consider as you tackle brand management at your company:

- **Be focused on your brand** - A manager rarely, if ever, thinks of the brand he or she is creating. It is important to stay focused on the fact that most of your decisions are in some way affecting the value of your brand. Have a brand strategy to help you maintain the focus you need to optimize the financial return from your brand. Make someone - probably you - accountable for the success or failure of your brand. Brand excellence will result from a strong brand focus.

- **It is all about customers** - Studies have consistently shown that not only will customers pay a premium to buy from a known brand company, but also that they will make faster buying decisions. The most successful brands are built by establishing lasting positive emotional experiences among customers and are sustained by consistently creating positive feelings among those same customers. When a brand occupies a distinctive position in a customer's mind it is very hard for a competitor to dislodge it. In other words, relationships matter!

- **Create a brand personality** - Know what your brand stands for and position it so there is a perception of a positive difference between your brand and others. It is OK to use emotion to build your brand's personality. In fact, I read somewhere recently that emotions trigger the brain 3,000 times faster than rational thought. You should be trying to develop a brand that gains the acceptance, friendship and lasting loyalty of your customers.

- **Focus on value creation** - Even if you don't plan to sell your company any time soon, you can create a substantial amount of value by building a strong brand. Focusing on this value creation will also help you keep a long-term focus with your business. Again, keep in mind that this value creation is totally dependent on the perception of your company within the minds of your customers. Build a good track record for your brand with your customers and you can create a lot of value.

- **Consider some market research** - My fellow columnist Wanda Kenton Smith can help you in this area more than I can. However, consider doing some market research to determine exactly where your brand is positioned in your market. The information you gather is certain to provide some surprises.

I believe today's top managers are those who are proficient in brand management. They realize that a brand left idle will soon become worthless. They also realize that good brand management not only creates short-term profits but also a significant amount of long-term value.

If you would like to improve your brand management skills, and are interested in some additional reading on the subject, e-mail me and I will be happy to recommend some excellent books I have read. They will help you, I'm sure.

In the meantime stay focused on building a quality brand. You will be creating an asset that will last well beyond your tenure. Both you and those who follow you will reap the benefits of your wisdom for years to come.

Chapter 80
THE MANAGER OF THE FUTURE WILL EXHIBIT THESE QUALITIES
December 2002

I find it hard to believe that 2003 is here. The years seem to be moving along too fast. Soon we are going to look up and it will be 2010.

On page 28 of this month's Soundings Trade Only, there is an article about a presentation I gave in October at the National Boatyard and Marina Conference. The presentation was entitled, "What Does the Future Hold? Global Trends and How They Will Impact Both You and Your Company." During the presentation I tried to describe major trends that will affect all of us, both professionally and personally, over the next 25 years.

If you heard my presentation or already have read the article, you will probably agree that life in the future is going to be much different from today. Luckily for us, many of the trends that are forming our future are very positive.

Since we have so many changes on the horizon, I would like to identify the attributes I believe the effective manager of the future must have to properly deal with what is coming. We can use this information to help prepare ourselves for the challenges that lay ahead.

Here are some of the attributes that will be needed by the effective manager of tomorrow:

- **An understanding of trends** - In the future, change will occur much faster than we are accustomed to experiencing it. Just look back a few decades and compare the pace of change today with what it was then. The change cycle will just keep speeding up. The most effective managers will develop an ability to identify and react to trends before they become major issues for their businesses.

- **Great employee management skills** - Labor markets will remain tight as the economy grows and the population of the developed world decreases. In addition, both your employees' work ethic and their loyalty to your company will be dropping, just as they have from the last generation to this one.

  These employee issues are going to require great management skills. The best employees will have many opportunities to walk away from micromanagers or companies that don't treat them right. Tomorrow's effective managers should be doing everything they can today to be developing the skills they need to manage tomorrow's workforce.

- **A global perspective** - Tomorrow's manager will be forced to get outside of his or her comfort zone. The world is getting smaller on many fronts. We will need to be able to recruit skilled employees from anywhere in the world. The Internet is eliminating all kinds of barriers in all areas of our businesses. We need to be able to negotiate strategic alliances anywhere in the world. Spend some time today getting outside of your comfort zone to help you prepare for the changes that are on the way.

- **An understanding of technology** - The advances in technology will be significant over the next few years. They will affect all aspects of our organizations and they will put some people reading this column out of business. We all need to be reading books, taking classes and doing anything else we can do to keep up with technology in our businesses.

- **A willingness to change** - If you are not willing to change in the future the implications will be even more dramatic than they are today. The effective manager of tomorrow will not only embrace change when it comes but also look at change as a wonderful opportunity.

- This willingness to change must even extend to our sacred cows, including our company cultures. Generation Xers and those following have different values from the baby boomers and their predecessors, and we will need to adjust for that.

- **An ability to deal with the government** - Since 1996 the U.S. government has enacted more than 14,000 new regulations, and the trend shows no sign of slowing down. We can either complain about the new regulations or use that energy to comply with them. Tomorrow's manager will have to be effective at understanding and implementing regulations issued by all levels of government.

- **Great planning skills**- While it is important to understand trends that will affect us, it is even more important to be able to prepare a plan to deal with them. Crawford Greenwalt once said, "Every moment spent planning saves three or four in execution." This will be even truer in the future as we deal with change at an ever accelerating pace.

As managers we have a responsibility to do all we can to prepare both ourselves and our organizations for the future. Obtaining these skills for you and your team will go a long way toward helping your organization avoid "future shock" as it deals with the inevitable changes on the road ahead.

Finally, you can summarize much of this by saying we all need to have a strong emphasis on continuous improvement. Change is coming and it is coming faster than we have ever experienced it before. Let's all keep focused on improving both ourselves and our organizations in ways that will give us a competitive advantage in the exciting days ahead.

Chapter 81
CATCHING A VISION OPENS UP A WHOLE
WORLD OF POTENTIAL
January 2003

For nearly 10 years, I have been fortunate to sit on the board of Hospice of Palm Beach County, an organization considered to be among the creme de la creme of our local companies.

Just over four years ago, however, Hospice went through a pretty significant transition. Our CEO - someone we regarded very highly - resigned to accept a great opportunity in another part of the country. I was asked to serve, along with three other board members, on a search committee to find her replacement.

After a few months and a nationwide search, we chose a new CEO. Dave Fielding came to us from another Hospice organization outside of Florida and, luckily for us, brought to our team a completely different and fresh approach.

Until Dave came on board, our business paradigm had been one of retrenchment. We were cutting costs and looking for opportunities to protect our organization from what seemed to be a very uncertain and volatile health care environment.

Dave's paradigm was completely different from ours. He believed we were operating far below our potential, and that we should be a much bigger organization serving many more people. Instead of retrenching, Dave encouraged us to invest in our organization and to reach the people who needed us but were not yet benefiting from our service.

He sold us on a growth vision, and four years later we truly have been transformed. We have increased our employment from around 160 people to nearly 600. Four years ago we were serving 200 patients a day; today that figure is up to nearly 700 - all because of a big vision.

I don't believe this is an isolated incident - rather, I view it as a great example of how an organization can be transformed by vision.

I can't think about the Hospice experience without wondering how many companies in the marine industry are failing to achieve their potential, and could be transformed if someone caught a big vision. I am convinced the results at many of our companies could be significantly improved.

What exactly is vision?

It is the ability to get out of your day-to-day box and see the world through a new set of eyes. It is the ability to dream about the big picture and all of the potential that goes with it.

Many times during presentations I have used a beach ball to help people understand vision. In fact, the beach ball presents such a powerful analogy that I keep one in my office to help me remember to have a big vision.

Picture a beach ball. It is large and has panels of different colors. The one in my office is red, green, white, orange, blue and yellow.

Now, imagine the beach is your world - much bigger - and you are standing on it. If you are on the blue panel, what color will your perspective be? Blue, of course. You will see your world blue and argue with others, especially those standing on other colors, that the world is blue.

Unfortunately, that is precisely what happens to most managers. They have not developed the conceptual skills necessary to see the whole picture; they see it from the perspective of where they are standing.

The best managers - those with vision - are able to step back and view the whole beach ball. They are the managers who get extraordinarily good results for their companies.

Enlarging your vision is important but it can also be difficult. Luckily there are steps you can take. Here are a few:

- Think big, really big. Allow yourself to dream.
- Break out of your old paradigms. Try to think of your businesses in a new way.
- Forget about the way it used to be done. If you find yourself thinking, "But this is the way we have always done it" - watch out!
- Forget about all the reasons you can't do it. Imagine what you could do with no restraints.
- Think global. The world is getting smaller and we all need to be ready for a more global business environment.
- Get "out of the box." Look for new experiences and technologies. Encourage new ideas in your organization.

Stretching yourself in the manner I have suggested can be a very uncomfortable exercise. You may be one of those who believes we shouldn't try to fix what "isn't broke." Most of us are built the same way, and it is much more comfortable to stay in the same old routine than it is to initiate change.

However, if you want to effectively compete in the years ahead you need to revisit your vision. Is it expansive enough to help you and your organization achieve the success you deserve? If not, start thinking big today!

Chapter 82
WORK AS A TEAM: SEND YOUR BUSINESS
TO THE BIG LEAGUES
February 2003

During last year's baseball season, on a day off for the Florida Marlins, I had the unique opportunity to participate in a Major League Baseball fantasy camp.

I was part of a group of about 25 South Florida business leaders who were invited to go to Pro Player Stadium and pretend we were big leaguers!

While it was a "fantasy" camp, I came away impressed with the reality of the experience.

Our group of middle-aged business people was taken into the locker room, given Marlin team jerseys and hats, then led to the Marlins' dugout for our instructions.

Our first task was to run a lap around the field - an exercise that was followed by the actual warm-up drill the Marlins go through before each game. Fantasy camp quickly turned into "Survivor," as many of the normally desk-bound guys struggled to make it through a workout with the Marlins trainer.

Next, we were separated into three groups and given pitching, fielding and batting instructions by Marlins players and coaches. Finally, we were split into teams and played a game. While I didn't set any records, I was pretty proud to have hit a single just over second base.

As I spoke with the Marlins players and coaches that day, I couldn't help but be reminded of the importance of teamwork on the ball field and, more importantly to us, in our businesses. Success in baseball requires people to be in the right place at the right time and work together as a team. Our businesses are no different. Just as teamwork (or lack thereof) can determine the success or failure of a big-league team, it can have a significant impact on our companies.

Shortly after my baseball experience, *The Wall Street Journal* ran an article on the attributes company recruiters are looking for when they are interviewing graduating MBA students. I found it interesting to note the degree of importance the recruiters place on the ability to work in teams.

In fact, the article concluded, being a team player is just as important to a recruiter's assessment of a candidate as are the "hard" skills such as financial or marketing knowledge.

Almost everyone acknowledges that teamwork is important, and almost everyone understands that organizations are more effective when each person is pulling on the same end of the rope. Why then do so few organizations operate as true teams?

One of the reasons many organizations are not more team focused is that their managers simply don't allow that to happen. You've heard the phrase, "We have met the enemy and they are us." Unfortunately, many a manager is his or her own worst enemy when it comes to promoting teamwork.

Sometimes managers are afraid to give up control. While they intuitively understand the importance of teams, down deep they would rather operate like a dictatorship.

This approach to management only can hurt the organization and the manager in the long run. As managers, we must encourage teamwork in our organizations and do what we can to facilitate the formation of teams.

Facilitating teamwork can mean many things. We do it by hiring good people, setting group goals, and rewarding employees based on how they perform as a team. Of course, it also helps to emphasize teamwork on a regular basis in your employee meetings.

Creating effective teams also requires being willing to hire people who think differently than you do. While ultimately someone in your organization must make the final decision, a big benefit of effective teamwork is being able to see things from many different perspectives.

When you have people in your organization with different perspectives, you have the opportunity to create synergy. Synergy takes the different perspectives of the people on your team and creates an idea that is much bigger than the sum of your individual ideas.

Teamwork also is about using each teammate's strengths and covering for his or her weaknesses. If everyone on your team has the same strengths your organization probably has a huge weakness.

Managers should hire good people with different perspectives. After bringing these people aboard, encourage them to operate as a team. Then, even more importantly, let them operate as a team.

Those of us who have played team sports know there is little in life more exciting than being on a winning team. With a little effort you can catch that feeling at your company.

Try some of the above and watch as both your winning percentage - and more importantly your profit - improves.

Chapter 83
DO YOUR RESEARCH BEFORE
YOU COME TO YOUR DECISION
March 2003

While I am certainly not a scientist, I do have a strong affinity for the subject. I love to read about new theories and developments, especially those that have a direct impact on our future. I also enjoy coming across fresh scientific findings that disprove what almost everyone has, until now, accepted as fact.

Despite the fact that most scientists are highly intelligent, they struggle with a problem that can hamper their productivity significantly and - in extreme cases - can ruin their careers. The problem is called **confirmation bias.** It can be equally devastating to companies and careers.

Confirmation bias occurs when a scientist attempts to prove a theory with a test that is almost certain to generate the outcome he or she expects or desires. Whether knowingly or subliminally, the scientist frames questions or designs experiments in a way that predetermines the outcome. The result of this manipulation is a conclusion that confirms what the scientist believed to be true from the start.

Fortunately for us, science has a built-in mechanism to overcome this problem. Modern scientific methodology requires that a second researcher duplicate the original test results. If it is a capable scientist who is conducting this second set of tests, he or she will quickly detect confirmation bias - even at the expense of embarrassing the original scientist.

Unfortunately, confirmation bias is not limited to the world of science; many managers suffer from it, too. The trouble here is that managers normally don't have that second set of eyes looking over their shoulders to catch the confirmation bias, and stop an action before it causes difficulty. As managers, we have to live with our decisions.

In the business world confirmation bias occurs when managers know what they want to do but ask others for opinions - either to make the other person feel involved or to make themselves feel better for asking. They structure their questions so the desired answer is either obvious or the only real way of responding to the question.

After getting the answer he or she wants, the manager feels smug about having achieved the desired objective - even though it was done by subtly manipulating the employee. Despite what the manager might think, the employee almost always understands exactly what has happened.

Managers have heard for so long that they should involve employees in decision-making that many times they are simply going through the motions. The manager ends up feeling good while the employee whose ideas have been solicited leaves feeling demotivated. In fact, it is better to not even ask your employees what they think than to ask them in a manner that reflects your bias.

From an employee's perspective, there is nothing to gain from disagreeing in this situation. It's a lot easier to go with the flow and tell the boss what he or she wants to hear. The desired answer is so obvious that the employee just utters it and moves on.

Besides de-motivating the people who work for you, bad enough in itself, there is another huge downside to asking employees for input in a way that demonstrates your bias. By tainting their feedback you lose a goldmine of potential ideas and energy, bottled up inside of your employees just waiting for the right situation to come out. Most managers never tap into even a small percentage of this resource.

Many times while speaking on this subject at conferences I have used a boat analogy to help managers understand what they are potentially missing. Imagine for a minute that you are in our new 42-foot Rybovich just outside the Palm Beach inlet. It is a beautiful day and you want to run to the Bahamas, just 50 miles away. You could throttle up the twin 660-hp engines and be there in about two hours.

Or, you could forget about those big engines and start paddling instead, more than likely never getting to the Bahamas. This may sound like an absurd example but it is exactly what many managers do on a daily basis. Through their employees they have access to wonderful engines representing ideas and creativity that they never tap, preferring instead to do it all themselves.

The best managers use those engines. They genuinely appreciate and ask for employee input. They don't always do what the employees suggest, but they do give them a legitimate opportunity to add their perspective.

If you are guilty of confirmation bias in your dealings with others, or if you are not getting the input of others at all, you are missing a great opportunity. The most effective managers solicit the opinions of others and they implement the best ideas, regardless of who came up with them. Stop paddling and use those engines - both you and your company have a lot to gain!

Chapter 84
ALL WORK, NO PLAY SELDOM BRINGS THE DESIRED RESULT
April 2003

Do you work hard? Really hard? Are you totally focused on your career?

If so, you could be past the point of diminishing returns. And, more importantly, you may be missing out on an excellent opportunity to achieve success in a better way - actually getting more from less.

Sound interesting? Would you like to get better results from less effort and enjoy your life a little more? Before I let you in on the secret, a little background.

Recently, I was intrigued to read an article in "Psychology Today" dealing with two researchers who analyzed the lives of Nobel laureates in chemistry. The researchers compared their distinguished subjects to other equally well educated and positioned, but less decorated, scientists in the same fields. They made this comparison in an effort to identify the difference that may give an edge to the most successful scientists. Their findings were fascinating.

The researchers discovered that almost all of the Nobel laureates had a hobby of significant interest outside of their work in chemistry. Correspondingly, (and this is what I found extremely interesting) very few of the less successful scientists had such outside interests.

The researchers went on to point out examples - discoveries that were made not in a lab but while scientists were away from their normal work surroundings. Similarly, they discussed a related study, which claims that more than a third of the MacArthur Genius Grant recipients acknowledge having built creative worlds in their own minds. A separate Yale study determined that children with vivid imaginations learn faster. Once again, these are examples of people stepping out of their normal surroundings to achieve really big things.

There is another example that wasn't mentioned in the magazine article. It is well known that Isaac Newton, arguably the greatest scientist of all time, attributed many of his most significant discoveries to time off when the European plague had forced the closing of Cambridge University, where Newton worked. Luckily for us, Newton went back to his farm in Lincolnshire to wait it out. While waiting on the farm he made many amazing discoveries.

So how does all this apply to us as managers?

Have you ever had a brainstorm while you were on the beach, fishing, playing golf or just relaxing? For most people, the answer probably is yes. Many times we can see the trees best when we step back from the forest.

It is all about balance. You do need to work hard to be successful, but you also need to give your mind an opportunity to step back and get out of its normal surroundings.

Perhaps for you it is a course of study totally unrelated to what you do. Maybe it's a vacation in some exotic location or just hanging out around the house.

I can't count the number of times I have experienced this principle. I never come back to work from a few days off without a list of job-related ideas I came up with while I was away.

It's not that I spend my vacation time thinking about work; I do not. Usually I am totally involved in whatever activity I am sharing with my family.

However, when we relax in a different environment or enjoy some actlvlty totally unrelated to our jobs we subconsciously see things from a different perspective. Often this different perspective will provide new answers to some old problems.

It amazes me how many managers - particularly business owners and their top executives - are willing to make a type of Faustian bargain to achieve success. In this business version of the story, however, the manager plays both Faust and Mephistopheles, convincing himself or herself that selling out to the job will bring the desired success.

Unfortunately, many of those managers lose it all. They sacrifice family, health, personal development and relationships, and (as Faust was doomed to never be satisfied) they rarely obtain the success they covet. And even when they do, it comes at an exorbitant price.

Remember, it is results we want. And many times getting those results requires stepping back and spending some time with your family or in some type of personal development or relaxation. I am convinced that most of the time, the managers who get the best results are balanced.

There is no easy way to achieve the success you desire - and I don't in any way mean to insinuate that you don't have to work hard. Of course you do. But, it is also important to ensure you have balance in your life.

Chapter 85
E-MAIL IS A WONDERFUL TOOL IF YOU USE IT THE RIGHT WAY
May 2003

We have become a culture of e-mail junkies. If you are like me your computer beeps regularly, signaling the arrival of a new email message. Even when traveling e-mail is easy to get - even for those few who don't carry a laptop computer.

Personally, I love it. E-mail has significantly improved my communication with people both inside and outside our company. I exchange messages regularly with people with whom I would have been playing telephone tag just a few years ago. I also am much quicker to either ask questions or offer assistance when it can be done with the ease of email.

I have started new friendships and had other friendships enhanced. Finally, and maybe most importantly, I believe e-mail has improved both my productivity and time management. It is a wonderful thing!

Unfortunately, even though e-mail has been around for a few years now, many people still struggle with the right way to communicate electronically. People who have done very little writing throughout their careers now find themselves writing every day. And, in many cases, the way they handle their email is hurting their professional image.

Here are 12 tips that can help you with your email and, hopefully, also help you establish and maintain the professional image you want for both you and your company.

- **Use a salutation** - Email salutations tend to be a little less formal than those used in letters. For instance, I might open a letter with "Dear Tom." In e-mail it's more likely to be "Hi Tom."

  Whichever you use, it is still nice if the message has a salutation before you get into the meat of your note. And keep in mind it doesn't make sense to open an email with "Good morning" since you often have no idea when the recipient will be reading it.

- **Be concise** - Email is best used as a quick communication tool. When using it, get right to your point.

- **Be careful of your tone** - It has been said the most important element of most communication is the nonverbal portion. Some studies, in fact, say it is as high as 93 percent of all communication that is nonverbal. Your reader has no way of knowing your frame of mind when you are writing. Therefore, don't infer tone; let your words speak for themselves.

- **DON'T USE ALL CAPS** - when you do this, your reader gets the impression that you are yelling at him or her. And, besides, it looks unprofessional.

- **Don't assume your message is private** - Emails get forwarded all over and can very easily be sent to someone you did not expect to be reading it. I have heard many examples of emails getting forwarded, intentionally or by mistake, to an unintended recipient with negative consequences.

- **Use threads** - A thread is a series of emails that have been sent back and forth on a subject. By using threads you help the reader keep track of the context.

- **Use complete thoughts** - I frequently receive emails that read like the sender started writing halfway through a thought or idea. The reader is probably picking your note up cold and has no idea what was in your head before you wrote. Use complete thoughts to help the reader get the whole picture of what you are trying to communicate.

Sometimes I will get a reply email that will say something like "Yes I agree." Unless the reply comes back immediately after I sent the original note, I have to figure out what the person is agreeing to, which sometimes requires finding the original email I sent. Don't be wordy, but when replying to an email give enough information to keep your reader from having to figure out what you are saying.

- **Respond quickly** - Because email travels so fast, a sender expects a quick reply. Respond to emails quickly even if it is just to say that you will get back to them soon. Many e-mail programs have automatic replies you can use when away from your computer for a few days.
- **Send an acknowledgment** - When someone sends you a note by email that does not require a reply it is still nice to send a quick note of acknowledgment or thanks.
- **Proofread** - I regularly get emails that have obviously not been proofread. It is a bad reflection on the writer to send out a note with obvious mistakes. Take a second and read over your e-mails before you send them.
- **Resist the urge to send notes "urgent"** - Some people send all their email out urgent. This is a quick way to lose credibility.
- **End with your name** - End your email with your name, even if it is one of the pre programmed endings with your name, telephone number, etc.

How you communicate may be the biggest part of your professional image. E-mail communication is no exception. Adopting the suggestions I have outlined here can help you project an image that will help both you and your company achieve the success you deserve.

Chapter 86
A POSITIVE OUTLOOK IS KEY TO MANAGEMENT SUCCESS
June 2003

The older I get, the more I realize that happiness depends less on a person's circumstances than on the way each individual chooses to view those circumstances.

Some people always seem miserable, regardless of what is going on around them. Others appear to see the positive side in most situations and have a more upbeat attitude. These are the people I like to be around.

I believe the way a person thinks has a great impact - both on success as a manager and in one's personal life. People who are optimistic and think big tend to be much more successful than those who don't.

Unfortunately, many people limit themselves significantly by the way they think.

Imagine a full-size hula-hoop lying on the ground. Now imagine a regular-sized rubber band lying in a perfect circle in the middle of that hula-hoop. Think of the hula-hoop as a representation of the potential most people have and the rubber band as the limits of what they actually achieve.

What are the restraints that keep most people trapped inside that rubber band?

Most people are their own biggest impediment. The way they

think prevents them from stepping outside that little rubber band. The phrase, "We have met the enemy and he is us," could not be more true. A combination of what we heard as kids, failures and setbacks over our lives, and a lack of self-confidence keeps many people from achieving even a small percentage of their true potential.

Luckily our thinking can be changed. Here are some ideas that can help you ensure your way of thinking is an ally and not an adversary:

- **Think big** - I have written before that people who think big are the ones who get the big results. Imagine where you want to be in five years, then multiply that dream by 10 times. If you want to accomplish something big, the first step is to start thinking big - really big. Have a big vision for both your company and yourself.

- **Take risks** - If you are like me, you may be somewhat risk-averse. However, the people who accomplish the most for themselves and their companies tend to be those who are willing to take some chances. Not foolish chances, but calculated risks that have a reasonable chance of success. If the thought of making a mistake has you paralyzed, you probably are missing out on some big opportunities.

- **Use your right brain** - The right side of your brain is the home of your creativity. Unfortunately, it is probably the lesser-used side for most managers. Albert Einstein, arguably one of the smartest people who ever lived, said imagination is more important than knowledge. At the risk of using a cliche, get out of your box and try something creative. Go to an art museum and walk around or try drawing something yourself - try to get those creative juices flowing.

- **Use visualization** - Years ago I read that Jack Nicklaus attributed much of his golfing success to imagining every shot in his head before he made it. Since then I have read about many people who attribute their success to visualization. Take some time to sit back and imagine yourself living out your dreams. It will improve your odds of making those dreams come true.

- **Avoid intellectual incest** - Try to fill your head with diverse information. Each month, in addition to the normal business publications, I try to read magazines of all kinds. I read *People, Sports Illustrated, Scientific American* and *Psychology Today,* among others. When traveling, I like to pick up magazines that I don't usually read just to learn something new. Broaden your horizons by reading new material every month.

- **Avoid "stinking thinking"** - A friend of mine uses this phrase often to describe people who are always coming up with reasons why things can't be done. We can be conservative without being so negative that we never accomplish anything. If you frequently find yourself being negative or focusing on why things cannot be done, it probably is time for a paradigm shift.

- **Be positive** - In his book "Learned Optimism," Martin Seligman clearly demonstrates that the most successful people are those who have a positive outlook. I like to think of it as a results orientation or a "can-do" attitude. I believe that a results orientation may be the most important characteristic in distinguishing the very successful from the less successful. People who believe they can accomplish something are much more likely to actually do it.

Are you limiting either your personal achievement or your company's results by the way you think? If so, don't feel alone, you are in the majority of managers.

The good news is that by changing your mindset you can also improve your results. Try some of the above suggestions and watch as both your personal effectiveness and your company's potential are quickly enhanced.

Chapter 87
SIGNIFICANCE AND SUCCESS: ONE LEADS YOU TO THE OTHER
July 2003

"The Generosity Factor" is an excellent book co-written last year by Ken Blanchard, author of "The One Minute Manager."

In a nutshell, the book is a parable of an investment broker who learns from a new friend that there is much more to life than getting and taking. He learns about the considerable benefits that come from being willing to give something back to the world around him.

"The Generosity Factor" makes many convincing points but, most importantly, it distinguishes between success and significance.

According to Blanchard, most people spend their lives trying to obtain success, which they define as wealth, achievement and status. Unfortunately, as corroborated by Tim Kasser's recent book "The High Price of Materialism," this emphasis on the elements of success is off-track. When people center on those objectives, they miss out on the opportunity to be significant, which the book describes as the source of real happiness.

People who are striving to be significant focus on generosity, service and relationships. They show by their actions that they care about those around them, and work deliberately on developing good personal relationships. They are willing to give to their communities, regardless of whether or not there might be some direct benefit for them.

What's really interesting is that the people who endeavor to be significant usually also achieve success as a by-product. In other words, seek significance and you will find success as well.

Seeking significance requires a charitable mindset, and money is the first thing that usually comes to mind. But there are far more important things we can contribute - time, talent, treasure and touch.

Our company tries to be a good corporate citizen. We donate both money and time - not only to local nonprofit and civic entities but to marine industry organizations. We support kids' ball teams and provide funding for organizations that our employees are supporting with their time.

I sit on the boards of our local university, the area hospice, the economic development committee and several marine industry organizations. We believe our company and our people benefit both extrinsically and intrinsically from supporting good causes. I am sure we could do more, but we are striving to do what is right.

How about you and your organization? Are you giving back to the community? Everyone reading this column has time, treasure, talent or touch they could use to help others. Strive for significance and odds are that success will follow.

"The Generosity Factor" is just one of the many books I have read in the past few months. Since many people know I love to read, I am frequently asked to recommend good books.

In fact, on two prior occasions I have used this column to recommend good management books. (If you are interested in getting a copy of those past columns, e-mail me and I will be happy to send them to you.)

Meanwhile, here are some books I have read recently that you might find interesting.

- "The New Psycho-Cybernetics," by Maxwell Maltz and Dan Kennedy. I read the original 25 years ago, and I thoroughly enjoyed this updated version that explains how to keep an effective mindset as we go through life. This book and its original version have served as mental turbochargers to many of today's most successful people.
- "Life Script," by Nicholas Wade. A great overview of the past 10 years of development in biotechnology and a summary of what we can expect in the years to come.
- "Vision," by Gary Hoover. A good book on both the importance of vision in your career and how you can develop it.
- "A Genie's Wisdom," a short fable about a genie who knows everything about marketing. A simple and fun book to read that is packed full of great marketing advice.
- "Full Steam Ahead!" by Ken Blanchard. Another book by Blanchard describing ways to develop and implement an effective vision for your company.

Besides the above, here are some books on global trends that I found outstanding. If you're interested in the world's future, these books are for you:

- "Global Trends 2005," by Michael Mazarr.
- "Global Trends and Global Governance," by Paul Kennedy, et al.
- "It's Getting Better All the Time," by Stephen Moore and Julian Simon. "What the Future Holds," by Richard Cooper and Richard Layard.

Finally, a couple of non-business books I have read recently that can help you expand your thinking:

- "The Greatest Minds and Ideas of All Time," by Will Durant
- "A History of Knowledge," by Charles Van Doren.

There is perhaps no better way to improve yourself than by reading good books. I hope you try some of these.

Chapter 88
MANAGING THE INTANGIBLES:
A TRUE MEASURE OF SUCCESS
August 2003

It probably comes as no surprise to learn that most managers are much more comfortable managing things they can see and touch. But did you know that, ultimately, your success as a manager depends on how well you manage the things you can't see or touch?

I believe the people who are most successful in their careers are proficient in managing the intangibles.

Intangibles are as important to your success as any facility, financial statement or product line. In fact, many times intangibles are ultimately the most important driver of an organization's worth.

So what are intangibles? While there are many examples, I will try to address a few.

At the top of the list would have to be leadership. I have said for many years that everything rises and falls on leadership. My experience is that effective leaders have vision, talent and focus. Vision is the ability to look ahead and think big; talent is the ability to communicate, interact with people, organize your time and continually improve; focus is the ability to identify what is important and then keep your attention on it.

Effective communication is another important intangible. When you get to the bottom of almost any management problem it is almost always a communication problem. An important point to keep in mind, especially if you are having communication problems at your company, is that the communication level of an organization never rises above the trust level.

Brand management is an intangible that can significantly affect your financial results, especially over the long run. (Last November I wrote about brand management in this column; if you would like a copy of that column email me and I will be happy to make certain you get one.)

Your reputation is another intangible that has a significant impact. I am always surprised by how many people and organizations are willing to sacrifice the long-term benefits of a good reputation on the altar of the immediate. I believe that operating ethically and fairly pays huge dividends over the long run.

At our company, we also believe that relationships and networking are important intangibles that should be cultivated. We work hard to develop relationships within our industry, with our customers and with the professionals we use. I cannot even begin to measure how much these relationships have helped us over the years.

Other intangibles that can have a big impact on your long-term results include corporate alliances, how you think, technological edges, corporate culture, people management, and both your personal and organizational creativity.

I recently read a new book on the topic of intangibles called "Invisible Advantage," by Jonathan and Pam Cohen Kalafut (Perseus Publishing, 2002). It is a great book that I highly recommend to any manager. It concisely articulates the importance of intangibles to both your career and your business. The book does a great job of identifying and defining the key intangibles that drive both an organization's performance and worth. It also tells the reader how he or she can go about addressing those intangibles in their business.

Some of the suggestions the authors of "Invisible Advantage" make include:

- **Identify your organization's intangibles** - The list above identifies several intangibles and the book has even more. Go through the lists and select those that can have the most impact on your business.
- **Decide how to measure them** - Almost any aspect of your business improves when you begin measuring it, and intangibles are no exception.
- **Use benchmarking** - Find out how other companies, both inside and outside your industry, are handling the management of their intangibles.
- **Focus on improving the intangibles you have identified** - Once you have identified your intangibles and determined how you will measure them, start the process of improving in these areas.
- **Communicate what you are doing** - If you want your organization to focus on improving its management of intangibles, you need to communicate that to your team. You won't make any progress in this area if you keep it a secret!

As an aside, whether or not you are interested in selling your business, you might be interested to know that smart business evaluators are now taking into consideration more than just historical financial performance (EBITDA) and asset value. Smart business evaluators realize that while past results and asset value are important to an organization's value, they may not be as important in the long run as an organization's intangibles.

Finally, it is obviously very important to effectively manage a process, read financial statements or carry out a task. However, the best managers are those who are proficient at managing the intangible aspects of their businesses. Take the time today to review how this information applies to your organization. By focusing on the intangible aspects of your business, you should be able to identify the advantages that will give both you and your organization the competitive edge you are looking for.

Chapter 89
THE LEADERSHIP INVESTMENT THAT
WON A SUPER BOWL TITLE
September 2003

Once again it's football season, and excitement is building among fans across the country over the prospect of a home team championship.

Fans of last season's NFL champs, the Tampa Bay Buccaneers, are no exception - eager to see if their team can duplicate that success. When you factor Bucs' coach Jon Gruden into the equation, not many people are betting against them.

Gruden's record of success gives me another opportunity to engage in one of my favorite pastimes: identifying the characteristics of highly effective leaders.

The attention visited on Gruden's leadership ability and the impact it has had on the Bucs is remarkable. Sportswriters and commentators credit him with giving the team the edge it was lacking. Many, in fact, say the $8 million the Bucs' owners paid to pry him away from the Oakland Raiders was a bargain.

As I read about Gruden's leadership attributes, I couldn't help but think about how we in the boating industry could apply those characteristics to our jobs. Here are some of the qualities that helped Gruden guide the Bucs to the top:

- **Giving credit where credit is due** - I was impressed to see

Gruden applaud his predecessor, Tony Dungy for what Dungy had done to build the team. Gruden did not have to do that, the fact that he did has earned him respect. As managers, we should take pains to acknowledge those who help us reach our goals. It's easy to take credit yourself when things go well, but in the long run, you are much better off sharing the accolades.

- **Hard work** - Coach Gruden claims to start each day at 3:17 AM. As a marine manager, you don't have to go that far, but you do have to work hard if you are going to succeed.

- **A positive attitude** - Jon Lynch, one of the Buccaneers' stars said, "From Day One Jon Gruden came in and told us we were winning a championship." An attitude like that will have a big impact on both you and your team. Negativity can become a self fulfilling prophecy.

- **Contagious energy** - Many people have spoken about the contagious nature of Gruden's energy. As a manager, you set the tone. If you are down, so are those around you. If you are "high energy," that too, rubs off.

- **Inspiring confidence** - One sportswriter put it this way: "Some of Gruden's best work occurred not on a blackboard, but between the ears." The Bucs were a talented team before Gruden came to Tampa and taught them to believe in themselves. Confidence may have been the missing ingredient.

- **A laser-beam focus** - I have written before about the importance of focus in the leader hip formula. In order to focus effectively, you have to identify what is important - both to you and your organization. When you've done this, don't get sidetracked by other non-important matters.

- **Grace in victory** -Though it was his old team he defeated for the championship, he threw no bards in the direction of Oakland for letting him go. If you plan to keep playing the game, you'd better be gracious when you win.

- **Continuous improvement** - Within 24 hours of winning football's top prize, Gruden already was talking about making the Bucs even better. Scary thought for the rest of the NFL, huh?

As we review these characteristics, it is important to acknowledge the importance of an incremental approach. The Bucs, as I said earlier, were a good team before Gruden arrived, Super Bowl champions after. Small, positive changes can bring disproportionately positive results.

We are not football coaches, but I believe Jon Gruden's example can make us better managers. His winning attributes carry over into the world of management. Start internalizing them and see if they don't help you achieve success.

Finally, don't be overwhelmed. Remember the old saying about how you eat an elephant? One bite at a time! Look back over the list and pick one item you can start working on today. When you have that down pat, pick another and then another until you have mastered the whole list. Become the "super" manager you have the ability to be.

Chapter 90
THERE'S MORE TO A BUDGET THAN AN ANNUAL HEADACHE
October 2003

Can you believe 2003 is three-quarters over? I can't. I find it hard to come to grips with the reality that we are only three months away from another new year.

For many of you reading this column (but not for those of us here in Florida), October means your busy season is winding down. You now have a minute to catch your breath, think about the season just ended and start planning your future.

That's my way of saying now is a great time to start thinking about your 2004 budget.

Don't quit reading yet. I realize that many managers dread budgeting. They consider it little more than metaphorically jumping through hoops before the start of each fiscal year. Unfortunately, these people are missing out on the many advantages this fundamental financial tool makes available to them.

A good budget can be a great help to your operation. Here are some of the things it will do for you and your company.

- It forces you to look ahead. You should always be focusing on your future, but many executives don't. The budgeting process provides you with a tool that forces you to do it at least once each year.

- It forces you to review all your operations. A good budget will cover every aspect of your business. Once again, this is a forced review of what you should be considering anyway.
- It gives you a standard against which you can measure your results. It is hard to know if you are doing well in a vacuum. Your budget should be a benchmark that helps you measure your success.

Sometimes just the process of preparing a budget is as much a benefit as the document itself - in some cases, even more so. It is an exercise that can be a significant help to both you and your business. If a budget is so helpful, why don't more businesses have one? I believe it' because they are not sure how to effectively prepare and use one.

So, whether you are preparing your first budget or whether it is something you do every year, here e some tips:

- Do the budget in your standard financial statement format. This will make it much easier to compare your actual results to what you have budgeted.
- Start with your core revenues. At our company, that is billable hours; at yours, it may be dockage revenue, boat sales or some other line of income.
- Estimate other revenues. These are your non-core income items.
- Identify your gross margin. See if you can improve on the past. At many companies, a 1-percent improvement in margin will have a big impact on the bottom line.
- Identify the staffing levels necessary to achieve your budgeted objectives. If your company is like ours, payroll is a big part of your budget. You must determine how many people it is going to take to get you where you want to be in revenue terms.

- Estimate pay changes. Are you going to give raises during the year? If so, generally how much?
- Look at expenses with a zero-sum approach. Avoid the temptation to review your expenses only on a historical basis. Look at each of your expenses from a different perspective - What would happen if I did not spend this money at all?
- Get input from as many people as possible. Tap the members of your team for information.
- Make a stretch. Don't make your review target a "slam dunk." Make it something you will need to strive to reach.
- Communicate the budget. Share your budgeted objectives with your team. Your people can't be expected to exceed the company's revenue projection if they don't know what it is.

Now that you have completed your budget and effectively communicated it to your team, you can begin using it. The most important aspect of using your budget on an ongoing basis is variance analysis.

Variance analysis is a monthly exercise that identifies all of the significant differences between your budget and your actual results. Of course, identifying them isn't enough. Once these differences are pinpointed, you must then determine why they occurred. And don't review only your negative variances. It is important to investigate both the positive and negative differences to pick up trends or other changes you might otherwise not have been aware of. You can use the information you come up with to make any necessary operational changes.

Sometimes the variances you identify may not require any such changes. But at least variance analysis gives you a tool to help identify an alteration that does need to be made.

Variance analysis cannot help but improve your profit throughout the year by forcing you to pay more attention to all aspects of your business.

Budgeting is fundamental - not only for ensuring good financial management but also for providing you with the operational information you need to run your business. Try using some of these ideas to either implement a budget if you don't have one or to improve the process if you do have one.

Chapter 91
YOU CAN'T CHANGE OUTCOMES
WITHOUT CHANGING METHODS
November 2003

Thucydides, the Greek considered by many to be the father of history, was the first to put forth the theory that the future can be predicted through the understanding of the past.

In other words, if we do the things that historically have generated certain results, we can pretty much count on those actions producing the same results in the future.

More than 2,000 years later - during the 1800s - this concept of learning from the past was further solidified by the Scottish scientist James Hutton. In his Law of Uniformitarianism, Hutton declared that forces that produced a particular set of results in the past would produce the same results in the present.

I firmly believe the teachings of Thucydides and Hutton apply to us today as managers in the marine industry. Simply put, we need to be willing to learn from our pasts.

You probably have heard someone say, "You cannot keep doing the same things over and over, and expect to get different results." There's a ton of management wisdom in that statement.

Unfortunately, many managers don't understand these principles. They are not happy with the way their organizations have been performing, yet they hope to bring about improvements by doing the very things that generated the disappointing outcomes in the first place.

Is that the case at your company? Are you doing the same things over and over and expecting to get different results? It's not going to work. If you really want to change your company's performance, you are going to have to come up with ways of doing things differently to improve.

You cannot expect results to improve unless you do something to make that not happen.

It is important for managers to stay focused on the future. Many, if not most, get so stuck in either the present or the past that they never take the time to plan ahead. But while it's important to avoid getting stuck in the past, we still have to be willing to learn from it. A commitment to doing so is a critical part of staying focused on the future.

In order to learn from your past, you have to have good information about it. Your company should have solid financial and information systems that provide you with an accurate and timely picture of your results.

Each month's financial statements should be distributed by the 10th of the following month. In many instances, however, even that is too late. You need information on your critical indicators every day. At our company, for example, we track two key indicators - cash flow d billable hours - on a daily basis.

Next, you have to have a benchmark against which you can compare your information. Historical results and budgets can be good benchmarks, but many times outside comparisons are even better. At our company, we compare our financial results to industry data at least once a year. Trade associations can supply you with general industry information you can use for this exercise. I also rely on the Almanac of Business and Financial ratios as a good source of outside information.

In learning from your past, it is not enough to be willing to change - you should be anxious to change. People who resist change get so stuck in the past they just watch their competitors pass them by. The world is changing faster today than at any time in history. To keep u with that change you need to look back just long enough to identify ways to change for the better.

Finally, you need to make a specific effort to learn from your past. After a busy season, completion of a big project or the end of a production run, be sure to undertake a post-mortem while your performance is still fresh in your mind. Get your team together to discuss how you could improve your results the next time. You should be doing this even if things went well. Many times, learning from your past is just a matter of focusing on what happened and what you could have done better.

Maybe you're happy with your results and think this column does not apply to you. Well, you don't get off the hook that easily. Thucydides also had some wisdom for those of you who think our companies are performing just fine.

The historian maintained that success is almost always followed by failure. Successful people, he maintained, tend to develop both arrogance and pride that inevitably leads to their downfall. Interestingly enough, history is full of examples - both inside and outside of the business world - proving his point. If you feel you are doing just fine - watch out! Many times a complacent mindset is the first precursor to failure.

The bottom line? Learn from your past, be willing to change and continuously improve. If you do these three things, you'll be well on your way toward developing and maintaining the perspective you need to achieve success in both your personal and professional lives.

Chapter 92
IT'S THE SEASON FOR LISTS:
HERE'S ONE FOR MANAGERS
December 2003

We are winding down another year and the season is upon us. No, I don't mean the holiday season; I am referring to the "list season."

It happens at the end of every year, and 2003 will be no exception. You're surely familiar with them - the 10 best movies, the 10 most important people, the 10 top news stories and so on. Anything that can be put in a list will be appearing in one over the next few weeks.

So, in the spirit of the season, here, in no particular order, is a list of 40 things everyone should know about management:

1. Teamwork is about synergy - one plus one CAN equal three.
2. Teamwork is NOT hiring people who think just like you do - teamwork is hiring people with different perspectives and building off one another's strengths.
3. Hire good people and then get out of their way.
4. Don't micromanage.
5. Employee performance evaluations are not about the past; they are about the FUTURE.
6. Invest in your employees. It is better to train them and lose them than to not train them and keep them.
7. If you have to fire an employee, do it with dignity.

8. Sharing financial figures with employees improves results.

9. The basis of almost every management problem is a communication problem.

10. The most important part of communication is the non-verbal aspect.

11. You must think big if you want to accomplish big things.

12. Allow yourself to dream.

13. More important than doing things right is doing the right things.

14. If you are not continually improving both yourself and your company, you are falling behind.

15. Optimistic people are usually successful.

16. Results-oriented people are almost always successful.

17. It is important to know what to do but it is more important to do it.

18. The most effective corporate cultures equally emphasize employees, customers and owners.

19. It is almost impossible to achieve success without well-defined goals and objectives.

20. After setting a goal, take steps toward reaching it.

21. A mission statement and strategic plan are great tools that will help keep you focused; however, they are the first steps, not the end.

22. Constantly ask yourself, is what I am doing right now consistent with my objectives?

23. A small improvement in time management can make a big improvement in your life.

24. Your customer does not care about your problems.

25. It is the customer, not you, who is the judge of good customer service.

26. The key to customer satisfaction is exceeding expectations.

27. Focus on the important - not the urgent.

28. Focus on areas within, not outside, your control.

29. Happiness is not a result of your circumstances; it is a result of how you choose to view those circumstances.
30. Planning is important; dollars are committed to projects long before they are spent.
31. Be willing to change. What we accept as truth today will be debunked tomorrow.
32. Learn from the past but stay focused on the future.
33. Think long-term.
34. Relationships are important - treat people right.
35. Dealing with integrity is always right.
36. Successful people are proficient in managing the intangibles.
37. Doubting yourself becomes a self-fulfilling prophecy.
38. Marketing is all about differentiation. You must communicate why you are better.
39. Remember the four P's from Marketing 101: Product, Place, Price and Promotion. Marketing is much bigger than just ads.
40. Your competition is probably much broader than you think.

One more year-end list! I hope you found it helpful.

Chapter 93
NEW YEAR'S RESOLUTIONS:
WHY GOAL-SETTING CAN FAIL
January 2004

It's the start of a new year and, as we've done throughout history, people everywhere are making resolutions.

New Year's resolutions frequently target some type of future personal or professional achievement, and for that reason, I think they're great. Goals are a crucial element to success, and the New Year's resolution can be effective in helping people focus on positive change.

But if you accept the premise that most resolution-makers approach the venture seriously - fully intending to achieve their mission - then you have to wonder why so few actually do.

As we see each January, most New Year's resolutions quickly fall by the wayside. In fact, a couple of years ago I read that, on average, they last less than six days! You cannot help but wonder why people who really seem to want to improve themselves - and go to the trouble of setting goals to do it - give up so easily.

I believe the answer lies in our approach to goals in general.

Over the years, I've run into people at my presentations who are not first-timers - people I know have heard me speak on the same topic before.

Why have they come back? When I speak with them after the presentation, the explanation goes something like this: " I got all fired up to change my ways the last time, but within a few weeks I got off track and slipped back into my bad habits. I'm here for a refresher."

What these people experience is not uncommon - in fact, it's a problem many encounter in both their personal and professional lives. They regularly set worthy goals for themselves or their or organizations, but are unable to turn those goals into reality.

At some point, they may even give up on goal setting because of past frustration or failures.

So, why do people so often fail to reach their goals? There are many reasons. Here are some of the more significant:

- **Failure to take steps in the right direction:** It amazes me how often I see someone set a worthy goal and then take no actual steps to achieve it. It's almost like these people equate goal setting with goal accomplishment. People like me put so much emphasis on the importance of goals that I sometimes think our listeners believe that setting goals is all they have to do to get what they want.

  That could not be further from the truth. Goal setting can be very powerful if you then take steps to reach the goal. The whole process, however, becomes totally toothless if you merely set the goal and then sit back and wait for it to happen. Goal setting is a beginning, not an end.

- **Self-image:** How you visualize yourself is critically important to whether or not you achieve your goals. Many people fail to reach their objectives because they do not think of themselves as the type of individual who can become what he or she is trying to be. They have a built-in failure mechanism that keeps them from being successful.

  If you doubt your ability to reach your goals, it can become a self-fulfilling prophecy. Start thinking of yourself as the person you want to be. Visualize yourself living your dreams. Believe in yourself - it makes achieving your objectives much easier.

- **Focusing on the past:** One of the primary reasons people don't achieve the futures they want for either themselves or their organizations is that they cannot let go of the past. You must let go of the past, whether good or bad, if you want to achieve your goals or the future.

  Don't stay focused on either how good you were or how badly someone hurt you. You haven't put those things behind you. To have success in the future you need to focus on the future.

- **Focusing on what can't be controlled:** We all have many factors in the world around us that we cannot control. If you spend time focusing on these, you will never accomplish your objectives.

Focusing on what you cannot control reduces the number of things you actually can control. If you want to increase your span of control you need to stay focused on the things you do have the power to control.

Many people try to reach their goals through sheer willpower. While it's a big plus to have that kind of determination you cannot reach your goals through willpower alone, you must set yourself up for successes.

Therefore, as you strive to reach your goals for 2004, be sure you are taking the four points listed here into consideration. If you do factor these things into both your personal and organizational goal setting, I believe you will find this year's objectives a little easier to achieve.

Chapter 94
CHOICES YOU MAKE TODAY ARE KEYS TO YOUR FUTURE
February 2004

Since I am not a fatalist, I find it a little frustrating to hear someone say, "It must have been fate" - or, "It was meant to be."

Obviously, there are times when things happen with total unpredictability. Most of the time, however, our life situations can be explained by a series of past choices.

As a friend of mine often says, "You can choose your choices but you cannot choose the consequences of those choices." Our companies' futures (or lack thereof) are determined, directly by the choices we make today.

As managers, we are responsible for shaping the future. Despite this clear obligation, many managers don't even make an attempt to be proactive - to influence the destiny of their companies. Instead, they choose to wait and react to events as they happen. We need to be focused on helping our companies reach their potential by making great choices now.

Here are just a few of the perspectives that can help you position your company for a bright future:

- **<u>Focus on Your Choices</u>** - we need to keep reminding ourselves of the importance of trying to make wise choices that will positively impact our futures. Technically a mathematical term, singularity is used in science to describe a point at which everything becomes uncontrollable, for good or bad. It is a great way to describe our choices. We can control our choice for a-while but at some point, the result of these choices takes over and we are left to deal with the consequences. That's why as managers we cannot let up. We must stay continually focused on making good choices because eventually those choices will come back to us in the form of consequences we cannot control.

- **Teamwork** - Get input from others, both above you and below you in the organizational hierarchy. Functioning as a team brings out the best in almost everyone.

  I recently read that Roger Bannister, the first human to run a four-minute mile, used teamwork to break a barrier that most people thought was unbreakable. I had always pictured him going out in his track shoes and breaking the barrier all by himself. Instead, he did it with a team of three.

  Bannister ran the first half-mile behind a runner who helped him start and get his speed going and the second half-mile behind another runner who helped him maintain the p e. What I had always thought of as an awesome individual feat actually was the result of people working together as a team. This is a great analogy to how we should

- **Focus on the Future** - As important as it is to learn from the past, it is even more important to stay focused on the future.

  The story is told of Robert E. Lee traveling through Virginia after the Civil War and meeting a Southern belle, who pointed out a war-ravaged tree in her front yard. It had been damaged by Northern troops as they passed through and she told Lee she intended to let it stand as a memorial to how badly the people of her area had been treated. His response, "Cut it down, madam, and forget about it."

Making good choices about the future sometimes means letting go of the past, whether good or bad.

- **Respect others** - USA Today last year published an interesting article on the tendency tardiness of chief executive officers when meeting with their employees.

  In a nutshell, it points out that CEOs are late for 60 percent of their meetings with subordinates. Besides a host of other problems, which are documented in the article, this shows a lack or respect for the employees.

  It's just a small example, but one that carries a big message: showing respect to our employees will reward us many times through additional motivation and lack of

- **Work Toward Your Goals** - The Romans used to say "Initium dimidium facti." If you've forgotten your Latin, this means, "The start is half the deed."

Many people set goals and objectives and never take steps to achieve them. If you want a bright future for your company it is important to set goals but it is equally important to take steps toward reaching them.

Do you take responsibility for the results of your company? If you don't then who does? Recognizing that you have to be personally responsible for results is the first step to ensuring the bright future that both you and your organization deserve.

Chapter 95
PROJECT MANAGEMENT:
IT'S NOT AS SCARY AS YOU THINK
March 2004

The Six Phases of a Project

1. Enthusiasm
2. Disillusionment
3. Panic
4. Search for the Guilty
5. Punishment of the Innocent
6. Praise for the Non-participants

You are probably familiar with the above Phases of a Project. If you're like most managers, you probably have lived them at some point.

Project management, which I define as a focused undertaking with a finite lifespan, can be extremely frustrating. Whether the project is a short one or one that promises to stretch out over a longer period, keeping it moving toward on-time and on-budget completion can be a real challenge.

Despite those obstacles, however, there are many substantive reasons to make project management a priority. Successful project management can help you ensure higher profits and lower costs, a better-quality product, and a quicker completion of your project. In the end, these are things that not only will help you exceed your customer's expectations but also keep your employees' morale high.

It all adds up to a better reputation - both for your company and your brand.

Since the benefits are so potentially great, we are fortunate to have some specific things we can do to improve the odds that our projects will be completed in the way we envisioned at the start.

Before we review the elements needed for successful project management, let's look at what project management is NOT:

- **Project management problems are not unique.** Many managers struggle with project management, and the difficulties you may be encountering most likely are the same ones other people are coping with. Resist the temptation to think, "We are different," or, "No one has the issues we do." The type of project you are managing may be unique, but the project management process and issues are the same. I believe the "we-are-different" mentality is just a cop-out to avoid really focusing on and trying to solve your particular problems.

- **Project management is not "foolproof."** While you should understand up front that project management might not be your "silver bullet" it is also important to recognize that it can significantly improve your odds of success. No matter what, don't let yours get caught up in the "we tried-that-once-and-it-didn't-work" mentality. Better project management can improve your chances of success, but you may have to work at it. There are no quick fixes.

- **Project management is not a magic formula.** Many managers consider project management a mystery that they personally will never solve. To many managers, it's overwhelming. But the truth is that project management is neither a mystery nor overwhelming; it is a lot of little things that, combined, create a positive project synergy well in excess of their individual elements. It's a kind of synergy that can really help your company's results.

- **Project management is not GANNT charts, PERT charts or Critical Path Method.** Many managers avoid project management because they are intimidated by quantitative methods and analysis. Though GANNT, PERT and CPM can be useful tools, they are a small part of project management. If you do choose to use these tools, they are probably easier to learn than you think and, fortunately, there are plenty of software programs to help you. But don't be intimidated; these tools are a small part of managing successful projects. Don't worry if you really don't understand them yet.

So now that we know what project management is not, what are the key elements of a successful undertaking? I have defined them as follows:

- **Planning** - Though most managers hate to plan to the extent needed, planning is an important element of successful project management. Every hour spent planning at the be inning saves many multiples of that hour later on.
- **Team considerations** - Most projects require more than one person; this makes the team elements of project management critically important. To borrow an old phrase, you want everyone on the project pulling on the same end of the rope!
- **Communication** - I have said many times that when you get to the bottom of any management problem it almost always is a communication problem. That truth may be even more relevant in project management than in other areas of management.
- **Control** - Control is what most people think about when the subject of project management is mentioned. It includes

variance analysis and also the quantitative techniques I mentioned earlier here. The various aspects of project management control can be critical elements to the management of a successful project.

Obviously, we have just scratched the surface of these four elements. In future columns, I will discuss each of these elements and, more specifically, how each relates to project management.

Improving your project management process can improve your results. Next month, we will look at planning and how it can be used to get the results you want from your projects.

Chapter 96
SOLID PLANNING BEATS OUT A CRYSTAL BALL EVERY TIME
April 2004

"Prediction is very difficult, especially about the future."- Neil Bohrs, Nobel laureate in physics

Generally, prognosticating is risky business. However, as a manager, there are some things you can do to forecast and control your company's future - and few things affect your company's future more than planning.

Last month in this column we looked at the importance of successful project management. The column identified four items that can significantly affect your success on projects. Those items were planning, team considerations, communication and control. This month I want to specifically look at the first of those items, planning, and how it can help you better manage your projects.

You have probably heard the phrases, "Lack of planning on your part does not constitute an emergency on my part" or, "Failing to plan is planning to fail." Planning is so basic it is like opening your mouth before taking a drink or taking off your shoes before your socks. However, despite all of this many managers still fail to make an adequate commitment to planning.

Managers need to invest in planning if they want any chance to remain proactive throughout the life of their projects. In many ways, the process itself is as important as the plan document. The process helps keep you looking forward.

Additionally, from a financial perspective, the single best way to keep your costs down on a project is through effective planning. Unfortunately, our traditional accounting systems, with their historical perspectives, fail us in this area. Most managers get really focused on saving money on a project when their accounting reports tell them their costs are running high but, unfortunately, by then it is far too late. Planning saves money and the reason is simple: The costs of a project are almost always committed well before they are spent.

So, if planning is such an important process, how can we do it better? Here are seven planning steps that can help.

1. Define the project/objectives - To properly define your project you must be certain you are crystal clear on your customer's expectations. Excellent customer service can only occur when you exceed your customer's expectations, and it is hard to exceed those expectations if you are not sure what they are.

2. Define the tasks to complete - Most of the time, you should be as detailed as possible when you are listing the tasks necessary to complete a project. The tasks should be listed in a linear manner that easily provides the road map you need to undertake and finish the project.

3. Identify critical items - While all of the tasks identified in step number 2 are important, they may not all be critical. You must identify the tasks that are absolutely essential to the completion of your project, and pay particular attention to those items.

4. Prepare schedules and budgets - Once you have identified the items to complete, including "critical" items, you need to prepare a schedule for your project. Objectives are important in project management; therefore you must prepare a time goal (budget) for each element of the project. If you have previously

done similar projects, your files can be a source of helpful history when completing this step.

5. Prepare a "risk" or "what if?" analysis - Try to think ahead and prepare for contingencies. Brainstorm with your team and try to identify problems that could hamper the project, including difficulties with past projects. Then, proactively figure out a way to keep those contingencies from becoming realities.

6. Include participants in the plan - Getting employees to "buy-in" on the plan can have a big impact. "Buying in" will improve understanding and reduce communication problems, as project participants try to affirm the validity of "their" plan. At the end of a successful project, morale will be sky high as everyone jointly celebrates that accomplishment.

7. Communicate the plan - As with all aspects of management, for your plan to work it must be communicated to everyone. It is hard to over-communicate in project management.

Finally, because each project you work on has its unique attributes, each plan should be unique. While historical background can be helpful, resist the temptation to use a "cookie-cutter" plan that has worked for you in the past. Be sure to give each project plan the unique attention it deserves.

You can predict your future. Whether you are using planning for project management, or for the general management of your organization, effective planning today helps you identify and implement the necessary steps to significantly improve your future.

Chapter 97
FOLLOW THESE SIX POINTERS TO BUILD AN ENERGIZED TEAM
May 2004

Working effectively with others is critical to success in all aspects of your business. Most of the interaction within your organization does not take place through systems or things; it takes place through your team. The most effective managers realize it is not them, but their teams, that determine their success.

This is the third column in a series on the importance of successful project management. My March column ended by identifying four items that can significantly affect our success on projects: planning, team considerations, communication and control. Last month (April) we reviewed planning. This month we will look at teamwork and how it can help you better manage your projects.

The benefits of teamwork are tremendous. Teamwork creates an energy that springs from synergy and can transform your organization. This team-driven energy will create a more productive environment, which will immediately result in higher quality, lower costs, quicker completion of projects, and, ultimately, greater customer satisfaction.

Before I review some specific ways you can build better teams, here are some general team concepts that you should recognize:

- **Differences between team members should create synergy-** In most organizations, differences between people create conflict. In contrast, an effective team considers its differences an important element of its success. People who make up this type of team learn to accept their differences as a competitive advantage and play off one another's strengths to create synergy (1 +I =3).

- **Teams don't naturally occur** - If you want your people to operate as a team, you need to be focused on building that team. Staff meetings, social events and daily interaction all can be used effectively for team building. Remember, to be really successful, what your people think about you is not as important as how they view themselves.

- **The project leader must maintain a team spirit** - Do your employees leave their interactions with you energized or do they go away stripped of motivation? You must learn to become a source of energy for your employees. Use positive reinforcement and encouragement to keep them operating at peak efficiency.

1. **Get a "buy-in" from your team** - Communicate from the very beginning with your employees in a way that gets them determined to complete your projects on time and on budget. Remember, this has to happen before Day One of the project. If you don't start getting a "buy-in" from your employees early in the process, you will have people working with you who are involved in the project but not committed to its

2. **Assign people to jobs that match their skills** - Don't throw people at a job just because they have available time. We all have strengths and weaknesses. Match people with assignments that take advantage of their strengths. If you put people on jobs that don't match their strengths, those employees will be frustrated

with the work, you will be unhappy with the time and costs of the project and the customer will probably not have his or her expectations exceeded.

3. **Hold people accountable/responsible** - You must be prepared to deal with poor performers. I personally lose sleep over having to terminate an employee, but occasionally it must be done to protect everyone's jobs.

4. **Be accessible to your team** - You need to be reachable and "on the job" all of the time. Don't micromanage, but do make sure you are available to help solve problems when people need you.

5. **Maintain a sense of urgency** - Last year on ESPN's SportsCenter, I heard an athlete say,"It takes me a long time to make a quick decision." (Really, I'm not making this up). Don't fall into that trap, the longer you delay decisions the more it costs your team.

6. **Celebrate accomplishments** - As a leader, you should be using positive reinforcement much more often than you are correcting employees. Look for opportunities to praise both your team and individuals. When you reach significant milestones on time and on budget, don't hesitate to throw a little celebration.

Teamwork is important in all aspects of your businesses, and project management is no exception. Figuratively speaking, every part of your business will operate most effectively if everyone is pulling on the same end of the rope.

It is your job as manager and leader to make sure your group is operating to its potential as a team. When that is happening, it is certain to have a positive impact on your results.

Chapter 98
THE BEST LISTENERS MAKE
THE BEST COMMUNICATORS
June 2004

"At the bottom of almost every management problem is a communication problem."

In March I began a series of columns on the importance of successful project management. The column ended by identifying four items that can significantly affect your success on projects: planning, team considerations, communication and control. The importance of each is obviously not limited to project management; they can affect all aspects of your business.

This month I want to focus on communication and how it can help you better manage your projects.

When most people think about communication, they think of someone talking. Talking, to be sure, is part of communication; however, the best communicators are also good listeners. They try to learn from the perspective of others, which helps them be more productive themselves.

Good listeners have several traits that are easily identified. They look at others when they speak, don't rush people or interrupt them, react responsively with a nod or smile, repeat some of what they've just heard and, finally, ask questions - either to show concern for the speaker's feelings or to clarify some point.

A poor listener, in contrast, interrupts frequently, finishes others' sentences, is inattentive (wandering eyes, poor posture), fidgets nervously and is quick to jump to conclusions.

Poor listening is not only disrespectful to the person talking, it also robs the listener of an opportunity to learn something - an idea or perspective - that could help him or her achieve specific goals. And if you're still not convinced, consider this: People enjoy being with a good listener.

When managing a project, you usually have five communications constituencies. They are:

- **Customers** - In most cases, you cannot over-communicate with a customer. I know I appreciate it when my car or boat is being serviced and I get a call telling me the status of the work. On the other hand, it never ceases to amaze me when I show interest in a purchase and get no follow-up from a salesperson. Remember, it is your responsibility to communicate with the customers, not their responsibility to contact you.

  When you are communicating with an existing or prospective customer, know your facts and figures, and be sure to guard against emotional reactions. And bear in mind: Customers, with few exceptions, aren't the least bit interested in your problems.

  Finally, be sure to communicate how a specific change will affect the customer's cost and deadlines. Remember, nobody likes to be surprised - especially when the news is bad.

- **Employees** - When dealing with employees, you probably have information that needs to be shared to keep them informed. However, more than likely, the employees also have information that you need to know. Employee communication is a two-way street

  Have an initial project meeting to educate your employees

and share the project's objectives. Then hold regular meetings - both to give your employees updated goals throughout the project and to allow information to pass in both directions.

Finally, always shoot straight with employees. The communication in your organization will never exceed the trust level.

- **Materials suppliers** - If you are undertaking a project that will require materials, don't wait until the last minute to inform your purchasing department. Keep the people who handle your buying in the loop. It will help ensure that you not only have the materials you need when you need them, but also will allow the buyers to get the best possible price.

- **Peer** - Maybe there is another project manager with whom you must share resources. If so, you need to be talking with this person regularly about your upcoming resource requirements and how you both can get what you need to keep your projects moving toward timely and cost-effective completion.

- **Bosses** - Remember, bosses do not like surprises, either - especially negative ones. You shouldn't have to update the boss on every little detail, but you do need to be very sure you keep him or her generally informed. And that you don't spring any big negative surprises.

Finally, don't forget the importance of non-verbal communication. Earlier, I emphasized the importance of being a good listener, and that is one part of nonverbal communication. The way you handle your body when you are communicating is important. Many studies have indicated that the nonverbal element is the most important part of communication. Luckily, there are many books that can quickly help you in this area.

When people are asked to identify a leader or a charismatic person, they'll almost always point to someone with good communication skills. Anyone can improve in this area and move closer to becoming the leader he or she wants to be.

Try implementing some of these ideas and see if they don't help you achieve more of your goals and objectives.

Chapter 99
5 STEPS TO HELP YOU KEEP A PROJECT UNDER CONTROL
July 2004

This is the last in a series of five columns focusing on effective project management techniques. While the umbrella of project management has provided the context for the management principles I have outlined in these columns, their effectiveness is not limited to that field alone. They can help you in all aspects of your business.

During the past four months we have considered not only general project management concepts but also the planning, team and communication aspects of project management. (If you missed any of these columns, e-mail me at wey@rybovich.com and I will be happy to send you copies).

This month, we wrap up the series of columns by looking at the importance of project management control. Control is the aspect that most people connect in their minds with project management, but also the aspect of project management that gives people the most anxiety. However, if you have followed the steps we have covered in the previous months, especially as it relates to planning, then the control phase of project management should be easy. Don't let yourself get overwhelmed; just take it one step at a time and execute what you already have planned.

There are five key elements to project management control:

1. **Prioritization** - Much of project management control relates to priorities. You must be working on the right thing at the right time. You should keep a hot list of key items that have to be completed and the dates for when they need to be done. Continually and relentlessly follow up on these items. Make sure you are particularly focused on the items you have identified to be on your critical path to completion.

2. **Manage change** - Many projects end up being something different than the project they started out to be. Many people allow a project to change once it has started but fail to make the necessary adjustments to that change. It is important to realize that change will affect your project; costs, deadlines and customer billings will not go on as if nothing happened. It is important that we communicate to our customers how change will affect a project. We must also make the internal adjustment our organization needs.

3. **Variance analysis** - It is imperative that you continue to compare your actual results to your original plans and appropriately deal with any variances. This is especially true when labor hours are a large part of your project. Comparing hours spent to the actual percentage of the job completed can serve as a great "early warning system." Typically variance analysis is executed by laying out on a spreadsheet what your expectation is compared to your actual results. The difference is the variance. And remember, it is important to identify the variances but it is much more important to use that information to get your project back on track.

4. **Project notebook** - Be sure to keep a notebook - either the old-fashioned way in a Joos -leaf folder or on your computers. List all the daily issues, both good and bad, that you have to deal with during the project. This diary will help you both during the project by keeping certain information that you

need at your fingertips, and after your project as you sit down with your team in the post mortem review process to discuss the aspects of the project that went both well and badly.

5. **GANTT, PERT, CPM and other software** - GANTT, PERT and CPM charts are a great way to help your team visualize how the project is going. For those not familiar with the terms, a GANTT chart is a bar chart that graphically displays work being done on a project, a PERT chart shows basically the same thing but in a more sequential line format, and CPM - critical path method - is the path that has to be followed on the PERT chart to make sure all tasks are completed on time. All three are closely related to good project management.

    Many project management software packages have the ability to produce these charts.

    At our company, we use Microsoft Project to help produce this information and find it very helpful.

When trying to control your projects, bear in mind that most projects get a lot of attention at the beginning and a lot at the end, but it's that middle part that can get you in big trouble. Effective project management requires relentless attention to making sure the project is going well at all stages of completion.

At our company, we have done well on some projects and not so well on some others. When we have followed the steps I outlined over the past few months - and have had one person specifically responsible for making sure we didn't deviate from them - we inevitably have done well. When we slip away from what we know we should be doing it almost always leads to problems.

The project management topics we have reviewed these past few months: planning, team, communication and control, can help you in all aspects of your business. Take this information and apply it to your organization today - it will help you achieve the productivity and effectiveness you desire.

Chapter 100
100 COLUMNS IN 3 WORDS:
VISION, TALENT AND FOCUS
August 2004

A hundred columns. Wow!

It's hard for me to believe that what you are now reading is my 100th management column written for the marine industry - most of them published here in Soundings Trade Only. Is it just me or does that seem like a lot of columns?

Writing 100 columns has led to at least as many speaking engagements, literally all over the world - from Australia to Europe and South America, and all over the United States. I appreciate the trust our industry's leaders have put in me to, hopefully, bring something worthwhile to their organizations.

I have been privileged to speak at conferences, boat shows, dealer meetings, conventions, association gatherings and every other kind of marine industry meeting imaginable. These gatherings have given me the opportunity to meet with and learn from many of you.

The countless emails, notes, calls and personal comments I have received over the years from people in our industry have all been a real encouragement. I appreciate how gracious many of you have been. Despite your kind words, I know I have learned more from all of you than I could ever communicate back in this column.

As I think about meeting many of you I cannot help but wonder what I have learned these past few years. What makes some managers very successful while others struggle? How can I sum up 100 columns in one column?

I would summarize the first 100 columns in three words: vision, talent and focus. Interestingly, the column to which I received by far, the biggest reader response was written in September 2001 on these three essentials of highly effective leadership.

So what are vision, talent and focus?

Vision is the ability to think big - really big. It is the ability to see the whole picture and think outside the box. The biggest factor that keeps people from achieving the success they desire is not their competitors or any other outside factor, it is themselves. More specifically it is the way they think. Most people sell themselves way short. They would accomplish much more by thinking bigger and really believing in themselves.

Talent is the ability to be a good communicator, supervisor and time manager. And, maybe more importantly, it requires a continual focus on improvement. Over the years I have written a lot on each of these topics.

Focus is the ability to keep doing what is important and not be distracted by the unimportant. It requires a strategic plan, mission statement and even a personal mission. You will not be able to focus on what is really important if you don't first take the time to identify what that is.

Another attribute, closely related to focus, that has a big impact on success is having a results orientation. Most managers get so bogged down in irrelevant details that they forget what they are actually trying to accomplish. John Maynard Keynes, the famous economist, once said, "I would rather be vaguely right than precisely wrong." While it is very important to do things right, it is much more important to do the right things. A results orientation is not a "win at all cost" mentality but it is a continual focus on what you are actually trying to accomplish.

Optimism is another characteristic shared by many of the very successful. If there is one thing I have learned it is that happiness in life is not so much based on circumstances, as it is on how we choose to look at those circumstances. Choosing to view your challenges from a positive perspective can make your job and life a fair bit easier.

Finally, I couldn't write this 100th column without again reflecting on the importance of integrity. Actually, I have tried to weave the importance of integrity throughout all of my columns. If you finish the race and lose your integrity along the way, you cannot be a winner no matter what else you accomplished.

I have written about many other topics that are also very important to both our personal and or organizational success - among them, customer service, teamwork, employee issues, financial management and dealing with change.

I appreciate you all allowing me to share my perspective on these issues, and more importantly, I appreciate many of you taking the time to share your perspective with me.

Thanks for reading!

Chapter 101
THE CHRONIC COMPLAINERS:
THEY'RE NOT ALWAYS WRONG
September 2004

Have you ever known someone who was perpetually negative? I have, and while I consider myself a pretty friendly guy, I frankly don't enjoy being around overly negative people.

We have all had to deal with these kinds of situations in the work environment. Years ago I worked with a woman who was so negative I would cringe when I saw her coming. I knew that no matter what was going on, she was going to find the negative aspects of it and be sure to let me know about them. Almost every time we talked, she was either complaining about a co-worker or pointing out something wrong. More often than not, it was a minor problem, but one that in her opinion, deserved a great amount of my time and attention.

The interesting thing is that many times she was right!

Maybe they were minor issues or matters that were not high on my own priority list, but problems and issues in our businesses need to be dealt with - and something negative happens almost every day.

Unfortunately, when something does go wrong there are those who will generalize and assume everything is going wrong. Usually, these people are not intentionally trying to harm the company; but the problem, whatever it is, gets built up in their minds into something that is not at all close to what is really happening. This situation is particularly dangerous if the "Chicken Littles" in your company find nothing at all wrong with spreading their negative opinions.

One of your jobs as a manager is to make sure these daily setbacks don't get extrapolated into something bigger than they actually are. If you are not careful to properly manage setbacks, your organization's culture can become one of tension, rumors and instability. Clearly, those are not elements you want entrenched in the culture of your company.

So, what can you do? Here are some suggestions to help you manage setbacks:

- **Be proactive** - When you have a setback, address it with your employees. Many times the rumors can be much worse than the truth. Being proactive is almost always the best way to deal with setbacks. Don't wait until the problem festers to the point that you are forced to deal with it.

- **Tell the whole story and be honest** - Always shoot straight with your employees. It makes no sense to lie or to give the story a "spin". The truth always comes out eventually, and when it does, you want to be sure your credibility is intact. As important as it is to communicate with your employees, not communicating with them is always better than misleading them. Your credibility is one of the most important management tools you have. Don't lose it!

- **Restrict the scope of the problem** - Reassure your employees that the problem will be dealt with and everything else is going to be fine. If appropriate, reassure employees about other specific areas of your business they might be concerned about and restore their confidence that the problem won't affect those areas of the business, too.

- **Look to the future** - Keep your team focused beyond the immediate problem and looking forward to a bright future. Keep reminding everyone that the current situation is temporary and that you will soon be back on track. You'll be amazed how quickly your immediate problem can go away if you shift your team's focus away from today's predicament and get them to think about a positive future.

- **Look for a bright side** - This point may be the hardest to understand or appreciate, but I know it is true. Time after time in my life I have seen people, including myself, grow and become a better person when times were tough. While none of us want to go through tough times, the reality is that those tough times frequently prepare us for a much brighter future. Most of us do not grow or learn much when everything is going great, but almost everyone grows exponentially when things are tough.

If you can truly internalize this principle it will change the way you view setbacks. In fact, it can become very empowering. You may never get to the point where you look forward to setbacks, but it will definitely have a constructive effect on your mindset when you are going through them. I believe this more constructive mindset will shorten your tough times by helping you navigate through your setbacks much more efficiently.

If you are not careful, some people (maybe not intentionally) in your organization will use the inevitable setbacks to poison, not only the current atmosphere, but potentially the entire culture of your workplace.

We all deal with setbacks, but the best managers limit those setbacks to what they really are - temporary speed bumps on the road to where they want to go. The next time you have a setback at your company try implementing the approaches I've outlined here and see if it doesn't help you quickly get your organization back on the path to success.

Chapter 102
LEARN PUBLIC SPEAKING SKILLS;
IT'S A SURE-FIRE STATURE BUILDER
October 2004

Would you like to learn a secret that will help you appear to be much smarter than you actually are? Thought so.

The secret is this: Learn to be a good public speaker. If you can speak well, people inevitably will attribute to you more brains, wisdom and common sense than you actually have!

At this point you're probably thinking, "Yes, but that's not so easy." Well, it's easier than you may think. While some people have a natural talent for it, it's a skill that can be learned.

Most people hold themselves back; they determine in their own minds that they are not good speakers, and it becomes a self-fulfilling prophecy. This self-limitation will cause them to miss out on opportunities that could propel their careers or personal lives forward in dramatic ways.

Over the years I have had the opportunity to speak at hundreds of management conferences, literally all over the world. I have made pretty much every mistake that can be made. So, to help you avoid some of those mistakes, I've compiled a list of things I have learned:

- **Don't be afraid** -A survey was taken asking people about their fears, and the results were astonishing. The No. 2 thing people were afraid of was death. No. 1 was public speaking! Don't let fear keep you from reaching your potential in life, and don't let fear box you into a negative stereotype. Others will respect you for being willing to speak. Don't hold yourself back.

- **Don't forget your non-verbal communication** - Gestures, eye contact, voice tone and posture are as important as the words you use. Be natural and relax. Too many people - most, in fact - let their nerves take over during their presentations.

- **Don't be pretentious** -A little humility and self-deprecating humor can go a long way with your listeners. You do need credibility, but being full of yourself is a sure turn-off to your audience.

- **Tell stories** - People love to hear them. An interesting story that helps you make a point can be a very effective way to communicate.

- **Master the "one-point" outline** - Many speakers attempt to cram far too much information into their presentations. Have one or two key points you want to communicate and build your presentation around them. And remember, short is always better. It is much better to have your listeners wanting more than to have them wonder when you are going to end.

- **Provide energy** - Be upbeat and energized. You want people to leave motivated to take some sort of action. If you are energized, it will rub off on your audience.

- **Be personal and build rapport** - Come across as friendly. If at all possible, get physically close to your audience. Walk around a bit and try to avoid standing behind a podium.

- **Have a good opening and closing** -A presentation is often judged by its opening and closing. Work particularly hard on the preparation of these two elements.

- **Use hidden notes** - Frequently I have people ask me how I can give an hour-long presentation without referring to notes.

What they haven't noticed is that my PowerPoint presentation serves as my notes. Good visual aids can both add to your presentation and serve as your notes. If you cannot use PowerPoint, giving your audience handouts can work much the same way.

I know from experience that these ideas can help you. They have worked for me. If you still would like more help with your presentations, there should be organizations accessible to you, including Dale Carnegie, that offer speaking courses. Look for them, or at the very least, buy some books that can help you improve in this area. Most people can dramatically improve their speaking just by focusing on it a little bit.

Finally, if you improve your public speaking skills, a by-product of that effort will be an improvement in all areas of your communication. So, even if you don't plan to go on the lecture circuit, becoming a better speaker will help you in many areas of your life - both professionally and personally.

Don't wait. Take steps today to make yourself a better speaker. You'll be glad you did.

Chapter 103
DELAYED GRATIFICATION: TAKING PROFITS NOW CAN COST YOU LATER
November 2004

I enjoy reading books on raising kids. For the past 14 years, I have read countless parenting books and collectively, they have supplied me with much-needed insight into the raising of my two daughters, Erin and Amanda.

Hopefully, all that reading has helped make me a better dad. There's another interesting by-product of reading parenting books. They have taught me many important management principles that can be applied in the workplace. I find the correlation fascinating.

One of those principles is the concept of delayed gratification. Teaching our kids the importance of delayed gratification is critically important, one author wrote - so much so, that he considers it the single most important character trait we can teach our children.

We all want our children and grandchildren to invest in themselves by making decisions that will enhance their futures. With the principle of delayed gratification in mind, I have often said to my daughters, "Only fools sacrifice their futures on the altar of the immediate."

As managers, we also need to be making decisions that will enhance the future of our organizations. Many times this requires a willingness to make decisions that cost us in the short-term, but are focused on the future.

William Wrigley, who founded the chewing gum company and baseball's Chicago Cubs (and is the namesake of Wrigley Field), understood the importance of taking actions today that would cost him in the short run but would have a great long-term payout. When Wrigley, clearly one of the most successful businessmen and entrepreneurs of his time, was asked to identify his single most important business philosophy, he responded, "Restraint in regard to immediate profits."

William Wrigley certainly understood the benefits of making decisions that have a return positively disproportionate to the current costs. He was not going to sacrifice the future of his organizations to the temptations of the immediate.

Earlier this year I had an excellent opportunity to see the concept of delayed gratification in action within our industry.

John Schopman of Forever Resorts (one of our industry's "William Wrigley's") runs a large group of marinas and houseboat rental operations that are spread all over the United States. I have known for years that Forever Resorts was a highly respected organization, but earlier this year I got a close-up look at how it operated and I was impressed.

John invited me to speak at the Forever Resorts' annual manager's meeting in Arizona. Because of my friendship with John and my respect for him, I accepted his invitation, despite the fact that it didn't really fit into my schedule. I flew to Arizona from my home in Florida on a Friday night, spoke twice to John's managers on Saturday and flew home on Sunday. It was a brutal trip but I sure am glad I went. It gave me an opportunity to see an example of how things can be done right in our industry.

Each year John takes about 50 of his top managers and flies them to a location where they can meet for a week and focus solely on how they can improve themselves - both individually and as a team. They have internal classes and bring in outside speakers such as myself. They spend an intense week investing in their futures by trying to make themselves better managers and people.

I cannot even begin to imagine how much this week of training costs John's organization. All of the managers' salaries, their travel expenses, the expenses of the speakers, administrative costs, and the cost of lost business opportunities due to having all of his managers out of their regular jobs for a week must be tremendous. I am sure it is a big number on the Forever Resorts' annual financial statement. John not only invests in this annual program, but I have also seen John's managers at other programs all around the country. I know that several of the Forever Resorts' marina managers have been through the training required by the International Marina Institute to become certified marina managers. John himself has done that.

Despite the fact that the cost of this training represents a substantial number on the annual financial statement, John is smart enough to know that the return on the investment is many multiples of the cost. He is delaying the gratification of more immediate positive financial results in order to improve his organization's future. That is smart.

Training is just one example of how we can focus on the future. Research and development, investments in facilities and smart marketing are other ways in which we can brighten our organization's futures by making smart decisions today. Each of our organizations is different and we individually have to decide how to apply this concept where we work.

Unfortunately, this concept can be tough to apply. While the general concept of delayed gratification may sound simple, we as managers are frequently under significant stress to get results today. However, if we are going to be successful in the long run, we must have the courage as leaders to make the right decisions today that will benefit our organizations in the future.

Chapter 104
KEEPING EMPLOYEES SAFE
KEEPS BOTTOM LINE HEALTHY
December 2004

Imagine you're a contestant on "Who Wants to Be a Millionaire?" You have one final question to answer, but no lifelines. Get this last one right and you win a million dollars!

The question: "How much does your company spend each year on workers' compensation insurance?"

Do you know? Would you win the million dollars?

If not, there's a good chance workers' compensation - and more specifically, employee safety - could use more of your attention.

Workers' comp expense is a cost that affects your organization in many ways, both tangibly and intangibly, and some of them are not really obvious. Usually, your workers' comp expense is directly related to your organization's focus on employee safety.

The most important aspect of employee safety has nothing to do with its financial impact, however. Workplace accidents have a big impact on the lives of your employees and their families - particularly if the accident leads to a permanent disability, or heaven forbid, a fatality. We owe it to our employees and their families to do everything possible to keep our workplaces safe. It's the right thing to do.

Though not as damaging as the impact on your people and their families, workplace accidents also directly influence your organization's financial results. One big way in which workplace accidents affect your bottom line is through their impact on your workers' comp premiums. The more your insurance company pays out in claims, the more you pay the insurance company in premiums. What's more, it's not just a one-year thing; most accidents boost your premiums for many years.

Finally, as if the impact on your employees, their families and your financial statements were not enough, workplace accidents may be affecting you in even more subtle ways. These less obvious and more-difficult-to-quantify impacts include the costs of having vital employees out of work and the overall impact of accidents on morale.

Fortunately, there are ways to reduce both the frequency and severity of workplace accidents. Here are some things you can do to make yours a safer operation:

- **Focus on safety.** Discuss it at every opportunity, including in your management meetings. Being more safety-conscious will help you, as a leader in your organization; make decisions that can protect your employees. By demonstrating that you value safety, you create a ripple effect throughout the organization.
- **Raise employee awareness.** Use workplace signs, employees' newsletters, paycheck notices, employee meetings or any other means you can to raise safety awareness. Something as simple as: "Think Safety" signs around your facility will produce a subtle message that may save someone's life.
- **Reward safety.** No one is going to avoid hurting themselves for a cup of coffee and a donut. However, rewards - even small ones - serve as one more method of reinforcing the importance of safety. They help people maintain a "safety mindset".
- **Have a safety committee.** Every few weeks get some of your employees together to discuss safety issues. It's okay if the committee is made up of different people each meeting. The

purpose is to identify ways in which all of your employees can work in a safer environment.

- **Welcome inspections.** Don't resist safety inspections. View them as an opportunity to make your facility better and safer. If you don't have someone from the outside periodically inspecting your facility, set up a procedure for conducting inspections internally.

- **Train.** I have heard that most on-the-job accidents are a result of actions, not the workplace environment itself. Make sure all of your people are thoroughly trained in the safety procedures related to their jobs.

- **Follow up with injured employees.** Many employers make little if any contact with those who have been injured on the job until the employees make contact with them. There are many good reasons to follow up with employees who have been hurt. First, it's the humane thing to do. Second, you should learn from the individual what caused the accident and implement any necessary changes immediately. Finally, the employee is a lot less likely to seek outside help if you are doing a good job of keeping him or her information about benefits and rights.

- **Keep clean.** Keeping your workplace clean can have a direct impact on accident prevention. When items are left lying around, the chances of an accident increase. A clean workplace also has a psychological benefit; it creates a more productive working atmosphere.

- **Use available resources.** Your workers' compensation company or local safety council probably will have invaluable resources you can use to help create and maintain a safe workplace. If those sources don't have what you need, key in "employee safety" on an internet search engine. You 'II find a plethora of resources.

Employee safety, or the lack thereof, can affect your employees and your organization in multiple ways over many years. Taking the right actions today can have a direct and positive impact. Try implementing some of these ideas at your company. You may find the benefits even greater than you expected.

Chapter 105
OUR INDUSTRY'S FUTURE RIDES ON
FEBRUARY JOBS SUMMIT
January 2005

Is your company finding it difficult to attract "good" employees? Are the people you are hiring less skilled and qualified than you might wish? Do you ever worry about where you are going to find well-trained employees in the future?

If you answered yes to any of these questions you are not alone - many companies in our industry are facing the same issues. Unfortunately, the problem is only going to get worse. Our nation is facing a convergence of demographic and economic trends that is going to make it even more difficult to find the kinds of people you need. A growing economy, baby boomer retirements, slowing birthrates and changing work ethics are coming together to make the future challenging for those of us who depend on good people to keep our businesses successful.

This increasing lack of talent will have an impact; it is going to force all of us to become trainers. It's only logical. If we can't find the people we need, we will have to develop them ourselves.

Fortunately, the marine industry offers many good training opportunities. The International Marina Institute, American Boat Builders & Repairers Association, American Boat & Yacht Council, National Marine Electronics Association, Marine Retailers Association of

America, state and local associations and individual companies all are making a valiant effort. I had the opportunity to speak at programs sponsored by each of these organizations, and have seen first-hand their excellent work.

But while each is offering excellent training opportunities, there is no overall coordination of the training. Most of these organizations are operating in a vacuum. If we are going to ensure the future vitality of both our individual businesses and the industry as a whole, we are going to have to work together. Fortunately, there are some leaders in our industry, led by Skip Burdon and his team at ABYC, who fully recognize this and are doing something about it.

The COMITT participants will include, not only the providers of training - the organizations listed above as well as secondary schools, colleges and vocational schools - but also many executives who are concerned about the future of our industry. We will have an eclectic brain trust that can work together to develop new and creative ideas.

The conference will include general sessions, which I have been asked to moderate, that will give everyone the opportunity to work together. These general sessions will address such broad subjects as the status of training programs, the importance of certification, how other industries address training and what our goals should be.

There will be breakout sessions in which people can discuss such topics as training needs by industry segment and how we can apply education in our workplaces. These breakout sessions will focus specifically on the different types of companies and educators within our industry. They will give you the opportunity to brainstorm with others who are facing the same issues as you are.

The marine industry in the United States faces many potential threats, not the least of which is overseas competition. If we are going to effectively face these threats we need to work together to make our entire industry better.

Focusing on training from an industry-wide perspective is one way we can work together. If we can lay a foundation that helps us ensure a well-trained workforce we all will benefit. I am excited that our industry has leaders with a vision to tackle this important issue.

COMITT will be a great opportunity for us all to work together toward a common and mutually beneficial goal. I expect it to be a huge success.

Don't be left out. Join me and many other industry leaders the first week of February in Fort Lauderdale. If you need more information on how you can participate, call ABYC at (410) 956-1050 or visit www.abycinc.org. Not only will this be a great event, but Fort Lauderdale isn't a bad place to be the first week in February! See you there.

Chapter 106
HELP KEEP CATASTROPHE AT BAY WITH
AN UPDATED DISASTER PLAN
February 2005

As you probably know, those of us who live in Florida had a very un-usual August and September. Four significant hurricanes in a six-week period shook the state in an immense way. Almost no part of the state was left unscathed by what seemed to be an endless conga line of storms.

The news was filled with pictures of marine facilities on Florida's east coast that had been destroyed. Fortunately, our boatyard and marina, which is on the Intracoastal Waterway near the Palm Beach inlet, was one of those that sustained the least damage. We didn't get off the hook entirely however, particularly in the marina. A combination of good luck and good planning helped minimize what could have been a catastrophic event.

Part of the reason we faired so well is that we didn't leave the outcome to fate. For many years now we have had a hurricane plan that addresses the operational and administrative issues we need to consider when coping with a big storm.

Your organization is probably vulnerable, too. Even if you're not in a hurricane-prone region, you should have an emergency plan. A fire, tornado, earthquake, flood or other type of disaster could devastate your business. Unfortunately, these things come with little or no warning.

Your plan should cover both preparation and recovery. For fire or other types of disaster where there is no advance warning, the emphasis should be on recovery.

Most people learn about the importance of a disaster plan the hard way. However, there is a lot of evidence, including my own personal experience, to indicate that damage can be mitigated by a good emergency preparedness and recovery plan.

So how do you prepare one? Here are some things you should consider:

- **Get staff input.** As with most things in management, you are less likely to overlook an important element of a disaster plan if you get input from people throughout your organization. Don't try and do it alone - you will forget something.
- **Identify threats.** You probably know what types of disasters are likely in your location; however, go ahead and identify them in your plan anyway.
- **Prioritize.** It goes without saying that human safety is always the top consideration, and your plan should clearly reflect that fact. However, after ensuring personal safety you need to identify the property and equipment that are most vital to your operation.
- **Protect key documents/functions.** You will need the proper administrative systems available to promptly get things up and running again. Of course, it is always important to protect your insurance information, too.
- **Describe the steps to be taken.** Don't worry about the little details; just make sure you cover everything.
- **Assign responsibility.** If you don't assign names to specific tasks, everyone will think someone else is taking care of key steps and they will not get done. Our plan goes as far as identifying who will film the property and who will order food for those working.

- **Set aside basic supplies.** At our company, we have a "hurricane box" that my assistant, Cindy maintains. The box includes many of the supplies we would need to cope with a hurricane.
- **Identify recovery plans.** If the worst happens, you must have an idea regarding how and where you would reopen. Make sure you consider this for your plan.

Write the plan. Once you have all of your information gathered, write your plan in a format that is easy for your team to follow.

- **Review it regularly.** Once the plan is complete, you should distribute it throughout your organization and then periodically update it. Make sure everyone knows what he or she is supposed to do.
- **Conduct a "post-mortem".** If you do have to execute your plan it is imperative to review it afterward to make sure it is adjusted for anything you may have learned from the experience. Over the years we have been regularly revising our hurricane plan.

These thoughts are just the tip of the iceberg when it comes to disaster planning. Luckily there are many resources available to help you. There are many websites that can provide you additional resources or even offer consulting services to help you prepare your plan. You can also go to an internet book store such as Amazon.com and find a wealth of material on this topic.

You can't eliminate all of your risks, but with the right planning you can minimize them. Save yourself a lot of heartache by investing the time to prepare your disaster and recovery plan today. With any luck, it will just sit in a file unused, but if the day comes when you do need it, you'll find it invaluable.

Chapter 107
DIAGNOSING AND STEMMING YOUR COMPANY'S BRAIN DRAIN
March 2005

Would it surprise you to learn that you may not have a handle on - or even be aware of - one of your company's most significant annual costs?

Would it surprise you even more to learn that this cost is so pervasive it affects almost every division and department in your organization - a cost so significant it can put a company out of business without the owners ever realizing what happened?

Would you be amazed to learn that this cost is not specifically identified on your operating statement or anywhere else in your financial data? Oh, it's reflected in your financial statements in a big way, but it's so surreptitious you probably had never focused on it!

What is this cost that manages to stay below the accounting radar? It's called employee turnover, and it may be hurting you far more than you realize.

Various studies have tried to accurately quantify the cost of turnover, and they've produced a wide range of findings - anywhere between 25 percent and 200 percent of the terminated employees' annual compensation. Those are high percentages, and even at the low end of the range, the actual costs to your organization can be very damaging.

Many people, until they focus on all of its elements, don't realize that turnover cost can be such a high percentage of terminated (either voluntarily or involuntarily) employee compensation.

Some of the factors that increase this percentage include the costs of administering the turnover, the costs of advertising or otherwise trying to attract candidates to the open position, the costs in time and resources to qualify and select a new employee; the productivity losses related to losing their terminated employee (including his or her lost knowledge); the cost of orientation and training of the new employee; and finally, any costs of relocation or pre-employment testing of the new employee.

Unfortunately, none of those tangible expenditures included what may be the most damaging cost of all - the lost business and lack of focus caused by the turnover.

How can you calculate employee turnover and its related cost at your organization? Let's do the math.

Inventory turnover can be calculated by dividing the number of employees who left your organization for any reason (either voluntarily or involuntarily) during an entire year by the total number of employees employed at the beginning of the year.

The cost of employee turnover can be calculated by taking the total annual compensation of all employees who left your organization for any reason during an entire year and multiplying that total by a turnover cost percentage. The employee turnover percentage you select can be anywhere in the range noted above (25 percent to 200 percent). However, I tend to stay on the lower end of that scale. Try making the calculation for your organization; odds are, you'll be surprised by the result.

Now that you realize how high the cost of employee turnover can be, how do you reduce it? The root causes of employee turnover vary by company, and therefore, so do the solutions. However, here are some general ideas that may help you minimize the problem:

- **Recognize good work.** Many studies have shown that the biggest motivators for most employees are not pay-related; they are intrinsic rewards. One study of 1,500 employees, conducted by Wichita State University, revealed that, "The most powerful employee motivator is personal, instant recognition from their manager." Rarely do employees want to leave organizations that make them feel good.

- **Review your selection process.** If you make the right hiring decisions initially, it is a lot easier to keep people. Unfortunately, no approach to hiring is foolproof; I know I have made my share of mistakes. But while there is no sure-fire method of ensuring only good people are hired, there are ways to improve your odds. A good application, comprehensive reference checking and a pre-employment temperament test (we use Predictive Index) can help you.

- **Review your benefits package.** If you are losing employees because your benefits are inadequate, it may be less expensive to beef up your package than it is to keep paying the costs of turnover. Ask your current employees as well as those who are leaving to identify those benefits that are important to keeping people. You might actually save by spending a little more on employee benefits.

- **Develop and communicate a clear mission.** Most employees want to be part of any organization with clear objectives. Try to build a sense of camaraderie; everyone likes to believe they are on a winning team.

- **End first-year turnover.** Many companies find much of their turnover problem results from the departure of recently hired employees. Consider offering a bonus to a new employee to be paid on their first anniversary. Once new people get past their first anniversaries, they start getting rooted in your organization and are less likely to leave.

To successfully reduce your organization's cost you must be willing to focus closely on employee turnover and the reasons for it at your organization. If you do, the benefits can be significant. In fact, it may be the easiest and fastest way to improve your company's financial results.

Chapter 108
DON'T PERSONALIZE CRITICISM EVEN IF IT'S NOT CONSTRUCTIVE
April 2005

I firmly believe that most people achieve only a small percentage of their potential. There are many factors that contribute to this achievement gap, and most people could give you a list of reasons (read: excuses) for not being all they could be. Most people tend to blame others, their boss, unfortunate circumstances or a host of other factors holding them back.

If you know me well, you know I don't mean to be unkind. However, I believe that the biggest thing holding most people back is nothing but themselves. It is not others, their environment or unfortunate circumstances; the reason many people don't reach even a small percentage of their potential is that they hold themselves back. That's right; many times we are our own worst enemies.

There are many ways we can hold ourselves back but few are as self-damaging as the tendency to personalize criticism. The personalization of criticism can be totally paralyzing to some people and a major hindrance to accomplishments of many others.

A good example is the boss having a bad day. Your boss wakes up late, has a fight with his or her spouse over breakfast, then gets a speeding ticket on the way into work. Not surprisingly, this is a person who arrives in a bad mood. An employee happens to walk in and ends up on the receiving end of all that frustration. I am not exaggerating when I say that a situation like that can affect the self-confidence and performance of some employees for months - even longer.

Another example relates to customers. Unfortunately, we have all had to deal at one time or another with an irate customer. Sometimes those people can be really mean. Many times their buildup of anger is not at all related to you or your company. However, you happen to be at the end of a regrettable chain of events so you have to take it. If you are not careful it is easy to take the customer's venting as a personal affront.

In each of these examples, you have to realize that the other person's problem is not of your making - you just happen to be in the line of fire. (If the problem relates to your company, obviously it is your problem, but all of the issues that caused the customer to over-react probably are not.) The worst thing we can do in those circumstances is to increase the intensity of the situation by taking things personally and responding personally. Just as destructive is internalizing the situation by taking it personally even if we do not say anything.

Here are a few things that can help you when you are personally criticized.

- **See the other side.** Try to understand the perspective of the other person. If that is not possible, just assume the person has problems you don't know about or understand.
- **Look for opportunities to learn.** If someone criticizes something you did (behavior) there may be an opportunity to learn something. However, if someone criticizes you personally, try not to let it affect you. This is really hard to do for most people, but the best thing you can do many times is to look for a possibility to improve yourself from the situation.
- **Don't get defensive.** This rarely helps you and almost always

hurts you. It is tough to resist, but sometimes it is better to take the high road and not say anything.

- **Come back to the situation at a later time.** If it is a boss or co-worker, let the person being critical settle down, then go back and encourage him or her to give you legitimate comments that focus on behavior- not you personally. Usually, it is better to just let the criticism pass and not bring it up again. However, if it is particularly harmful you should wait and address it when you both have cooler heads.
- **Believe in yourself.** Just because someone makes a comment about you does not make it true. You let people have a tremendous amount of control over you when their negative words have an appreciable effect. You will rarely achieve more than you believe you can achieve, so think big!

While we should try not to personalize criticism ourselves, as leaders and bosses we should also keep in mind how paralyzing criticism can be to those around us if it is not given constructively. I have written about these topics before and some of the writings are available in my book "Yeargin on Management" (VTF Publishing 2003). The short version is that we need to be diplomatic and constructive in our criticism.

Don't let real or perceived criticisms keep you from achieving all of your potential. If you are not careful, personalizing criticism will become like a bag of rocks you carry around, weighing you down for years and years. It has to be a tough feeling to be at your retirement party knowing that you have only achieved a small percentage of your potential. Don't let that happen to you.

Believe in yourself and forget about what others think. Not only is it a liberating feeling, but will also put you on the path to success.

Chapter 109
IN BUSINESS AS IN SPORTS, CAPTURE
THE MOMENTUM
May 2005

For many years, I had the privilege of coaching my daughters' soccer teams. Throughout that experience I found myself amazed at how much I was able to learn about teamwork and the workplace, while coaching youngsters who had never worked a day in their lives.

One thing that stands out in my mind is a phenomenon well known to anyone who follows professional sports. It's called momentum.

You've seen it many times. Visualize a close game in almost any sport. Suddenly one team gets a break. The team capitalizes on it and the momentum starts. The team that has the momentum can do no wrong and the team without it can't catch a break.

As a coach I would experience this phenomenon almost every week. Things would be going well and in no time our girls were bursting with confidence. They'd start playing above themselves and everything would be going right.

Of course I saw it the other way, too. When the momentum turned against us, it took every ounce of my ingenuity to stop or reverse it.

The concept of momentum is not limited to sports. As managers and leaders, we have to manage momentum in our businesses.

A few months ago in this column I wrote about the importance of limiting setbacks, or to put it another way, limit negative momentum. This month we will focus on how we can build our success.

When something good happens at your company you should do everything possible to extrapolate that success into momentum. Sometimes this can be done through little things. For instance, at our company we've had parties when jobs have gone well, and doughnuts and coffee when we've gone a while without accidents. I have taken groups to lunch or dinner to show my appreciation for a job well done.

These are easy examples, but your ability to build on success may be limited by the culture of your organization. If it's one of negativism or skepticism, the odds of getting any momentum going are slim.

Here are some things you can do to create a culture that will allow you to build on your success.

- **Create a positive environment.** A zillion words have been written (many of them by me) about the importance of a positive environment in the workplace. A positive environment allows people to think the best, a perpetually negative environment encourages them to think the worst.
- **Celebrate accomplishments.** When things go well make a big deal of it. Many managers are quick to tell their employees when they mess up, but say little or nothing when the employees do something exceptional. Let them know you appreciate their efforts. You like to hear about it when you achieve something and your employees are no different.
- **Be trustworthy.** Trust is so fundamental to effective management that it shouldn't even need mention. You will never be able to create a positive environment that builds on success if you are not trusted. Integrity is foundational to any management success.
- **Have goals.** People working toward well-defined goals are less likely to focus on the negative and much more likely to

accentuate developments that reinforce their belief that they are going to reach or exceed their goals. A results-oriented environment will help your team stay focused on its goals and encourage positive thinking.

- **Create a future.** Make sure your employees know they have a future with your company. If you have big plans, share them. People who feel good about the future are much more likely to look for positive development that is in line with your long term view.

- **Communicate.** If you are not communicating with your employees, either someone else will be giving them information that is inaccurate (and almost always negative) or they will come to their own conclusions about what is happening (many times, it too, will be negative). Through better communication, you can help create an environment in which you can build on the good things that happen.

- **Do it daily.** Acknowledging success is not a monthly or quarterly event, it is an everyday necessity. Look for the small victories to celebrate.

If you want to capture some of the energy that momentum can bring to your organization you must look for ways to do it. Most likely, it won't happen by accident, it will require proactive action by you.

Positive momentum can be a powerful tool to help you and your team achieve your potential. Try some of these steps and watch as your organization capitalizes on the energy that is created by building on your successes.

Chapter 110
ARE YOU DROWNING IN DETAIL AND MISSING THE BIG PICTURE?
June 2005

"He who considers too much will perform too little." - Johann van Schiller

Recently I was in my car, stopped for a light, when a bicycle tire at the side of the road caught my attention. As my eyes zeroed in on the tire, my daughter Erin said, "I hope whoever was riding that bike is okay."

I replied, "Maybe the tire has just fallen off a truck. I was somewhat embarrassed when Erin pointed out that there was more than a tire - there was a mangled bike lying a few feet away. I had totally missed it. I was so focused on a detail (the tire), that I had failed to see the big picture (the mangled bike).

The bicycle example is a variation of what I have often called the "beach ball effect." Sometimes we get so focused on one color of our figurative beach ball that we forget the ball is multicolored. When we get mired in detail (our panel of the beach ball, for example) our perspective and effectiveness are significantly reduced.

People who are very successful rarely get bogged down in this way. They have the ability to balance detail with the result they are seeking. They pay enough attention to detail to be certain a job is done well, but they don't let themselves get so immersed that they forget what it is they are really trying to accomplish.

Most people who get bogged down in detail are well-intentioned. They are conscientious - trying to do things right - and that is perceived by most people, including me, to be a valuable characteristic. That's why this issue requires balance.

Many times during speaking engagements I have said, "More important than doing things right is doing the right things."

Did you read that carefully? I always worry that someone will leave the meeting thinking I have said it is not important to do things right. It IS important. But it is MUCH MORE important to be doing the right things.

It doesn't matter how well we do if we are not doing the things we should be doing, even if it means sacrificing some of our desired precision. As the economist John Maynard Keynes put it, "I would rather be vaguely right than precisely wrong."

Many managers and their employees are spending their days trying to do things correctly, but they are missing what is really important. They are unknowingly and unintentionally wasting huge amounts of their organizations' resources "going through the motions."

Because I'm an optimist, I view this problem as a huge opportunity. If we can identify the things that are burying our organizations in unnecessary detail, and redirect those resources to more productive use, it will have a dramatic impact on our results.

So how can you step back and identify the things that may have you drowning in unnecessary detail? Here are three pointers that can help:

- **Take a fresh look** - Don't assume that anything you are doing is something that has to be done. Review each task you and your team is involved in and ask yourself, "If we stopped doing this would it really matter?" Most likely you'll find things that continue to be part of the routine only because they've been around so long they've taken on a momentum of their own.

- **Zero-sum approach** - Look at your organization as though you were starting from scratch. If you were establishing a new organization, would you include all of the tasks you are performing? Identify those that are critical and then, more importantly, use this process to identify and eliminate those that are unnecessary.

- **Get an outside perspective** - Very rarely do transformational ideas come from within an organization. The inside people are too buried in the details of "how we do it" to see the biggest opportunities for change. If you are happy with incremental change, look inside. But if you really want to transform the organization, an outside perspective can be invaluable. If you don't want to go totally outside the firm, have people consult one another across departmental and divisional lines. However, remember, "A prophet has no honor in his own country." Many times you will have to hire a true outsider to help you identify the biggest opportunities for positive change.

The key word here is balance. A focus on details is important, but it requires balance to ensure that your focus does not overtake your orientation and keep you from doing things that are really important.

Chapter 111
CLEARLY DEFINED EXPECTATIONS ELIMINATE OFFICE FRUSTRATIONS
July 2005

Which aspect of managing your employees do you find most frustrating?

If you're like most, people failing to meet your expectations is near the top of your list. Not only do these failures generate frustration, they frequently require a significant amount of effort from you to correct.

As managers it is natural for us to focus on our own frustrations. But you should be aware that in many instances where you are frustrated with an employee who has not met your expectations, the employee is equally frustrated with you - perhaps more so. That's right; in fact, often the level of frustration you feel is only a fraction of what the employee feels.

The source of all this management/employee frustration? Unspoken or unclear expectations.

People rarely achieve what they don't receive. By that I mean an employee's failure to meet your expectations often is not the employee's fault. It is a direct result of how you have communicated those expectations.

Most employees want to do a good job and want to please their bosses; they are conscientious, value their jobs and want to contribute to the success of their companies. Certainly there are exceptions (if you allow an employee who does not want to do a good job to stay with you, that is a different problem entirely - one that demands your immediate attention but is outside the scope of this month's column).

Fortunately, there are several things we can do to help resolve the problems that arise from unspoken or unclear expectations. Here are a few:

- **Accept responsibility.** As managers, it is very easy for us to pass the buck and blame employees when we, ourselves are at fault. You will never end your frustration over unmet expectations unless you accept responsibility for it yourself. It is completely unfair to blame your employees for something that actually is a shortfall in you own job.

- **Communicate clearly.** I have said many times that when you get to the bottom of any management problem it is almost always a communication problem. As the boss, you are the person responsible for proper communication. This is critical, you must be clearly communicating your expectations or your employees have no realistic chance of meeting them.

- **Communicate frequently.** It's almost impossible to over-communicate in the workplace. Talk to your employees often. Explain your expectations fully and clearly. Frequent communication minimizes misunderstandings. And there's a by product, morale goes up when your employees feel an increased sense of importance.

- **Ask for feedback.** When you communicate your expectations, be certain the employee completely understands them. Ask the employee to express his or her understanding of what it is you have asked for. If the employee can clearly communicate your expectations back to you, then you have succeeded in transferring the responsibility of meeting them to the employee.

- **Use an early warning system.** Observe the employee's actions to be certain they are consistent with what you both have agreed on. Don't wait until a project ends and then berate the person for having done it wrong. Look into performance early on and be effusive in your praise when the employee is moving in the right direction.

Finally, imagine for a moment you are in a bowling alley participating with your boss in a big-money tournament. There's a lot of money on the line. The boss looks at you, calls your name and says he needs you to pick up a spare to win the tournament.

You really want to do that and carry the day for your team. But when you pick up your ball and step up to propel it down the lane you discover there is a curtain in front of the pins. You have been given the job of picking up a spare but you have no idea which pins remain standing.

Just as the ball nears what you hope will be an impact point, the curtain lifts and you see you have completely missed the standing pins. Your boss is furious and frustrated. You know you have tried your best and you're equally frustrated. That's how your employees feel when you do not clearly communicate your expectations to them.

You have it within your power to eliminate a significant amount of workplace frustration by lifting the metaphorical curtain. Be sure your employees are clear on what you expect of them. If they fully understand your expectations, not only will you enjoy a less frustrating workplace, but you'll see significant improvements in results.

Chapter 112
EFFECTIVE COMMUNICATION:
A SKILL THAT CAN BE LEARNED
August 2005

Think of someone you consider successful, and odds are he or she is a good communicator.

Surveys in fact, indicate that a high percentage of successful people attribute their achievements to their ability to communicate. Only in rare instances do people achieve real success without strong communication skills.

Each of us has many different communication constituencies, as I call them - groups of people with whom we must regularly communicate. They include our company owners, our bosses, customers, employees, vendors and peers. If we are not able to communicate well with each of these groups, we are doomed to failure.

Fortunately, there are things we can do to develop communications skills. Here are some examples:

- **Be a good listener.** Did your mom ever say anything like, "God gave you two ears and one mouth for a reason"? Many people forget that communication is a two way street. You cannot succeed at it unless you are patient enough to listen to others.
- **Learn nonverbal communication.** This includes everything related to communication other than words: posture, eye

contact, tone of voice, body language. It is what we sometimes call charisma. Some studies have indicated that as much as 90 percent of communication is nonverbal.

Many people believe that the ability to communicate non-verbally is innate, but that is not true; it can be learned. There are many books available on websites such as www.amazon. com. Find one that catches your interest and read it. Even a small improvement in nonverbal communication can greatly increase your effectiveness.

- **Be energetic.** This is especially important when you are communicating with your employees. Think of yourself as a battery that provides energy to those with whom you are communicating. Even when you are having a bad day you need to remember that other people draw their energy from you. Sometimes you have to be energetic even when you don't feel that way.

- **Be Positive.** Do you prefer talking with someone who is usually positive or someone who is usually negative? If you are like me, you prefer to be around positive people. Studies have shown that effective communicators are positive in their approach. One good example of this is described in a great book called "Learned Optimism".

- **Know what you want to say.** Don't initiate communication without knowing what you want to say. Not only do you risk appearing incompetent, but you are also being disrespectful of your listener's time.

- **Be concise.** Use as few words as necessary to make your point.

- **Be direct.** Do you want people to be direct with you? Of course you do. You should also be direct with others. Many times we are so worried about what other people will think, that we beat around the bush. Be respectful and polite, but also be direct in making your point.

- **Ask for feedback.** There is no better way to ensure that your listener has heard what you have tried to communicate than to respectfully ask them to repeat what you have said. This will ensure that you have achieved a true "meeting of the minds".

- **Understand your listener's perspective.** This is particularly helpful if you are involved in conflict with another. Trying to see the perspective of the other person will go a long way toward effective communication with that person.
- **Give goals.** Goals are effective in many areas of management. Communication is certainly no exception.
- **Ask for action.** It is very dangerous to assume that another person will interpret a set of circumstances in the same way· you do. Therefore, it is imperative that you specifically ask people to do what you need them to do. Don't assume the other person knows what to do based on a scenario you have described.
- **Use phrases that promote.** "Good point", "Thank you", "Let's try it". These types of encouraging words can go a long way toward helping you achieve your objectives.

When you get to the bottom of almost any management problem, it is almost always a communication problem. No matter how smart we are, our ability to achieve is limited by our ability to communicate. Find some books on effective communication and try some of these suggestions to help both your communication and your overall effectiveness.

Chapter 113
YOU CAN GO WITH YOUR GUT,
BUT BACK IT UP WITH DATA
September 2005

Have you ever had a "gut feeling?" Or, more politely, have you ever made a decision based on intuition?

If you're like most leaders, of course you have. Sometimes when faced with a decision we choose the alternative that just feels right.

Most of us have based at least one important decision in our careers solely on intuition. Sometimes those decisions even end up being correct, and we're left wondering how we really "knew" which course to choose.

A friend once told me that what we call gut feeling is the accumulation of all our experience and education, expressing itself in a way that we cannot readily articulate. I believe there is some truth to that.

Despite our occasional successes with intuition (people are more inclined to remember the times they got it right); most of the time we need real information to make accurate decisions. In fact, most people find "gut feeling" works much better when they have sufficient information to review beforehand.

Don't misunderstand me; I am not suggesting that decisions should never be based on intuition. But many times we end up using our "gut" as a guide when we really need solid data. It's easy to use intuition as a copout when we really should be digging out the real pertinent information.

Much of Japan follows a management concept called "speak with data." The essence of this approach is that if you're going to propose a course of action you need to have the relevant and analyzed data to support your proposal. In other words: No facts, no decision.

Each of us should make sure we have all the relevant data before making important decisions. Here are some guidelines that can help you in this area:

- **Understand how your information is gathered.** Most readers of this column are not accountants of information system specialists. But it is important to have a basic understanding of how the information you are using was gathered. Understanding the accumulation process will help ensure you are reviewing the right information and that you are using it appropriately.

- **Be certain the information is relevant.** Sometimes we need to dig rather deep to get to the real root of the problem. Don't always accept the first bit of information you are given to explain a problem. Keep questioning your information and you may find the real problem is two or three levels below the issue upon which you are focusing.

- **Identify the source.** Many times we try to solve problems using information that is gathered far from the real problem. Or, the source may have a bias that could distort the true picture. Be sure you both identify the source of your information and are using information that is as close as possible to the problem you are trying to solve.

- **Make sure the information is accurate.** It's okay to be a little skeptical. Questioning the information you are given will do three things: First, it will help ensure its accuracy, second, it will help you understand it more thoroughly, and finally, it will help ensure that you get good information in the future by signaling that you will be questioning it.

- **Understand how the information has been analyzed.** We all look at everything in life from different perspectives and analyzing data for management decisions is no different. You must be sure you understand the paradigms of anyone who analyzed the information before it was passed on to you. Also, you need to be realistic about your biases or paradigms.

- **Verify the information.** Don't just rely on what you have been given; go take a look at the problem yourself. Often you will have a dramatically different perspective when you take the time to experience or view the problem with your own eyes. This takes a little more time, but to make the best decision you need first-hand experience with the issue you are trying to resolve.

- **Avoid "paralysis through analysis."** While it is important to get good information, don't let the pursuit of it serve as an excuse for delay. In many situations, you will never be able to get all the facts in a timely or cost-effective manner. This may seem contradictory to some of what you've read here but it is not. The key is to get all the relevant information you can in a timely and cost-effective manner and then use your intuition to make the right decision.

The extent to which you can carry out some of these steps depends on both the size of your organization and your position. However, whether your company is large or small, the principles are the same.

Finally, do you remember the phrase, "Show me the money," made famous by the movie Jerry Maguire? When making decisions we should be thinking, "Show me the data." Insist on getting factual support and the odds of making good decisions rise dramatically.

Chapter 114
TRY REVISITING "THE 7 HABITS";
IT WILL BE TIME WELL INVESTED
October 2005

I recently reacquainted myself with an old friend - not a person, but a book. It was Stephen Covey's perennial bestseller, "The 7 Habits of Highly Effective People."

I read "The 7 Habits" at least twice during the 1990s and since then have tried to follow the principles Covey has introduced to more than 15 million people around the world. I have woven those principles through many of my columns and speeches over the years and recommended the book to numerous people. Many of them have told me it changed their lives, both professionally and personally.

My most recent encounter with "The 7 Habits" came as I prepared to teach its principles to all of the employees at our company. As I worked to prepare my presentations, I found it hard to believe it had been several years since I had last read the book. I was reminded again of the power of its principles.

I'll let you buy the book for yourselves to discover all seven of Covey's Habits. However, to whet your appetite, here are a few principles that really stand out to me.

- **You have to take care of yourself.** Covey uses several examples such as Aesop's fable of "The Goose Who Laid the Golden Egg" and something he calls "sharpen the saw" to make his point. The key principle is that we have to both, take care of ourselves and continue to improve.

Taking care of ourselves requires balance that brings improvement in all areas of our lives; professional, mental, emotional, physical and spiritual. The Japanese concept of Kaisen contends that if we are not improving, we are going to fall behind. When you start feeling content and maybe a little smug, thinking you have it all together, that's the time to watch out. You could be heading for disaster. We need to be continually finding ways to improve - in all areas of our lives.

Most of you reading this column are busy people and I know you find it hard to always eat the right foods, exercise and do all the other things you know you should be doing. But when you are not caring for yourself today you are letting problems build up for tomorrow. Until you acknowledge this fact, you will continue to find excuses to avoid doing what you know you should be doing.

I have made it a priority and you should, too. I find it's a greater use of my time. I'm not only heading off future problems, but I feel great. My stress level is reduced and my energy increases to a level that more than compensates for the time I invested in myself.

- **Private victories lead to public victories.** Most everyone wants to be both effective and successful. But the difference between those who just talk about success and those who actually achieve it is initiative - taking the steps needed to achieve your goals. Most people hope success will just come their way. In reality, it requires what Covey calls "private victories" - many of them.

In sports, a team's success has less to do with what the players do on the field than it does with what they do in the offseason. Hitting the gym, studying the playbook and practicing with teammates are all critical to achieving success in the games (public victories). That's how it works for us, too. We need a string of private victories to lay the foundation for future public victories.

If we want to achieve public victories, either in our companies or in our outside lives, we must first have the private victories. Private victories for our organizations include management and employee development, strategic planning, upgrading our facilities and keeping them neat and clean and looking for ways to reduce waste in our operations. All of these steps are private victories that lead to public victories.

- **Be proactive.** Most people are reactive. They go through their personal and professional lives just reacting to whatever comes their way.

  Being proactive means looking ahead to identify two things. First, you want to pinpoint potential problems and what you must do to solve them before they become real problems. Secondly, you must identify the private victories you need today to achieve the public victories you want in the future. Don't just wait for life to happen to you, take charge of your career.

  The key to being proactive is focusing on the things you can control and not concerning yourself with those you can't. The beauty of this is that if you want to increase your influence in a certain area, focus on matters you can control in that area. People want more influence in their lives, but they waste their time focusing on things they cannot control. That actually reduces their areas of influence and leads to frustration.

I have barely scratched the surface of "The 7 Habits" in this column. It's a book worth reading (or rereading). Learning or relearning its powerful principles can change your life, both professionally and personally.

Chapter 115
DON'T BE A "DUMB" MANAGER; IT HURTS YOU, YOUR COMPANY
November 2005

I had to laugh while reading a People magazine article called "Dumb Criminals." It described how several inept lawbreakers had been arrested because, to put it kindly, they weren't too smart.

Some examples:

- The guy who robbed a pizza delivery girl and then called her back to ask for a date. He told her she was "cute".
- The regular on Howard Stern's radio show who bragged to the entire country about how he didn't pay taxes. It got him a year in jail.
- The carjacker who used a camera he found in the car to take his own picture at the wheel, and then left the camera in the car.
- And finally, the bank robber who showed up at his own branch, deposited $160 in his account, and then proceeded to pull a weapon and rob the teller.

You ask yourself, "How could these guys be so dumb?"

Unfortunately, many managers are guilty of doing things just as dumb. The difference is, the managers get away with it - or at least appear to. But in reality, they are hurting their companies in a big way.

Here are some examples of how we can be dumb managers:

- **By "knowing it all"** - Many managers believe that being in a leadership position makes them smarter than their subordinates. This results in a tremendous loss to a company. Employees are a wonderful source of ideas on ways to make a company better. In fact, their proximity to the front lines usually makes them better in this respect than their bosses.

- **By being content** - One of the primary responsibilities of managers is to constantly challenge their people (and themselves) to improve. No matter how good we are, we should always be looking for ways to do things better. For many managers, this will require a bit of a paradigm shift. It is easy for us to become satisfied with ourselves. But we shortchange ourselves, our employees and our companies when we become complacent. The best managers are always striving to improve.

- **By micromanaging** - We should hire good people and get out of their way. There is nothing as discouraging as a boss who micromanages. It slows down the employee and wastes the manager's time; neither person is effective. Weaning yourself from the tendency to micromanage may require developing your employees to the point where they gain your confidence. But most of the time, all it takes is a willingness to give up a little control.

- **By draining energy** - Like it or not, your temperament as a manager has a big impact on the energy level of your organization. Think of your boss - or maybe a previous boss. If he or she was in a bad mood did it affect you? Of course it did. And if you are in a grumpy mood it will slow down your entire organization. As leaders, we should think of ourselves as batteries - constantly energizing our organizations. Often, this requires that we be "up" when we don't really feel that way.

- **By failing to give goals** - Goals are one of the most powerful and least used tools in the management arsenal. It is foolish to assign a task and not give goals, but many managers do it every day. When the job is not done on time, or the employee fails to produce the desired result, the manager gets frustrated. Because the manager is in a position of authority, he or she can take that frustration out on the employee. As managers, we should always give clear goals.
- **By not demonstrating integrity** - If your employees see you cheating and lying you are sending them a clear message. You cannot expect employees to treat you ethically when they see you acting in a less than ethical manner. You must set a very high standard of integrity. In the long run, it's always smart to do things right.

Because managers are in positions of authority, they often get away with being dumb. But they are costing their organizations (and ultimately themselves) a tremendous loss in productivity.

It's not hard to avoid being a dumb boss. Most of the time it's as simple as treating employees the way you would like to be treated. Not only will they be happier, but you and your organization will benefit from a more productive workplace.

Chapter 116
DON'T LEAVE A CAREER BEHIND AT THE OFFICE HOLIDAY PARTY
December 2005

Once again the holidays are upon us, and you know what that means; company party season - the time of year when co-workers get together and let loose.

Unfortunately, it's also a season in which you can blow, both your reputation and your career in a single night.

Most of our organizations will be planning holiday parties during December. Not all of them realize that these seemingly innocent gatherings can have a significant negative impact on the team's long-term performance.

We've all heard the horror stories. Someone tells off the boss, gropes a co-worker, or with the help of a little too much alcohol, turns him or herself into a company laughingstock. There are even more glaring examples, but it's not just the obviously embarrassing lapse of judgment that cause problems. Sometimes even the smaller and seemingly innocuous acts can have a negative impact.

I first focused on this problem after graduating from college and working for an organization that, at the time, was the world's largest CPA firm. I was sent off, along with a couple of dozen other recruits, for a two-week orientation program. I don't remember much from that two-week period more than 20 years ago, but there is one thing that stands out as though I just heard it yesterday.

One of the partners came in and told us that more people destroy their careers at company parties than at any other time. They let down their guard and say or do things they never would say or do in the office. The price for those momentary indiscretions can be huge.

I am not opposed to company parties; they can be very enjoyable get-togethers and significant morale boosters. But when an employee crosses the line that defines professional behavior, company parties can spell disaster for individual careers.

To make certain it isn't YOUR career that is torpedoed; here are some points to keep in mind at this year's party:

- **It's still about business.** Although there clearly is a party atmosphere with food, drinks, and music, the company party is still about business. Save your party-animal instincts for a more appropriate setting. Stay professional at all times.
- **Avoid the alcohol.** Whenever there is a major career-busting event at a company party, it almost always involves alcohol. Enjoy a soda or bottled water but stay away from any drink that is going to increase the odds of you behaving in an unprofessional manner.
- **Dress professionally.** The company party should be about helping your career, not sinking it. Think professionalism. Save your Saturday night outfit for Saturday night on the town. Once again, be thinking professionalism.
- **Mingle.** Use the party as a time to speak with as many people as possible. Don't just hang out with the same crowd. Take advantage of the opportunity to tell people what you appreciate about them. Network with people in other divisions or departments.
- **Be appreciative.** Be sure to thank anyone who was involved

with putting on the party. Most people won't take the time to do that. Show a little graciousness, and it will go a long way toward reinforcing the professional image you want to portray.

- **Manage your timing.** You should be at the party on time, but don't feel you have to be the one who shuts it down. Arrive on time, mingle, eat, pay close attention to the / presentations and then leave.

If you are in charge of putting on the party try to remember the following:

- **Limit the alcohol.** Putting a limit on the amount of alcohol someone can drink may save yourself and your company a whole host of problems. Be sure someone is keeping an eye on how much alcohol is being dispersed to ensure no one overindulges.
- **Remember: People are different.** Not everyone likes the same music, food and drinks you do. Try to accommodate as many people as possible.
- **Make it first class.** The company party tells employees a lot about their company. If you want first-class employees, you need to treat them that way. Spend a little extra on the food and decorations to ensure the employees leave feeling they were treated well.
- **Keep speeches short.** It is fine to have speeches at a company party, just be sure they err on the short side. A brief update is great; a long-winded speech does nothing but make the employees wonder when you will quit talking.

One of the quickest ways to shorten a career is to blow it at a company party.

Remember that the company party is all about business. It's okay to enjoy yourself, but keep your reputation and your credibility intact. The day after the party, you'll be glad you did.

Chapter 117
ELIMINATE WASTE FROM YOUR OPERATIONS
January 2006

Recently a men's fitness magazine published an interesting article which claimed that people who go to fitness centers actually exercise only seven minutes of every hour they are in the gym.

At first, I found that hard to believe. But I was surprised during my next visit to our local gym; I watched and determined that the article was pretty accurate. I saw people doing everything but exercising. They spent a lot of time watching the TVs, hanging out at the juice bar, taking long breaks and chatting with other members, but very little time doing what they were presumably there to do: exercise!

As I began extrapolating this thought to other areas of my life, I couldn't help but wonder how much time most companies' employees actually spend doing what they are being paid to do. At many organizations you can see employees chatting with one another, eating, walking around and just about anything other than working productively. Additionally, we have all visited a business that seems to operate in an incredibly inefficient manner. Many companies in the marine industry, if they are honest with themselves, must admit that they too have a fair bit of waste in their operations.

There is a lot for us to consider on this topic, but before we further consider the potential waste in our operations, it is important that we understand two things:

- **Waste is not your employees' fault** - If you have waste in your business it is not because you have bad employees. Blaming employees is the easy, but incorrect, way to look at waste. Blaming employees only lowers employee morale, which in the end leads to more waste. Frankly, any waste in your organization is most likely a result of your systems and management, NOT the result of bad employees.

- **Waste is an opportunity** - You probably consider the waste in your organization a bad thing. Most people would agree with you. However, I challenge you to look at waste not as a bad thing, but as opportunity - a chance to improve your results. In fact, removing waste may be the easiest way to get the improvement you desire.

- In Japanese management, they have a word for waste; it is called "muda" (pronounced moo-dah). In a nutshell, there are seven kinds of muda.

- **Overproduction** -All muda is bad, but many consider overproduction the worst type. Instead of this type of noble effort to keep people busy, you might consider using that time to develop your employees or make improvements to increase future productivity.

- **Inventory** - If you have a large inventory, walk through your stockroom and think of all those parts as stacks of $50 bills. Sure, you want enough stock to do your work efficiently; however, many times excess inventory can be used as a method to cover up inefficiencies in operations.

- **Rework** - Redoing work costs you three times - once for the first time you did it, second for the second time and third-ly for the opportunity costs (lost sales, etc.) of doing it the second time.

- **Motion** -Any body motion that does not add value is muda. This does not mean we want to make people work harder; odds are your employees already work hard. It is about putting your brains together and figuring out ways to work smarter.
- **Processing** - This muda results from inadequate technology or planning. Can the time you are investing in certain tasks be dramatically shortened by investing in technology? Are you reaping the time savings that can be gained by investing in a little more time up front in planning?
- **Waiting** - Do your employees wait for job assignments, materi-als or another process to be completed? Employee waiting can have a significant cost to your company. You must figure out ways to reduce time your employees spend waiting for anything.
- **Transport** - Moving materials in your operation creates no value and runs the risk of damage. You should be looking for ways to reduce material movement through placing material closer to work sites or moving stockrooms to more centralized locations.

Imagine how much your results would improve if you were able to reduce waste in each of these areas. Chances are, the savings will be much higher than you might have first thought. Why wait? Starting today, look at each of these areas, squeeze out waste and you'll be im-proving your results in ways you may not have been able to previous-ly imagine.

Finally, remember that improving in each of these areas is not about working harder. You may actually end up working less, as you become more efficient and improve your productivity. It is about work-ing smarter.

Chapter 118
TECHNOLOGY AND GLOBALIZATION
September 2017

Technology and globalization are two trends that are combining with incredible force to significantly impact us all (and our industry). It does not matter if we consider technology and/or globalization as good or bad; they are both changing our world in a big way.

While bringing significant benefits on a global/macro level, both globalization and technology can also bring substantial uncertainty and disruption on a micro level. Change is happening much faster than the world has ever seen and it will materially impact peoples' lives. However, instead of resisting change and doubling down on the past, we need to look for ways to benefit from the inevitable change to come.

Globalization includes ideas and increasing connectivity that shrinks the world into smaller markets which, facilitated by ease of communication and travel, makes it much easier to do business anywhere and everywhere. The global economy is growing at a breathtaking pace and as I have traveled around the world I have seen this first hand. China sells three times as many cars as the U.S., is home to many of the world's largest public companies, and is doing a great job of establishing relationships around the globe that will allow them to control the world's most precious resources. The world's tallest building is in the Middle East, Macau is a bigger gambling destination than Las Vegas, India has the world's largest movie industry and refinery, and

95% of the world's consumers live outside the U.S. When visiting their countries I have often been asked by foreign government officials what they can do to attract one of our companies to their country; leaders around the world have embraced capitalism and are competing hard to develop their economies. There is no turning back.

The good news is that globalization is pulling billions of people out of poverty and many of those people want U.S.-made products. The even better news is that the global growth is not reducing U.S. growth or reducing our piece of the pie; U.S. wealth is growing significantly and globalization is making the overall pie MUCH bigger which benefits everyone.

Technology is also progressing at breakneck speed and will be advancing even faster:

- Artificial Intelligence (AI) is evolving quickly and will be accelerated by cloud computing which will automatically share what one AI system has learned with others. Vladimir Putin recently predicted that whichever country leads in AI will rule the world.
- Biotech, Biometrics, and Genomic advancements will soon significantly change both how we live and how long we live.
- Nanotechnology will offer us both better products and manufacturing processes.
- Robotics will eventually help us alleviate labor shortages, significantly improve productivity, and lower costs of products.
- 3D printing will not only lower the cost of production, but also dramatically speed up the time to get both industrial and personal goods to consumers.
- The "Internet of Things" will make the internet even more prevalent but significantly improve efficiency, health, safety, and information flow while lowering costs.
- Energy will change significantly as we phase out the

carbon-based products we have used for the past 150 years, resulting in lower costs and a healthier environment.

While these changes can be exciting, they can also be very disruptive. There will not only be a major reset of both companies and people with influence and wealth, but also a potential reset of world powers. Power won't primarily be a result of ships and planes, but who controls these new technologies. This will result in new entrepreneurs we have not yet heard of who will have major global influence. It will also allow small countries that today have little global influence, to become major powers.

All of this is not starry-eyed thinking – it is all happening today and heading toward a tipping point that will impact everyone. Trying to hold onto the past (like the videotape rental stores over a decade ago trying to keep their customers) just delays the inevitable and extends the agony. Most people will try to hang on to the past and even many of those who see the changes coming will not know what to do, but, those who are smart and forward-thinking will topple today's leaders (both people and companies). ***We need to embrace the inevitable and look for ways to take advantage of future changes instead of looking for ways to protect the past.***

So, what do we do? We need to embrace the inevitable, see our markets as global, make sure we have a technology strategy (where you are going to be on the innovation adopter curve) and stay aware of the upcoming changes. Knowing the world is changing and embracing it is half the battle.

Finally, as an industry, we should consider spending a day (like last year's Grow Boating Summit) to discuss the future and how we can protect and advance our position as the world's leader in recreational boat production.

Chapter 119
TECHNOLOGICAL CHANGE WILL RESET GLOBAL POWER STRUCTURE
July 2018

The world is changing very fast. Changes are coming from many different directions, including technology. Increasing computational power is driving exponential technological developments that will dramatically change the world in the next 10-15 years.

These inevitable technological developments will provide amazing opportunities unlike anything the world has seen but they will also be incredibly disruptive as they reset the economic landscape. If the U.S does not prepare today, these changes will also reset the global power structure; that's not hyperbole.

We are at an inflection point and how we react today to these changes will determine if the U.S. can maintain our economic security and continue to lead the world in the decades ahead. The U.S. should not only stay ahead of these changes but also see them as an opportunity to lead the globe in technological development.

The development of technologies like virtual reality, robotics, biotech, 3D printing, the internet of things, renewable energy and electric vehicles are already well underway and will create tremendous global business opportunities. Unfortunately, companies that don't lead in the adaption of these technologies risk being put out of business.

Then, of course, there are the three real game changers;

nanotechnology (manipulating atoms and molecules to create new materials and products,) artificial intelligence (increasing computer power reaching and surpassing human thinking,) and quantum computing (transition from current binary computers to new quantum bits which will make computers exponentially more powerful.) Further development of any of these three technologies could by itself potentially reset the geopolitical and economic power structure of the entire globe.

Countries around the world are working hard to develop these technologies with the goal of resetting their economic and global standing. However, no country is better suited to lead in each of these areas than the United States.

We need a bold vision for the United States that inspires us to look forward and lead in each of these areas. These technological changes will drive the global economy in the decades ahead and with the right leadership, the U.S. can develop and maintain our economic and military leadership position for a long time. This is an incredible opportunity to positively impact the next few generations of Americans.

This is not just an economic issue, it is also a clear national security issue. Current weapons will be as effective as bows and arrows when compared to the damage that can be done by some of these emerging technologies. Focusing on leading in the development of these innovative technologies is a certain way to ensure the U.S. remains strong.

As John Kennedy did decades ago with his call to put a man on the moon, I hope our current leaders will not only inspire us to look forward and be the clear leader in the development of these technologies but also direct the resources of the U.S. government to help ensure that happens. It would be a great gift to the next generations of Americans.

Chapter 120
READING = SUCCESS
March 2019

At Correct Craft and our companies, we have a reading culture that has significantly contributed to our success. We talk about the importance of being "learners" vs. "knowers" and reading plays a key role in our focus on continuous improvement; at pretty much any given time some group of our team is working through a book.

Our team knows I love to read and often I will recommend a book to someone if I think it will help them – it is what our team calls "getting booked!"

While I enjoy sharing books and having people share with me their suggested reads there is no way I could list the hundreds of books that have influenced me. So, I thought I would start this first blog (yep, look for at least one more book blog) with some of the books that have influenced me the most by providing the below list of what I consider "must-reads" for business leaders:

- *The Seven Habits of Highly Effective People* (Covey) – A classic I have read three or four times and taught numerous times. This book will change your life.
- *Start with Why* (Sinek) – A powerful book that set the tone for Correct Craft when we began expanding several years ago.
- *The Advantage* (Lencioni) – All Lencioni's books are great and

this one summarizes some of his key principles – healthy organizations have functional teams and clarity. As a side note, several years ago I sat next to Lencioni on a plane – what a great guy.

- ***Innovator's Dilemma*** (Christenson) – A classic that was written years ago but reading this book will help you realize how close you may be to going out of business. I spent a week at Harvard studying under Christenson and his theories will change your thinking in important ways.
- ***Mindset*** (Dweck) – An influential book that helps people realize that the biggest thing holding them back is their own thinking.
- ***Leadership and Self Deception*** (The Arbinger Institute) – By deceiving ourselves we limit our effectiveness and happiness – this book is a wake-up call.
- ***Being Wrong*** (Schultz) – An earth-shaking book that explains how we can feel so right while being so wrong – this book will expand your thinking in a big way.
- ***Derailed*** (Irwin) – When great leaders fail it is almost always for the same reason – pride. All leaders should read Derailed.
- ***Six Thinking Hats*** (de Bono) – Explains why we get trapped in our way of viewing things and provides a great tool for expanding the thinking of teams.
- ***Switch*** (Heath and Heath) – Helps companies understand why change is so difficult and gives tools to help drive transformation.
- ***How to Win Friends and Influence People*** (Carnegie) – A classic on how to deal with people.
- ***Good to Great*** (Collins) – This book has fallen out of favor because some of the companies featured have failed. However, it is still full of great principles that can help any business.

There are many great books and it was very difficult for me to pick a few of the top books business leaders should read. I am certain others would add or take away from the above list, however, these books have impacted me and I am confident they will change your life, your teams, and your business.

Chapter 121
GOOD THINGS WILL HAPPEN
March 2020

We are living in a time that reminds me of eras we read about in history books but never thought we would experience. During this challenging time, it might be hard to imagine any good coming out of what we are experiencing, but history teaches us that good comes out of even the most difficult situations.

Many years ago, I read a book called *The 100: A Ranking of the Most Influential Persons in History* by Michael H. Hart. The book was fascinating, and I was intrigued that the author identified the second most influential person in history as Isaac Newton.

Newton, one of the smartest people to ever live, was selected as number two in the book because he discovered many of the principles that modern science and mathematics are built upon. We would not live the life we enjoy today with modern technology if it weren't for Newton's discoveries, which triggered the scientific revolution.

What many people do not know is that Newton made his discoveries at home on his family farm in "quarantine," while England was ravished with the bubonic plague. His time alone to think during the plague resulted in the development of calculus, prisms, gravity and many more discoveries that changed the world dramatically.

Many people also don't realize that a few decades before Newton's discoveries, William Shakespeare was also sent home from London during a plague and did some of his most creative thinking/writing/ work during his "quarantine."

I am not in any way downplaying the suffering COVID-19 is creating and I clearly do not think what we are experiencing is good. It has been very sad to see so many people suffer and loved ones lost. I am deeply saddened for those affected and I will continue to pray for everyone hurt in any way by COVID-19.

However, there will be many significant and unexpected consequences of COVID-19 and some of them will be positive. I have written and spoken often about being a "learner" and, even during our challenges, there are opportunities to learn.

It looks like the weeks ahead will be challenging, but, while we cannot imagine it today, we can expect something good to come from this chaos.

Chapter 122
LEADERSHIP DURING CRISIS
March 2020

Crisis Leadership

The global community is dealing with a crisis unlike anything those of us alive have ever experienced. It feels like we are in some sci-fi movie with a pandemic slowly (or not so slowly) moving across the globe.

A crisis like what we are experiencing requires great leadership and, unfortunately, some leaders who are excellent in a stable environment can really, really, struggle in crisis.

If you think of it in terms of jet pilots, some leaders are like commercial pilots and others are like fighter pilots (a common analogy but bear with me). Commercial pilots are necessary and have an important job, but in a crisis like we are experiencing right now, we need leaders who are fighter pilots. Fighter pilots can fly commercial planes, but commercial pilots don't fly fighter jets.

So, what are attributes of leaders who are fighter pilots? Fighter pilots:

- **Move toward problems** – In times of crisis, leaders can either move toward problems, run away, or freeze. Fighter pilots fully engage and move toward the crisis. The worst thing a leader can do in crisis is freeze. If a leader runs away from a crisis at least they are getting out of their team's way but when a leader freezes, they just become dead weight for the rest of the team to carry.

- **Have a "can do" attitude** – Fighter pilots who don't have a "can do" attitude don't live long. Fighter pilots don't get emotionally hijacked by their environment; they see challenges as obstacles that can be overcome and then they do it.
- **Solve problems** – Fighter pilots don't drop problems in the lap of others – they take ownership of the situation or problem and do what they need to do. They don't wait for others to solve the problem.

Last week at one of our companies we had a great example of a team acting like fighter pilots. It started when we heard from a vendor that COVID-19 had unfortunately forced them into closing their business, not temporarily, but for good. This was a critical supplier who provided material "just-in-time" so this closing was going to have an immediate impact on this particular company's ability to build products. Within twenty-four hours some of our team had repurposed a bay, acquired the right equipment, built workstations, procured the raw materials, and started producing the product in-house. It was a great job by a group of fighter pilots getting the job done.

We are in an uncertain environment with our organizations and teams needing leaders who can function as fighter pilots. They need leaders people can trust to make good decisions on the fly while looking out for their team.

Chapter 123
DON'T RESTART - RESET YOUR BUSINESS
April 2020

Don't Restart Your Business – "Reset" It

These are extremely stressful times for business leaders. We are all wondering what we should be doing during this period of uncertainty. There is no playbook to read; we are writing it.

With the stress leaders are currently experiencing, it may seem too early to be thinking about reopening your closed (or soon to be closed business.) However, if you are not currently developing a reopening strategy, you are putting your business at a significant disadvantage and losing an opportunity for your business to excel in the upcoming decade.

When I assumed my current CEO role, our company was in a mess. I was the fifth CEO in five years, and much was broken. The first couple years in my new role were spent putting out fires, trying to develop a long-term strategy and navigating a company ownership change. Then, just when things seemed to be on track, literally on my second anniversary, the bottom of the economy fell out and we entered the Great Recession.

The Great Recession was excruciatingly difficult on our company but at the same time, it helped us create a foundation that resulted in a decade of record-breaking results. This foundation was laid because we were able to make several years' worth of changes in a matter of weeks, not years.

Leaders should view COVID-19 as an opportunity for a significant reset of your business. This is a rare opportunity to restructure your businesses in a way that your team will benefit from for the next decade. Specifically, think about what you could do to change your business for the better and do that during this time. You need to be sure that when you reopen your business it has processes and a cost structure that produces better results than before your shutdown. This is particularly important if you reopen at a production rate less than the rate you closed.

For instance, are there things you stopped doing during the shutdown that you do not need to restart? Or, can you reduce the number of resources needed for a particular job or function? Are there processes that would be tough to change in normal times that might be easy to change now? Make sure you reopen your business in better shape than you shut it down.

While this is a horrible health crisis that I don't want to minimize in any way, our current situation also presents leaders an opportunity unlike any they may ever get again. This is an opportunity to make changes that will ensure your organization's health for a long time.

Changes take energy and courage, but the current situation is an opportunity to make your business better, much better. If you do, your employees and company will benefit from it for the next decade. In a few months, we will be able to judge how well we all did at the "reset," so now's the time to act.

We learn a lot about ourselves and each other in times like we are now experiencing, and it takes an exceptional leader to not only recognize and grow from what they are learning, but to also look for opportunities to improve in the crisis.

Chapter 124
CRISIS MANAGEMENT
May 2020

Being Crisis Ready

The past one hundred years have been one crisis after another; WWI, the Spanish Flu, the stock market crash, the Great Depression, WWII, Korean War, flu's of the 50's and 60's, Vietnam War, Oil Embargo, inflation, sky-high interest rates, the '87 stock market crash, the Gulf War, 9/11, the Great Recession and now COVID-19. You'd think we would recognize that crisis is a regular occurrence; but, we don't.

Despite a clear track record of crisis on a consistent basis, we often get captured by the thought that when things are good, they will stay that way. Last year I read a book, called "This Time It's Different," which did a good job of explaining how we get captured by thinking our current situation is different than similar situations in the past and ignore lessons we should have learned.

As Mark Twain is reputed to have said, "History does not repeat itself, but it rhymes."

Since it is difficult to project what the next crisis might be or when it will occur, some of the best things we can do are:

- Expect that there will be a crisis even (maybe, especially) when you don't see it coming and remain flexible.
- Create a crisis business model that is flexible and can be adjusted quickly if needed. I am wired to be an optimist, so this is not negative, it is smart.
- Have a downturn plan ready. While you cannot predict the crisis, you can have a plan for how you will function when a crisis happens. This is not necessarily a detailed plan, but a model that helps you adjust your business for the unpleasant surprises that are inevitable. This needs to be a workable model with targets that are achievable.
- Once the crisis starts, assume a "fighter pilot" mentality. My CIA agent friend Michele tells me that CIA agents are taught that they have three options in a crisis (fight, flight, or freeze). She says the CIA teaches them the importance of "getting off the spot;" which means that of the three options, the worst choice is to freeze.
- Use the crisis as an opportunity to "reset." I have been repeating this with our team over and over since COVID-19 began. As much as we don't want to deal with this pandemic, it is a rare opportunity to make substantive change. No one wants a crisis, but teams need to see them as an opportunity.

Forming your team's thinking is more important than giving them a to-do list. Get your team to take on a fighter pilot mentality and embrace crisis as an opportunity; they will take care of the details.

In the last couple of months we have all had a crash course in crisis management, and, this particular crisis has been one with no playbook. We have all been writing the pandemic playbook on the fly. But despite the uniqueness of a global pandemic, the crisis principles are still the same; there are things we can do to prepare and respond well when the unexpected happens.

Chapter 125
THE WAY FORWARD
June 2020

I have been in the marine industry for over three decades and, so far, 2020 has been about as crazy a year as I remember. COVID-19, social unrest, and as I write this a dust storm approaching Florida, where I live, from Saharan Africa. And, of course, a big part of the country is starting to think about hurricane season. All we need now is to top it off with an alien invasion and 2020 would definitely be the most interesting year ever.

Of all that is happening, and despite good May and June retail sales, COVID-19 has been particularly tough for our industry. According to the NMMA, 81% of marine businesses have been impacted negatively by COVID-19 and the estimated economic losses for our industry from the virus are over $20 billion dollars. There was no playbook for a pandemic, so we have been writing the playbook as we go. Lessons from history are important but sometimes it is hard to know what lessons to apply to an event we have not previously experienced. Fortunately, we have a collegial industry and many of us have been working to help each other, even those of us are normally competing.

During a time like this, a leader's first job is to do what is necessary to "save the ship." Most leaders get this, so they have been trying to do that while also trying to be empathetic to concerns of employees, dealers, vendors, and of course customers. But to save the ship leaders have had to make some tough decisions this year, some very tough.

What may be not as intuitive to many leaders, is that crisis is a huge opportunity to improve. Our team has seen 2020 as an opportunity to "reset" and make several years of changes in a short time. As most smart companies have done, we have used the 2020 crisis to make changes in our organization and cost structure that will benefit our company for the long term. During the Great Recession, we made changes to our company that resulted in nine straight record years of growth and profitability. While we would never ask for it, if we must experience a crisis, we need to use the crisis as an opportunity to improve.

Also, as leaders, we have all learned a lot during this time.

- We have all been reminded that it is critical to have a great team we can count on, especially in times of crisis. At Correct Craft, we have a bunch of employees and they are almost all better at their job than I could ever be. Investing in a great team when things are good really pays off when things are tough.
- We have learned who the "fighter pilots" are on our team. We have learned who moves toward the problem, who runs from the problem, and who freezes. We have learned who sees crises as bigger than themselves and who sees themselves as bigger than the crisis and views it as an opportunity to make the company better, much better.
- Maybe most importantly, as leaders, we have learned a lot about ourselves. We have learned whether we can motivate and energize in crisis, whether we can provide clarity and reassurance, and we have learned how empathetic we are in a time when many are concerned.

It is great to learn these things, but it is much more important and valuable to apply these learnings to make both our organizations and us better. Looking forward from today, it is critical that we use what we have learned during this crazy time to improve and ensure we don't need to learn the lessons again.

So, what else should we think about looking forward?

- **Know that crisis will come, and it will come regularly** – One of the biggest mistakes I have seen people make over the years is to assume that because the economic environment is great, it will stay that way. However, if you look back at the past 100 years you know that crisis is a regularly occurring manifestation. WWI, the Spanish Flu that killed up to 100 million people, the stock market crash, Great Depression, WWII, pandemics of the 50's and 60's, social unrest in the 60's, inflation, oil embargo, sky-high interest rates, the first Gulf War, Y2K, 9/11, the Great Recession and finally 2020 all make it hard to find a decade in the last 100 years without a major crisis. Yet somehow it is easy for leaders to think "This time it's different." It is never different, so we need to always be prepared for challenges on the horizon.

- **Have a crisis plan** – Over a year ago we started working hard to develop an economic downturn plan with a financial model to help us understand how we needed to react when the next recession occurred. We didn't expect a pandemic, but the plan we had developed for an economic downturn was very useful and helped us react quickly instead of trying to figure out what we needed to do.

- **Be forward-thinking** – As leaders, we need to always be looking out on the horizon to prepare our companies for the future. This comes naturally to some leaders and is very challenging for others. Leaders who are enamored with "details" often have a hard time looking years ahead and this can create a big risk for their organizations. Unfortunately, leaders who are not wired to look forward and connect the dots on the horizon usually also have a hard time delegating that responsibility because it seems like the kind of thing the leader should do. Leaders who are not naturally wired to look out into the future, but also have the self-awareness to realize that, take the necessary steps to ensure someone in their organization has a forward-thinking perspective.

- **Expect big changes** – In the next ten years, we will see more changes than we have in our industry up to this point. The changes will primarily be technology-driven and will impact all areas of our businesses. Overall the changes will create great abundance but also create great disruption. There will be boating companies, but just not the same ones we have today. The reason is that most companies will have a difficult, almost impossible, time making the changes they need to make. All of today's boating companies have the opportunity today to adjust but most won't because we get trapped by our own thinking. We also cannot see the world differently than the way we know it. Leaders who are not consistently feeling like they are outside their comfort zone should beware, they may not see the tsunami of change coming their way.

Over and over throughout my career I have seen that crisis and change provide the best leaders an extraordinary opportunity to move their organizations forward. The best leaders embrace these situations and take their companies to new heights. That is the way forward.

Chapter 126
BUSTING THE CREATIVITY MYTH
August 2020

This blog, without hyperbole, could change your life.

First, imagine what your life would be like if you were more creative. Would life be more fun? Would people find you more interesting? Would you do better in your job? Make more money? Would you have a more positive impact on the world? I'll bet the answer to all those questions is an unequivocal yes!

So, if the benefits are so obvious, how can you be more creative? What makes the people who we consider creative the way they are? Does their brain just work differently?

I have come to believe that our creativity is a direct result of our self-perception. In other words, if you think of yourself as creative, you will be.

My wife Leigh has taught elementary school art for many years and works hard to encourage kids in their creativity. Years ago, she shared an article with me that claimed adults who consider themselves creative had their creativity re-enforced as kids. Sometimes it was just one teacher who told the child they were creative which sent the child's life on a completely different, more positive trajectory.

While it is hard to shift our paradigms, especially about ourselves, I believe that, no matter our age, we can still change our creative trajectory as adults. I am not saying it is easy, but it can be done, and the potential rewards are enormous.

Our self-image is how we think about ourselves and it can be changed; it does not have to be permanent. It is developed over our lives and is impacted by a lot of different experiences. Just like kids, our adult lives can be sent on a new trajectory because of positive reinforcement, but often as adults that positive reinforcement must come from ourselves. Fortunately, you can use your thoughts and self-talk to change your life. You have the power to change your entire life by thinking of yourself as creative.

Visualization is a tool used by many top tier athletes and it can help you too. Think ahead five years and picture what your life could be like if you were creative. Once you have a clear picture of the new and creative you then take it day by day. Tell yourself each morning that today you will be creative. Have a long-term vision and a daily plan and take steps to execute them.

I realize that many people reading this will think it's craziness. However, try it, there is little downside and the upside is huge. It will change your life.

Once you have changed your self-image, most of the work is done. However, to develop your creativity even further try the following:

- **Be a learner** – Read books that are written from a new perspective or which are written by someone with whom you disagree. Listen to a podcast from someone who can teach you something new. Visit new places. Expanding your thinking is one of the best ways to be creative.
- **Enjoy some quiet, nature time** – The older I get and the more I learn, the more I realize the benefits of spending time enjoying creation. My friend J. Nichols writes about this in his book *Blue Mind*. Time spent recharging in a natural setting

is not time lost, it is time invested in our creativity with very high returns.

- **Be courageous** – I often wonder what great art, inventions, new songs, or cures the world has been deprived of because people were not courageous with their ideas. Fear of looking stupid has probably robbed people of more success than any other thing. Creative people sometimes say things that don't make sense to others, don't worry about it and just step out of your comfort zone. As my friend and ex-CIA agent Michele Rigby says, "Nothing significant happens in your comfort zone."

Finally, I am a CEO, not a psychologist, so I don't want to get out over my skis. However, in my experience, it's a myth that some people are wired to be creative when others aren't. It's time to bust the myth. For decades I have seen that people who perceive themselves as creative, are creative.

Try it for the next ninety days; modify with your thoughts and self-talk to begin considering yourself creative. It will change your life for the better and who knows, maybe the next great idea will be yours!

Chapter 127
INNOVATION MADE EASY
August 2020

Get your resume polished up if your company is not highly innovative; soon you will be needing a new job. Companies that are not innovative cannot survive in the long run; they are going out of business.

Despite its importance, innovation is a mystery to many leaders. To some it is all about technology, some wonder how to innovate without disrupting their current business model and others want to innovate but are not sure how to get started. Innovation is critical to your organization and these hurdles are easily overcome.

More Than Just Technology

The first step to being innovative is creating the right mindset. Innovation is much more than just technology; it is an outlook that should impact every part of an organization. As leaders, we need to continually encourage our teams to look for new and creative ways of doing things and sometimes those new ways will include technology, but not always.

It seems simple, and obvious, to say we should encourage our teams to be innovative, but most leaders don't truly embrace that mindset. Most leaders are fixed in their thinking and the way they do things. Though it's cliché, so they would never say it, their thinking is "if it's not broke, don't fix it." The problem is that these leaders often don't realize that it is broken until it's too late to fix.

The risk of unforeseen change is a big problem today and while innovation should be viewed as more than just technology, technology does often play a part. Increasing computational power is driving change so fast that we will experience more transformation in the next ten years than most industries have ever seen. Leaders no longer have time to recognize change on the way and adjust; change today is coming so fast we need to expect it, and always be innovating.

Our team demonstrated their innovation mindset earlier this year when we were closed as a result of the uncertainty around COVID-19. Our leaders embraced a "don't reopen, instead reset" mentality that challenged them to reset everything we do and position us for success post-COVID-19. Our team is already seeing positive results from this innovative mindset and we will benefit from it for years to come. However, if we had not had an innovation mindset it would have been impossible to reset that quickly.

When organizations need an innovative culture, it is often too late to develop one; the first step to being innovative is realizing it is more than just technology and creating the right mindset with your team.

Fear of Self-Disruption

The business landscape is littered with examples of leaders who let concerns about disrupting their own organizations keep them from taking the obvious steps needed to survive. Kodak, Blockbuster, Blackberry, Nokia, Borders, and just about every retailer falls into a group of businesses who failed to act even when they knew it was necessary; they did not want to disrupt their own business model. Sadly, they all ended up as victims of disruption.

The interesting part is that almost every company that has

been disrupted out of business considered themselves innovative. Unfortunately for them, they focused on the wrong type of innovation.

Innovation falls into two broad categories, sustaining and disruptive. Many companies are good at sustaining innovation which, in short, is innovation that makes current products better. Because those companies are good at sustaining innovation, they often consider themselves "innovators" and that is a big, dangerous, trap that sets them on a path to going out of business.

The second type of innovation, disruptive, is named appropriately. Disruptive innovation transforms markets and how customers have their needs met. Companies that practice sustaining innovation make it tougher on their competitors, but disruptive innovators put their competitors out of business; that's a big difference.

Even leaders who understand the different types of innovation, often do not realize that it is almost impossible for organizations to be both sustaining innovators and disruptive innovators. Disruptive innovation often requires organizations to put their entire business model at risk; it becomes an existential problem, literally. Sustaining innovators are rarely willing to take the risk of disrupting their entire business. That is why disruptive innovation almost always comes from the outside, even though sustaining innovators may have the same ideas and better resources.

A great example of this is Kodak, a company that invented the same digital technology that put them out of business. Their team was so consumed with their then-current industry-leading technology and sustaining innovation that even when they considered marketing digital technology it was through the lens of their print business. Kodak invented a transformative innovation but could not see it because they were stuck focusing on their sustaining innovation. This mistake cost many Kodak employees their jobs and Kodak investors billions of dollars.

In order to mitigate this problem, companies need to set up an entirely separate organization fully devoted to disruptive innovation. Our company, Correct Craft did that, creating Watershed Innovation with the entire purpose of identifying, researching, and developing plans to implement disruptive innovation throughout our organization. Our Watershed Innovation team works on research involving electrification, IoT, robotics, additive manufacturing, virtual and augmented reality, and other opportunities in a way that is not threatening to the existence of all or any part of our other companies. So far, the results have been phenomenal.

How To Get Started

So, how does a leader who wants their organization to be innovative get started? Below are some thoughts:

- Read the book *Mindset*, written by Carol Dweck, with your team. Dr. Dweck explains not only how people get stuck in their thinking but also the ways that it limits a person's potential. It is nearly impossible to be innovative without a growth mindset

- After you and your team are done reading Mindset, read *The Innovator's Dilemma* by Clayton Christensen. This book is the Bible of innovation and clearly explains the key issues related to being innovative.

- Create tremendous clarity around the importance of innovation to your organization. Make sure everyone knows that transforming products and processes is important to you and the organization's future success.

- Consider how to separate sustaining and disruptive innovation within your organization. This is hard at small companies, so consider alternatives. At the very least ensure your team has a high awareness of the innovator's dilemma so they can be on the lookout for it.

- Be willing to fail. No one wants to do foolish things but having a high-risk aversion makes it almost impossible to be disruptively innovative.

Innovation is not mysterious; there are proven ways to help your company become an innovator. By implementing the above steps, it will take you and your company a long way toward being innovative and may even ensure your organization's survival.

Chapter 128
LEADERSHIP MADE EASY
October 2020

Most people think leadership skills are innate; either you have them, or you don't. While it's true that there are some people who are wired to be great leaders, there is also hope for the rest of us. We too can lead well and achieve great results.

However, leadership can be confusing. There are so many leadership books and consultants sharing their views that sometimes the whole concept can feel overwhelming. Besides that, most leaders are looking for the silver bullet that will make them great. I have spoken on leadership at conferences all over the globe and most of the people I have met at those meetings are hoping to get the one secret that will transform them from an average to an extraordinary leader. Leadership is simple, but unfortunately not that simple.

While there may not be a silver bullet, there are four things I have found leaders can do to ensure they are optimizing results at their organization.

Create Clarity

Management guru Peter Drucker said that there is no greater waste than being good at something that does not matter. Along the same vein, Drucker also said that managers make sure things are done right, but leaders ensure the right things are being done. An organization being good at something that does not matter or doing things that should not be done often results from its leader's lack of clarity.

It is essential that leaders provide clarity in the following areas:

- **The Organization's "Why"** – In his book "Start with Why" Simon Sinek explains the importance of "Why" much better than I can; I highly recommend every leader read it. At our company, we have embraced the "Why" of "Making Life Better" and it impacts everything we do. We want everyone we connect with to be better for having dealt with us and that includes our employees, customers, vendors, dealers, people around the world we serve through our philanthropy and even our competitors.

- **The Organization's Values** – Our team has a culture pyramid that clearly identifies our values. We talk about our values all the time and hang the pyramid around our facilities. We work hard to ensure no one must wonder about our values or what is important.

- **The Organization's Vision** – Every team needs to know where the leader wants to take them. Teams are much more effective when they are working toward a vision of the future. People respond well to goals; having a clear vision is energizing.

- **The Organization's Strategic Plan** – An effective strategic plan identifies the path a team will take to achieve its vision. It is usually a three to five-year plan that serves as a roadmap. If a strategic plan is both well developed and well executed the company will achieve its vision.

Build a Great Team

I hate to admit this but anyone who knows me well already realizes it; I am likely the least talented person on our team. To be successful, I need to be part of a great team and fortunately we have one at our company. I embrace hiring people who are smarter and more talented than me because I know we need them.

When you get the right team, everything becomes much easier. Unfortunately, some leaders hesitate to hire people who they perceive could be threatening to them or their leadership. They either want to be the smartest person in the room or are not willing to invest in the best people and it holds back their organization.

Building a great team, of course, starts with hiring the right people. We look for character, competency, and chemistry in a leadership candidate. The consistent mistake I have made over my career is overvaluing competency at the expense of both character and competency. I would never even consider hiring someone I knew had bad character or chemistry but I can become enamored with a prospective teammate's competency and not consider the other areas as much as I should; it always ends up bad and I hope I have learned my lesson.

Over the years our team has used tools such as Predictive Index, MBTI, and DISC to help us find the right person for a job. I have found that a combination of both MBTI and DISC helps me get a good understanding of the candidate and how they will fit on our team.

After hiring great people, great leaders develop them incessantly. Often we invest in hundreds of our employees so they can go back and get their bachelor's degree or MBA, obtain a useful certification, attend an executive education course, or participate in our Correct Craft University. Years ago, at a conference I heard Zig Ziglar say, "It is better to train your people and have them leave than not train them and have them stay;" that idea stuck with me and I embrace it.

Finally, your company will get the best results if your team is healthy and embraces constructive conflict. By far the best book I have read on this is Pat Lencioni's "5 Dysfunctions of a Team" and I would highly recommend every leader read it.

Move Toward Problems

New leaders are often surprised at how difficult it is to assume the responsibility of leadership. It is much easier to say what you would do than actually do it. Leadership can be both stressful and, unfortunately, the unique challenges of leadership often result in leaders avoiding problems and challenges. It is easy to think problems may go away on their own but hard to have the difficult conversations, but the best leaders move toward problems.

In his great book, Necessary Endings, Dr. Henry Cloud shares that sometimes it is even in everyone's best interest to end business relationships that are not working. It is difficult but to be an effective leader we need to make tough decisions, even when those decisions involve necessary endings.

While moving toward problems can be challenging for any leader, often it is even harder for introverts. However, regardless of our wiring, it is impossible to be a great leader without moving toward problems.

Provide Energy

Organizations require energy and leaders must be the primary source of that energy. It takes effort to provide energy to your organization but benefits to the organization, leader, and the team are immense. Unfortunately, while it takes effort to provide energy to an organization it is all too easy to be a de-energizer. To provide your organization energy, do the following:

- **Be Impact, Not Reward, Focused** – If your team believes you are focused on attention, money or other rewards it is de-energizing to them. When you are focused on making your team better by developing them and using your platform for good it energizes your team. Pat Lencioni does a good job of explaining the difference in his great book, The Motive.

- **Be a High Expectation, High Affirmation Leader** – When a leader sets high goals and affirms progress toward those goals it is highly energizing.

- **Believe in Your Team and Let Them Know it** - Make sure you let your team know you believe in them. If you don't believe in them see the section above on "Build a Great Team."

- **Be an Optimist** – Optimism is contagious and provides energy. Check out Martin Seligman's book Learned Optimism to better understand how being an optimist can help you be a better leader.

- **Be Humble** – As Tim Irwin explains in his great book Derailed, pride is at the root of almost every leadership catastrophe.

Leadership is not mysterious, there are things you can do to lead better and improve your results. Start with creating clarity, building a strong team, moving towards problems, and creating energy; both you and your team will be better for it.

Chapter 129
TRUTH OR CONSEQUENCES?
November 2020

Everyone reading this article is self-deceived; and so am I. We all believe things to be true that are not. We are all severely limited by our own experiences. And, finally, we are all especially bad at evaluating our own performance.

For those still reading after that opening paragraph, fortunately there are things we can do to expand our thinking and dramatically improve our results, our impact, and our world.

The depth of our self-deception is perfectly described in the interesting and classic book, *Flatland*, written during Victorian England by Edward Abbott. In the book, Abbott shares the story of a society that lives on a two-dimensional plane, appropriately called *Flatland*. We learn about Flatland from Square, who is sharing his story from prison. Square is in prison for revealing what he learned about a third dimension, which conflicts with the two-dimensional world the leaders of Flatland believe to be true.

The book also describes Square seeing Pointland, a universe occupied by its Monarch, Point, who believes he is the entire world. It describes Lineland, a society that lives on a one-dimensional line whose Monarch wanted to kill Square after Square tells him about the two-dimensional land where Square lives, a concept that seems impossible to the Lineland Monarch. And, finally, we learn about Spaceland, a three-dimensional world that Square visits and first learns that a third dimension exists.

This story from Flatland may sound silly but, despite its grounding in Victorian views of classes and gender roles that are much different than today's, the book is incredibly thought-provoking. It demonstrates in a clear way how very unusual it is for people to seek truth. We rarely seek truth, we seek validation.

I've been down this road enough times to know that most people reading this article agree with me in general; they just don't see how it applies to them personally. That's self-deception at its finest.

The reality is that most people are not learners, they are knowers. They would rather feel good about being right than seek truth. They don't want to consider any new information that might indicate they are seeing something incorrectly. They would rather ignore information that contradicts them and feel 100% right, even though there is a chance they are actually 100% wrong.

In her great book, *Being Wrong*, Kathryn Schulz tackles this issue head-on. Schulz uses studies and anecdotes to explain why it is so typical and easy to feel 100% right while, in reality, being 100% wrong. Schulz uses example after example to demonstrate her point. The book was an eye-opener to me, and I highly recommend it.

It is a huge challenge to resist being a knower. As much as I understand this idea and as many times as I have taught these concepts, I still struggle with it.

Nobel prize winner Daniel Kahneman explains this struggle in his interesting book, *Thinking Fast and Slow*. In his book, Kahneman explains that 90% or more of our thinking is fast thinking, what he calls Type 1 thinking, where we draw quick conclusions based on our existing perspective. In Type 1 thinking we use heuristics, or mental shortcuts, based on our world view or other biases we have picked up over our lifetime. As we learn in Behavioral Economics, a science pretty much invented by Kahneman and his research partner Amos

Tversky, those heuristics and biases are notoriously wrong, even when they feel 100% right.

In slow thinking, what Kahneman calls Type 2 thinking, we slow down enough to consider what we are trying to decide but even then we can be severely impacted by our biases. Like the people of Pointland, Lineland, and Flatland, it seems impossible that the world could be different than the way we see it.

And, speaking again of the book Flatland, remember the people of Spaceland who live in the three-dimensional world, like us? Once our friend Square became a learner, he asked the people of Spaceland about a fourth dimension and they replied incredulously, just as Pointland, Lineland, and Spaceland did when they were confronted with the thought of a new dimension. I am clearly not a physicist but that is something to think about, huh?

So, we can either become a learner, with a growth mindset, or suffer the consequences of being a knower; and those consequences are high. Knowers stay trapped in their own thinking which makes them feel good but also results in living a lie. Knowers not only fail to reach their potential but also go through life deceived. Who wants to live with those consequences?

So, what can we do?

- Acknowledge the reality of self-deception – The first step to changing your world in a big way is to acknowledge the problem of self-deception. This is really tough for most people because they feel so right; for those who want to improve in this area the books I mention above will help.
- Decide you would rather seek truth than feel good – This too is hard because most people believe what they already think is truth and it makes them feel good.
- Surround yourself with people who will disagree with you – Make sure your team knows you want their opinion and never

criticize, or even harder, don't get emotional with someone for sharing their perspective in good faith.

- Read items that broaden your perspective – I am a voracious reader and enjoy books that have a different perspective than me. People will sometimes hear me share thoughts about a book I am reading and wonder why I would read something so different than my normal perspective. I am not afraid of seeking truth and that perspective has materially helped me over the years.

- Travel to different places – I have had the opportunity to travel to about 120 countries and every visit to a different place expands my paradigms. You don't need to visit 120 countries but try to visit someplace different; you will be surprised how your view expands.

- Watch a different news channel – this point may be the toughest of all for some people. I am not a TV watcher but the past few months I have tried to watch different news programs, especially after a big event. The days of news programs actually sharing news are long over. They have become a big echo chamber and people listen to news channels that make them feel good about their views. Mix it up a little by watching something different.

There is tremendous opportunity to improve both yourself and your organization by being a learner. It is hard but once you start down the path of being a learner it is also exhilarating. The number one thing that holds most people back in life is themselves, and more specifically their thinking. Being a learner will go a long way to breaking free of self-deception and allow you and your organization to reach full potential.

Chapter 130
EXPECTING THE UNEXPECTED
November 2020

Despite many of us having an inclination toward hindsight bias, which is believing we saw things coming when we actually didn't, I haven't spoken to one person who claims to have predicted the events of 2020. We have lived through a pandemic, social unrest, an economy that is struggling and a crazy election; as I have often said the past few months, all we need is an alien invasion to make it the craziest year ever.

Even though we all deal with craziness when we must, most of the time we easily settle into our current environment, whatever it may be. In their excellent book *This Time It's Different*, authors Reinhart and Rogoff explain how we fall into the trap of thinking that our current situation is different from similar situations in the past, which means we failed to learn the lessons of history. As Mark Twain said, "History doesn't repeat itself, but it rhymes."

In another exceptional book, *Black Swan: The Impact of the Highly Improbable,* author Nassim Taleb explains how susceptible we are to unpredictable but highly impactful events. At Correct Craft, we have a risk matrix that attempts to identify potential risks to our company and the projected impact of those risks occurring but, frankly, we did not have a pandemic on the list of risks. The pandemic was a Black Swan event.

While it may have been tough to predict a pandemic, we all should have known something was coming. In the past one hundred years we have experienced one Black Swan after another. We had WWI, the Spanish Flu, and Prohibition which resulted in a crime wave. A stock market crash in 1929 followed by the Dust Bowl and the Great Depression. It took WWII to pull the U.S. out of the Depression followed by the Korean and Vietnam Wars. The world had flu pandemics of 1958 and 1968 both of which killed over a million people. The 1970's brought an oil embargo, high inflation, low economic growth and interest rates near 20%. The U.S. had another stock market crash in 1987, followed by the first Gulf War, Y2K, 9/11 and the Afghanistan and Iraqi Wars. Finally, the Great Recession and a world-wide pandemic bring us to today. One Black Swan after another; anyone else out of breath?

So, while we may not specifically know what is coming, we should always plan for the Black Swan. Some things that will help you are:

- **Expect the unexpected** – We need to be prepared for the next Black Swan. I hope it won't be as impactful as a pandemic, but within a few years there will be another Black Swan event that will significantly impact us. If we realize this will happen, we can be prepared.
- **Have a plan** – While we didn't plan at Correct Craft for a pandemic, we did have a downturn plan ready. Even when we aren't expecting a downturn, we have a plan ready to operate on significantly less business than normal. While the circumstances may vary, having a downturn plan ready really helps a business when the crisis happens; I know it helped us.

  A strategic plan helps too. When I came to Correct Craft, I was the fifth CEO in five years and there were a lot of things our team needed to do. One of the first things we did together was to develop our company's first strategic plan. Shortly after we finished our strategic plan the Great Recession hit, and the plan was an incredibly valuable roadmap of what we needed to do; just much faster than we planned. We had a plan that helped us make 10 years of changes in 10 months and set us up for a decade of record results.

- **Have a flexible business model** – Build a business model that keeps as many of your costs variable as possible. Keeping costs variable helps reduce the odds that a cyclical crisis will become an existential crisis. If necessary, pull out your old managerial accounting textbook from college and brush up on your cost accounting, it could save your business.
- **Don't waste a crisis** – No one wants a crisis, but they do provide huge opportunities. A crisis provides the opportunity to make changes that need to be made anyway but seem much harder in a normal environment. Any leader whose company does not come out of a crisis better than they went into it made a huge mistake.

I have no idea what the next crisis or Black Swan will be, but I do know there will be one. While we cannot lead in fear, it is also irresponsible to assume that we won't have another unexpected event that will impact our businesses. Following the above steps will help you prepare and thrive when that event occurs.

ABOUT THE AUTHOR

Bill Yeargin is CEO of Correct Craft, a 95-year-old company with global operations. Correct Craft's subsidiaries include eight boat brands, three engine brands, three water sports parks and an entity devoted solely to innovation. The company has manufacturing facilities across the U.S. and distributes into 70 countries.

Under Bill's leadership, Correct Craft has developed a unique culture of "Making Life Better." They have won all their industry's major awards and were recognized as Florida's "Manufacturer of the Year." One publication recognized Correct Craft as the boating industry's "Most Innovative Company" while another described the company under Bill's leadership as being "on an aggressive improvement path, the likes of which the marine industry has never seen."

A passionate lifelong learner, Bill has earned a bachelor's degree in Accounting and an MBA. He has also completed post-graduate studies at Harvard, Stanford, Villanova University, and the Massachusetts Institute of Technology (MIT). Bill is a Certified Public Accountant, Certified Lean Six Sigma Black Belt, and is certified in both Myers Briggs Type Indicator (MBTI) and DISC.

Bill has served on numerous for-profit and non-profit boards. Currently he serves on the Board of Directors of the National Marine

Manufacturers Association (NMMA), the Recreational Boating Leadership Council and the Florida Chamber of Commerce.

Bill has served both the Obama and Trump administrations on cabinet-level advisory councils and actively represents both his company and industry on a national and state level. He was appointed by Florida's Governor to serve on the board of the University of Central Florida and is a member of the Florida Council of 100.

Bill has been recognized with many of the marine industry's top awards including Boating Industry's "Mover and Shaker of the Year." Florida Trend magazine has recognized Bill as one of "Florida's Most Influential Business Leaders" and he is an Orlando Business Journal "CEO of the Year." Bill was also presented the "Governor's Business Ambassador Medal" by the Governor of Florida.

A prolific writer, Bill has been published hundreds of times and has authored two books. He has traveled to over 110 countries and is a sought-after conference speaker.